W9-BVV-587

Anglo-American Defence Relations 1939–1980

Anglo-American Defence Relations 1939–1980

The Special Relationship

John Baylis

St. Martin's Press
New York

St. Martin's Press Inc., 175 Fifth Avenue, New York, NY 10010
Printed in Hong Kong
First published in the United States of America in 1981

Library of Congress Card Catalog Number 81-50018

ISBN 0-312-03669-8

To my Mother and Father

Contents

Preface

The focus of attention of this book is on the defence relationship between Britain and the United States from 1939 to the present day. Defence is clearly only one dimension of Anglo-American relations but it is nevertheless one of the most intimate areas of cooperation and as such is seen by many observers as the core of what is often known as the 'special relationship'. The aim of this study is to chart the changing fortunes of the defence partnership and to determine how far these relations have reflected the trends in Anglo-American relations in general. For many contemporary observers the 'special relationship' is a thing of the past. For some it ended with the Suez débâcle, for others with the Cuban Missile crisis,[1] and for others still with Britain's failure to help the United States in Vietnam and the decision to withdraw British forces from east of Suez.[2] In the light of these interpretations and the generalized impressions of erosion which seem to be widely held, the study attempts to identify in what ways defence relations have been 'special' in the past, whether they remain so today, and what the prospects are for the continuation of close military ties between the two states in the future. Some consideration is also given to the various criticisms which have been levelled against the relationship on both sides of the Atlantic.

The phrase 'special relationship' is one which has very wide currency and yet remains somewhat ill-defined. The word 'special' usually refers to something which is 'exceptional', 'uncommon', 'peculiar to one thing' or 'additional to the ordinary'.[3] Its use therefore to describe relations between Britain and the United States suggests a relationship which is not only very close but one which is, in some respects at least, extraordinary or 'different in kind' from those with other states.

One problem which arises from this interpretation is whether there is such a thing as a 'standard' or 'normal' relationship between two sovereign states, to which all relationships between pairs of states more or less conform, with the sole exception of the Anglo-American relationship. A case can be made that the world is full of 'curious, interesting, particular relationships between states'.[4] Every bilateral relationship in a sense can be described as unique or special. As Arthur Campbell Turner reminds us, however, if we are going to think usefully about relations between states, some form of classification is necessary.[5] To argue that all states are unique is not particularly helpful. The nature of state relations is generally 'matters of more and less, with infinite gradations'.[6] As such, in order to understand these relationships broad classifications are not only possible and helpful but in many respects essential. Thus, as Turner has argued, 'it remains broadly true, subject to this and that qualification, that certain cases of relationship between nation-states are exceptional and stand out from the ruck of the run-of-the-mill international politics'.[7] It is also his contention, and one which is accepted by this study, that there is 'something inherently different, unique and distinctive' in the Anglo-American relationship which makes it stand out and justifies the use of the word 'special'.[8]

If relations between Britain and the United States can be regarded as being 'exceptional' then a number of questions arise. Have Anglo-American relations always been 'special' or is this a recent phenomenon? In what particular way does the relationship stand out as being 'inherently different, unique and distinctive'? What is it that gives relations between the two countries this 'special' quality?

For most observers of Anglo-American relations the origins of the 'special relationship' lie deep in the roots of history. To writers like H.C. Allen, the whole course of relations between the two countries from the eighteenth century onwards has been 'a ripening of friendship' and a 'persistent, even steady progress from mistrust to cordiality'.[9] For those like Professor Allen who hold this 'hands-across-the-sea' view, defence has traditionally been one of the most tangible and visible forms of the wider relationship between the two countries. The United States, it is argued, was only able to promulgate the Monroe Doctrine in 1823 and maintain her isolationism because of the dominance of the British fleet and the protection it afforded to the United States. British naval superiority is also regarded as being of decisive importance in allowing the Civil War of 1861-5 to be fought without the involvement of the European powers.

Another specialist observer, H. G. Nicholas, also emphasizes the long historical background of Anglo-American relations.[10] He argues, however, that it is only 'since World War I, that British governments have given the highest priority to establishing and maintaining a close understanding with the USA'.[11] Despite this emphasis on the more modern relationship, H. G. Nicholas, like Professor Allen, also highlights the important contribution of defence and security questions in bringing Britain and the United States closer together. He points to the growing awareness of the strategic interdependence of the two countries in the early years of the twentieth century as providing a solid base for the emerging partnership. This was particularly so in the naval fields and it was appropriate, Nicholas argues, that when the US entered the First World War in April 1917 a joint naval command was established under a British admiral. In this one area at least, collaboration was very close with British and American navies cooperating in convoy duties, the blockade and the war against the U-boat menace.

There are other observers of Anglo-American relations, however, such as Professor Coral Bell, who argue that despite the existence of the 'unavowed alliance' between the two countries from the Monroe Doctrine onwards, 1940 is a more appropriate date for the start of the especially close, 'special relationship'.[12] In this respect Professor Bell's views are similar to those of a joint British and American study produced by the Council on Foreign Relations and the Royal Institute of International Affairs in 1953.[13] In this study the authors suggest that it was during the Second World War that the intimacy of cooperation was raised to a new level 'never before realised or even approached' by other sovereign states. According to this work the post-war relationship, when each regarded the other as 'its most important ally', was a continuation, 'at a lower level of intensity, of their war-time collaboration'.[14]

This emphasis on the period since 1940 is also contained in Winston Churchill's famous speech at Westminster College, Fulton, Missouri, on 5 March 1946. In this speech, which is better known for his comments about the 'iron curtain', Churchill spoke specifically about the importance of the wartime partnership and the need for continuing instruments of cooperation between the two countries in the post-war period as the international atmosphere darkened. The continuance of the intimate relationship was necessary, he argued, 'as the only means whereby the safety of the parts of the world possessing free institutions could be maintained'.[15] According to Churchill:

> Neither the sure prevention of war, nor the continuous rise of world organization will be gained without what I have called the fraternal association of the English-speaking peoples. This means a special relationship between the British Commonwealth and Empire and the United States. . . . Fraternal association requires not only the growing friendship and mutual understanding between our two vast but kindred systems of society, but the continuance of the intimate relationship between our military advisers, leading to common study of potential dangers, the similarity of weapons and manuals of instructions, and to the interchange of officers and cadets at technical colleges. It should carry with it the continuance of the present facilities for mutual security by the joint use of all Naval and Air Force bases in the possession of either country all over the world.[16]

This speech is of particular significance not only because of the imagery of the iron curtain descending across Europe and the emphasis upon the importance of continuing military cooperation between the two countries, but because of the popularity it gave to the phrase 'special relationship'. Although the phrase was probably coined by some long-forgotten journalist, it was in fact its repeated and emphatic use in the Fulton speech which 'launched it effectively on the world and from that day on secured its wide circulation'.[17]

The view that the Second World War is a proper starting-point for a study of the 'special relationship' is one which is accepted by the present author. Although the roots or origins of the relationship can be traced back into history, it was only during the 1939-45 war and afterwards that the partnership became so close, intimate and informal in such a wide spectrum of political, economic and especially military fields that terms like 'exceptional', 'unique' or 'different from the ordinary' can be applied. The relationship can be said to 'stand out' largely because of the degree of intimacy and informality which was developed during the war and which continued in somewhat diluted form in the post-war period.

Besides the dispute over which period in the history of Anglo-American relations the term 'special relationship' refers to, there is also a disagreement in the literature over what it is that has given the relationship its 'special' quality. For some writers the particularly close nature of the alliance stems essentially from sentimental attachments, cultural affinities, historical traditions, similar institutions and a common language. According to this view it is the cohesion created by these 'family' bonds which have elevated the Anglo-Saxon relationship to a qualitatively different plane in comparison with most other international relationships. Sir Denis Brogan is one commentator of Anglo-American affairs who has written that 'the linguistic and cultural relationship between England and America is not paralleled in any other pair of relationships'.[18] In similar vein Arthur Campbell Turner has argued that 'the foundation of the special relationship between Britain and the United States is demographic, the basic fact is that to a considerable extent the population of the United States derives from British sources. . . . The common language is the basic thread of Anglo-American communion, the basis of the Anglo-American community.'[19] Even one of the more outspoken critics of the 'special relationship' in the United States, George Ball, has argued that 'to an exceptional degree we look out on the world through similarly refracted mental spectacles. We speak variant patios of Shakespeare and Norman Mailer, our institutions spring from the same instincts and traditions, and we share the same heritage of law and custom, philosophy and pragmatic *Weltanschauung* . . . starting from similar premises in the same intellectual tradition, we recognize common allusions, share many common prejudices, and can commune on a basis of confidence.'[20]

While these rather intangible factors are undoubtedly of immense importance, it is also true that in terms of history, culture and language both countries have very close ties with many other states as well. The United States is peopled by many continental Europeans as well as by those of British stock. Likewise Britain has particularly strong ethnic links with countries like Australia, New Zealand, Canada and South Africa. Why then has the 'special relationship', until recently at least, only applied to relations between Britain and the United States? The answer would seem to derive from the fact that closeness is not the same thing as importance or significance. And the term 'special relationship' seems to imply this extra ingredient of importance. For Britain it is undoubtedly true that since 1940 at least the relationship with the United States has been 'overwhelmingly more important' than with any other state. Similarly, although the relationship may have been less crucial to the United States it would nevertheless seem to be true that Britain has invariably been regarded as its closest ally.[21]

The question of importance is taken by some to indicate that interest is the major *raison d'être* of the partnership rather than history or culture. For those who hold this view each is thought to regard its relations with the other as being closer than with any third country because of the awareness of the mutuality of interests between them and in particular the contribution each can make to the other's security.

Whether history, language, sentiment *or* common interests are at the root of the 'special relationship' is, however, something of a sterile argument. Both have clearly played their part. The exceptional nature of the relationship is in itself a product of the particular mix of these factors rather than any one on its own. A common outlook towards the world and common values which derive from history and culture have helped to produce what one writer describes as 'a shared capacity to see the elements of common interests in whatever international storms the time may bring'.[22] Thus political calculation has often provided the compelling impetus for cooperation while a common history and culture have contributed to the interpretation of that calculation and provided an added dimension of warmth and intimacy which has helped to cement the alliance.

This 'shared capacity' has been particularly evident in the defence relationships between the two countries with which this book deals.

The term 'defence relationship' is also one which needs some clarification. In general it may be said to cover the myriad of different forms of cooperation in those areas relating to the security of Britain and the United States. It could no doubt be argued that almost every aspect of joint diplomatic and economic policy has been, in part at least, designed to enhance the security interests of each state and as such could quite properly be included in a study of this sort. This was obviously the case during the Second World War when almost every aspect of Anglo-American relations was directly or indirectly geared to achieve the war aims of defeating the Axis powers. There is a need, however, to be more specific. Although an attempt will be made to deal with some of the more important areas of the wider relationship as far as they relate to the security of both countries, attention in the main will be centred more sharply on four main areas of defence relations. These include:

(a) *The Political/Strategic Relationship* involving discussions and negotiations, particularly at the highest levels, designed to coordinate and harmonize the strategic policies of both countries (bilaterally and within a multilateral context like NATO).

(b) *The Technical Relationship* covering the exchange of information and cooperation in the procurement of conventional, chemical, biological and nuclear weapons and associated equipment.

(c) *The Operational Relationship* between the Services, Defence Departments and the Intelligence agencies, involving the conduct of military and security activity in both peace and war.

(d) *The Economic/Commercial Relationship* involving financial assistance and sales of defence equipment and weapons between the two countries.

Some of the wide range of contacts included under these headings have been the result of formal arrangements and binding agreements between the two governments. Many others, however, have been of a more informal nature. Indeed one of the characteristic features of the 'special' defence partnership (as of the 'special relationship' generally) has been the preponderance of 'gentlemen's agreements', 'secret unwritten arrangements', and 'Memoranda of Understanding' (MOUs) which have reflected the close personal working relationship which has been established. Nowhere was this more true than during the Second World War when the 'special relationship' in its purest form was developed.

The Introduction deals with the evolution of the partnership both before and after the United States entered the war in December 1941. The first section charts the development of the 'common-law alliance' between the two countries before Pearl Harbour. During this period a 'gradual mixing-up process' took place with cooperation involving such things as the lend-lease arrangements; the destroyers-for-bases agreement; the Tizard mission; the joint Staff Talks; and the beginnings of intelligence collaboration: all of which laid the foundations for the 'full marriage' to follow. The second part of the Introduction describes the formation of the joint war machine which developed rapidly after the American entry into the war. This began with the 'Arcadia' conference and the confirmation of the 'Germany-first' strategy, followed by the formation of the Combined Chiefs of Staff and the Combined Boards which together played such a crucial role in the direction and coordination of the allied war effort. By considering briefly the war against Germany, the war against Japan and two specific areas of Anglo-American cooperation in the fields of Atomic Energy and Intelligence, the attempt is made to highlight the extraordinary degree of cooperation which was achieved: 'the most complete unification of military effort ever achieved by two allied states.'[23] Despite the remarkable nature of the partnership, however, the Introduction also identifies various differences and strains which existed in certain areas (especially in the war against Japan). 'Special' the relationship may have been, but it is argued that this should not obscure the fact that Britain and the United States remained separate sovereign states whose interests could and did differ and conflict as well as coincide.[24]

A certain amount of friction also characterized the immediate post-war period. Chapter 1 considers the rapid break-up of the integrated war machine in 1945-6 with the abrupt cancellation by the United States of lend-lease, the winding up of the Combined Boards and the unilateral ending of nuclear cooperation by the United States. The chapter goes on, however, to describe the restoration of the military relationship with the forging of a wide range of defence links as the Cold War gathered momentum and a growing identity of view was established between the two countries about the Soviet Union and the emerging threat to their security. Despite this emerging partnership, one area in particular in the late 1940s remained outside the trends towards a greater harmonization of defence policies. This was the field of atomic energy. Despite minor amendments to the 1946 McMahon Act little was done to restore the range of co-operation which had existed in the wartime Manhattan project.

Chapter 2 considers the period from 1950 to 1956 when there were important movements towards even greater cooperation but also difficulties which at the end of the period shook the bilateral alliance to its foundations. In the early 1950s the pattern of progress towards greater intimacy in a range of defence fields, established in the late 1940s, was continued. Gradually, however, as the chapter attempts to show, problems arose in various areas with the difficulties over the recognition of China; the nuclear question during the Korean War; different interpretations over the Indo-China War; the EDC problem; and misgivings over the Baghdad Pact. The worst of these differences came with the traumatic clash over the Suez invasion in November 1956. Such was the hostility engendered by the crisis that the alliance between the two states which had been so carefully built up since the Second World War came close to collapse. Despite these areas of friction culminating with Suez, ironically, the one area of co-operation which had proved so difficult since 1946 began to show signs of improvement in the mid-1950s. In 1954 the McMahon Act was further amended, opening up, to a much greater extent than before, the flow of information on the characteristics of nuclear weapons and laying the foundations for more far-reaching legislation later.

Chapter 3 describes how, after Suez, this cooperation in the nuclear field became an important symbol of the desire by both countries to mend their fences. Important agreements followed the Bermuda and Washington Conferences in 1957 which helped to recreate the atmosphere of trust and spawn other agreements and a closer working partnership between the respective defence communities. The chapter also describes how the renewed intimacy was demonstrated by operational cooperation between the British and American Armed Forces in 1958 (with the landings in Lebanon and Jordan) in the very region where the partnership had recently so nearly foundered. Despite these close and intimate ties which had been forged by the late 1950s frictions and difficulties still remained. The chapter discusses the Skybolt crisis and tries to show that despite the favourable 'solution' reached at the Nassau Conference in December 1962, the growing disparity in power and diverging interests which were becoming evident between the two states at this time provided pointers to the future of the bilateral relationship.

The gradual cooling of Anglo-American relations in general during the middle and late 1960s is dealt with in Chapter 4. Despite the wide spectrum of cooperation, in the defence field as in other areas of the relationship difficulties were occurring with increasing frequency. Problems arose over such issues as the MLF and ANF, the war in Vietnam and the decision by Britain to withdraw most of her military forces from the east of Suez region.

Chapter 5 charts the continuation of this erosion in the intimacy of the partnership in the 1970s. Attempts were made in the early 1970s to restore relations but the continuing divergence of interests and increasing inequality between the partners helped to further slacken the bonds between the two countries as the decade progressed. As the US became more and more preoccupied with great-power problems such as relations with the Soviet Union and China as well as ending her disastrous war in Vietnam and the growing domestic difficulties with which she had to deal, so the close relationship with Britain must have seemed less and less important to American interests. For her part Britain had her own preoccupations, including severe economic problems and the determination to join the EEC after the two French vetoes in the 1960s. The chapter tries to show that as a consequence the attention of both countries tended to be deflected away from the traditional post-war priority given to relations with each other. In the defence field, this relative weakening of the bilateral relationship was reflected in such things as Britain's active role in the Eurogroup, her contribution to the creation of the Independent European Programme Group (IEPG), and the increasing collaboration with other European countries in the procurement of weapons systems. It is argued that the United States has also demonstrated a growing interest in dealing with the Western European states as a whole, especially over the question of burden-sharing in the alliance and the 'two-way-street' in weapon purchases.

Chapter 5, however, goes on to suggest that, despite the erosion of the defence relationship in certain areas, cooperation in a number of other important aspects of defence has continued throughout the 1970s as well. In the nuclear and chemical warfare fields, laser technology and intelligence, collaboration remains very close indeed. The chapter also argues that in many other areas, including the Services and defence communities generally, the long-standing close and intimate ties have been largely unaffected by the changes in Anglo-American relations in general. As such the chapter concludes that this residual defence partnership stands out as one of the few remaining symbols of the 'special relationship' of the past.

The final chapter reflects on the Anglo-American defence relationship over the period covered and considers the prospects for future cooperation. In general it is argued that defence relations have mirrored the trends in other areas of the relationship between the two countries. It is also suggested, however, that there have been times when defence has been somewhat out of line with the wider relationship and even that certain areas of military cooperation have on occasions been out of tune with the more general defence relationship itself. On the basis of a discussion of the advantages and disadvantages of defence collaboration the chapter suggests that on balance the benefits seem to have outweighed the difficulties for both states; although undoubtedly Britain has gained more and the relationship has, as a consequence, been regarded as relatively more important in Britain than in the United States.

Chapter 6 concludes by considering whether the bilateral defence partnership will erode further than it has done already to parallel more closely certain trends in Anglo-American relations in general and the possible future movement towards greater integration in Europe. As nuclear cooperation has been something of a barometer of defence cooperation as well as one of the most important areas of preferential treatment in the relationship some attention is given to the contemporary debate about the replacement of the Polaris component of Britain's nuclear deterrent as a pointer to the future. The chapter suggests that although Anglo-French cooperation may be possible and may in fact occur in some form in the future, nevertheless, the scale of existing cooperation with the United States and the likelihood of the purchase of another American missile to replace Polaris suggests that both governments regard close ties as enhancing their security interests. It is argued, therefore, that in the nuclear field, as well as in certain other areas of military policy, a 'special' residual defence relationship will continue in the 1980s and beyond. Such a relationship, it is argued, is seen by the British government in traditional terms as being complementary (rather than in opposition) to Britain's role in Europe.

John Baylis

Acknowledgements

This book arose out of a chapter I wrote in 1977 on 'The Anglo-American Relationship in Defence'. The chapter whetted my appetite for more research in a field which seemed to me to be of great importance, particularly in the light of the growing concentration of Britain's defence effort in Europe. The subject has been dealt with, in passing, in other books but not in the direct way I thought it ought to be covered. This work is in no sense a definitive study – it is an early contribution which in time I hope will be replaced by other more detailed and authoritative accounts. If it leads to other works on the subject, however critical of the present book, it will have achieved an important objective.

A number of individuals and institutions have been of enormous assistance to me in my research. I would like to express my thanks to my colleagues in the Department of International Politics at Aberystwyth who have had to put up with what must have seemed my rather boring ramblings on the subject. In particular I am grateful to Professor Ieuan John, Robbie Purnell, Brian Porter, Pete Wright and Ken Booth for their comments and insights in discussions on various themes covered by the book; to David Steeds who read the Introductory Chapter and made a number of invaluable suggestions on various improvements; and above all to John Garnett who not only listened with patience at times when I was preoccupied with various themes but who also helped refine my thoughts in frequent dialogues. The help of my colleagues has been invaluable but the mistakes and inadequacies of the book remain my own.

I would also like to express my debt to the following individuals with whom I have either corresponded or had the privilege of an interview: Dr Andrew Pierre; Dr C.J. Bartlett; Professor Peter Nailor; Professor Margaret Gowing; Admiral of the Fleet the Lord Hill-Norton, GCB; General Sir Harry Tuzo; Air Vice-Marshal S.W.B. Menaul, CB, CBE, DFC, AFC; Michael G. Macdonald and John R. Miley of the American Embassy; Jay E. Hines (Command Historian at RAF Mildenhall); John Roper, MP; Henry Stanhope (*The Times*) and Peter Kellner (*The Sunday Times*). In particular I wish to thank Mr Harold Macmillan for an interview which ranged widely over relevant issues during his period in office. The experience was one which I shall long remember. I also wish to thank those many other people who have helped but who prefer to remain anonymous.

The author also wishes to express his gratitude to the HMSO and owners of the Churchill copyright for permission to reproduce copyright material. I must also thank the Library Staffs in the Hugh Owen Library, UCW, Aberystwyth; the National Library of Wales; the National Defence College,

Latimer; the cuttings libraries at Chatham House and the International Institute for Strategic Studies. In particular a special word of gratitude is due to Jane Davis who has given up a great deal of her time in an uncomplaining and always cheerful way to assist with some of the research for the book. She has also compiled the index for the book. Thanks are also due to the following secretaries who have typed various drafts of the manuscript; Kay Critchley, Marian Weston, and in particular Doreen Hamer who has borne the brunt of the task.

Above all I must thank my wife Marion for her understanding and tolerance in enduring my frequent absences and changing moods while at the same time adjusting to her new role as mother of our newly-arrived daughter, Emma.

Aberystwyth
September 1979

John Baylis

The author and publishers wish to thank the following who have kindly given permission for the use of copyright material:

Cassell Ltd for the extract from a letter by Sir Winston Churchill; the Controller of Her Majesty's Stationery Office for extracts from *The Central Policy Review Staff Review of Overseas Representation* (1977) and other government publications; Hamish Hamilton Ltd for the quotations from *Allies of a Kind: The United States, Britain and the War against Japan* by Christopher Thorne; Michael Joseph Ltd for an extract from *The Labour Government 1964–70* by Harold Wilson.

List of Abbreviations

ABM	Anti-ballistic Missile
ALCM	Air-launched Cruise Missile
ANF	Atlantic Nuclear Force
BAOR	British Army of the Rhine
BCSO	British Central Scientific Office
BDSW	British Defence Staff Washington
BSC	British Security Coordination
CIA	Central Intelligence Agency
CIGS	Chief of the Imperial General Staff
COS	Chief(s) of Staff
CPC	Combined Policy Committee
CINCEASTLANT	Commander in Chief Eastern Atlantic
CINCWESTLANT	Commander in Chief Western Atlantic
DIA	Defence Intelligence Agency
ECM	Electronic Counter Measures
EDC	European Defence Community
FBI	Federal Bureau of Investigation
GC & CS	Government Code and Cipher School
GCHQ	Government Communications Headquarters
IEPG	Independent European Programme Group
IISS	International Institute for Strategic Studies
IRBM	Intermediate Range Ballistic Missile
JAEC	Joint Atomic Energy Commission
MAGIC	Code-name for the intelligence derived from the American ability to decipher Japanese codes in the Second World War
MARV	Manoeuvrable Re-entry Vehicle
MIRV	Multiple Independently Targetable Re-entry Vehicle
MLF	Multilateral Force
MoU	Memorandum of Understanding
MRV	Multiple Re-entry Vehicle
NID	Naval Intelligence Directorate
NPT	Non-proliferation Treaty
NRO	National Reconnaissance Office
NSA	National Security Agency
OSRD	Office of Scientific Research and Development
OSS	Office of Strategic Services
PES	Polaris Executive Staff
SALT	Strategic Arms Limitation Talks

SEAC	South-East Asia Command
SIS	Special Intelligence Service
SLBM	Submarine-launched Ballistic Missiles
SPO	Special Projects Office
ULTRA	Code-name for British operation to decipher enemy codes and distribute the intelligence derived to the appropriate headquarters during the Second World War
USAEC	United States Atomic Energy Commission
VTOL	Vertical Take-off and Landing

Introduction: The Wartime Relationship

> . . . any enquiry into Anglo-American relations during the Second World War must lead in the first place to a recognition of the remarkable nature of the partnership that was then achieved. . . . Whether the particular subject for examination is grand strategy, the economic substructure on which the war-effort was based, or an inter-Allied Command in the field like that of Eisenhower in Europe, what stands out initially is the attainment of 'a much higher degree of co-operation and unforced fusion than had ever before existed between two sovereign states.'[1]
>
> CHRISTOPHER THORNE

The creation of the 'Common-law Alliance'

For most observers the quintessence of the 'special relationship' between Britain and the United States is the partnership in arms developed during the Second World War. In terms of the intimacy of personal relationships, the strategic direction of forces, the allocation of war materials, the coordination of communications, and the cooperation between the armed forces and intelligence agencies, most writers agree that the wartime alliance between the two states was not only very close but perhaps unique in the history of war.[2] Although the full range and depth of the partnership only developed after the Japanese attack on Pearl Harbour on 7 December 1941, the first cautious steps were taken in the late 1930s and continued after war broke out in September 1939 when the United States remained officially neutral.

Discussions between the two countries about defence programmes, equipment and staff plans went back at least to the early months of 1937.[3] Notable amongst the early contacts were the Ingersoll Mission to London in January 1938,[4] followed by the secret visit of Commander Hampton to the United States in May 1939,[5] which marked the starting-point of limited Anglo-American naval conversations in the period before war broke out. In the summer of 1939 King George VI also visited the United States and Roosevelt outlined the help he planned to give Britain in the event of war. The President talked of an Atlantic patrol which would relieve Britain of responsibilities along a radius of 1000 miles.[6] Significantly in terms of subsequent negotiations which took place over American destroyers in 1940, President Roosevelt also indicated an interest in establishing US bases in Newfoundland, Bermuda, Jamaica, St Lucia, Antigua and Trinidad.

Despite the promising signs from Britain's point of view, however, military cooperation with the United States had yet to become a reality when war broke out in September. Between Hitler's invasion of Poland and the Japanese attack on Pearl Harbour American public opinion remained impaled on what H.G. Nicholas has called 'an agony of indecision' as strong isolationist sentiments prevailed in Congress.[7] It was, to a certain extent, the President's own indecision as well as his concern to take public opinion along with him which led to the adoption of a gradual cautious policy in the field of military collaboration with Britain.[8]

This caution was illustrated by Roosevelt's reaction to British attempts during the latter half of 1939 and most of 1940 to get information about various items of American military equipment. A number of enquiries, for example, were made about the Norden bombsight which, it was thought, would greatly improve the effectiveness of the RAF.[9] On 25 August 1939, Prime Minister Neville Chamberlain wrote to the President asking for details about the bomb-sight. In reply, however, he received 'a non-committal answer'.[10] To show British good faith, Churchill, as First Lord of the Admiralty, and a passionate believer in the need for Anglo-American cooperation, wrote to Roosevelt in mid-October 1939 offering information about Britain's ASDIC apparatus in anti-submarine warfare. 'We should be quite ready to tell you about our ASDIC methods whenever you feel they would be of use to the US Navy and are sure the secret will go no further,' he told Roosevelt.[11] Despite the formal request from the US Naval Attaché in London in early December for the ASDIC information and Lord Halifax's suggestion that the bombsight might be exchanged in return, Norden remained 'one of the most jealously guarded secrets' of the US Services throughout most of 1940.[12] It was only in September 1940 when the Battle of Britain was at its height and when Britain had succeeded in stabilizing her own automatic bombsight that the US replacement of the Norden bombsight, the Sperry bombsight, was released to the British Air Commission.

Despite the US caution over such things as the Norden bombsight the areas of Anglo-American cooperation widened gradually but surely during late 1939 and 1940. As one of the official British historians, J.R.M. Butler, points out, 'the world now knows to what extraordinary lengths, inconceivable from the standpoint of the traditional law of nations, President Roosevelt could stretch assistance to one belligerent without provoking the active hostility of the other'.[13] In November 1939, after a long struggle in Congress, the President finally managed to secure a revision of the Neutrality Act which lifted the arms embargo and substituted in its place 'cash-and-carry' arrangements. This revision was particularly beneficial to Britain (and France). It was followed by the setting up of the British Purchasing Commission under a Scots-Canadian, A.B. Purvis, who, until his death in August 1941, developed a close and extremely fruitful liaison with the US Secretary of the Treasury, Morgenthau, in the vital field of supply.[14] In many respects the Morgenthau-Purvis combination during this period was the forerunner of the Anglo-American Combined Boards which were to play such a vital role in the joint war effort later. Significantly, President Roosevelt was able to use this vital link to turn over surplus weapons to Britain after the losses at Dunkirk in May and June 1940.[15]

During the dark days of Dunkirk, Winston Churchill, now as Prime Minister, saw American assistance as the only hope of victory, or, indeed survival.[16] Not surprisingly this was a view also shared by the British Chiefs of Staff. In their appreciation on 25 May 1940 the COS based their hopes for the future on the assumption that Britain 'could count on the full economic and financial support of the United States of America, possibly extending to active participation on our side'.[17] Churchill himself had been one of the earliest to realize the importance of Anglo-American cooperation and in his correspondence with Roosevelt from September 1939, as Naval Person to POTUS (President of the United States), he constantly urged greater assistance for Britain. His first telegram as Prime Minister to the President on 15 May contained an impassioned appeal for what Britain wanted immediately. In particular he asked for forty to fifty over-age destroyers to sustain Britain's effort in the Battle of the Atlantic. Faced with the threat of invasion and the vulnerability of Britain's shipping lanes to German U-boat attack, Churchill saw the need for the destroyers as a 'matter of life or death'.[18] Legal difficulties and problems of public and Congressional opinion, however, still made the simple transfer of even over-age destroyers difficult for Roosevelt to sanction. The Prime Minister nevertheless kept up a barrage of requests throughout the summer and finally managed to circumvent the constitutional difficulties by offering the United States the kind of base facilities President Roosevelt had mentioned to the King in July 1939 in return for the destroyers. The 'destroyers-for-bases' agreement was concluded on 2 September 1940 and gave the United States air and naval base rights in the form of 99-year leases in Newfoundland, Bermuda, the Bahamas, St Lucia, Trinidad and British Guiana. In return Britain received the destroyers she needed.[19]

For some the agreement was seen as 'a hard bargain for Britain,'[20] but as the official record of the war cabinet shows, the arrangement was 'not looked at merely from the point of view of the exchange of destroyers . . . for certain facilities by way of naval and air bases'.[21] It had much greater significance. It was generally thought that it would 'prove to be the first step in constituting an Anglo-Saxon bloc or indeed a decisive point in history'.[22] With an election in November, President Roosevelt was able to justify the agreement as enhancing the national defence of the United States.[23] Nor was this merely a rationalization. As with most of the other areas of cooperation, American interests were very much the determining factor.

The sale of destroyers to a belligerent power, however, was hardly a neutral act and, from Britain's point of view, it represented a significant move by the United States to joining the war on her side. Churchill emphasized the inexorable momentum of the two states becoming more and more closely aligned in his speech to the House of Commons on 20 August 1940. 'This process', he said, 'means that . . . the British Empire and the United States will have to be somewhat mixed-up together.'[24] He emphasized, however, that, he did not 'view the process with any misgivings'.[25] Lord Lothian, British ambassador in Washington from August 1939 until his death in December 1940, likewise saw the significance of the agreement. For him it involved an important American acceptance of the British-based fleet as the outer line of defence of the United States. Hence the need to strengthen the British fleet with the destroyers. Lord Lothian saw the offer of bases in the British transatlantic islands, on the other hand, as a recognition by Britain that these islands were 'the inner circle of American defence'.[26]

The 'mixing-up' process, which Churchill referred to, was also taking place in other areas as well. Agreements were reached between the Air Forces of the two countries on the training of air crews in the United States in September 1940, and arrangements were made to repair damaged British warships in the US.[27] Of even greater importance, however, was the start of Anglo-American military staff talks on the formation of a joint grand strategy in the event of American entry into the war. In mid-August 1940 a military mission headed by Admiral Ghormley (the US Naval attaché in London), General Emmons (of the Army Air Corps) and General Strong (of the War Department), was sent to London ostensibly to sit on a committee of the 'Standardization of Arms'.[28] The talks which took place were essentially exploratory but they ranged much wider than just the standardization of weapons. In fact they covered the whole field of strategy with the British deciding 'on a degree of frankness with the Americans', which, the official historian, Duncan Hall, suggests, 'was probably unprecedented in relations between a belligerent and a neutral'.[29]

As a result of these talks, Admiral Stark, the US Chief of Naval Operations, produced his famous memorandum on the 12 November recommending full military cooperation with Britain should the United States be drawn into the war.[30] 'Plan Dog', as the Stark Memorandum was known, advised the President to authorize confidential and formal conversations with the British. In response President Roosevelt agreed to secret staff talks to be held in Washington between 29 January and 29 March. At this conference between the military authorities of both countries, plan ABC-1 was produced which laid down the grand strategy to be followed in the event of American entry into the war.[31] Significantly in terms of future disputes the main recommendation of ABC-1 was that in the event of a conflict with both Germany and Japan priority should be given to defeating Germany first. The plan also provided for a continuation of Anglo-American talks after the conference ended through the creation of military missions which would facilitate both an exchange of information and where necessary a coordination of plans. In line with this recommendation the British Joint Staff Mission was established in Washington with the US Special Observer Group in London which provided the basis for the Combined Chiefs of Staff Committee which was set up shortly after Pearl Harbour.

The Washington Staff talks were not the only secret measures being taken in private while the United States remained officially neutral. The 'mixing-up' process was taking place in two other vital areas as well: scientific information and intelligence. Following a visit by a British scientist, Professor A.V. Hill, to Washington in November 1939, a Scientific and Technical Information Mission led by Sir Henry Tizard was sent to the United States in August 1940. Tizard was told to tell the Americans '*everything* that Britain was doing in the scientific field'.[32] Remarkable as this seems, from Churchill's point of view it was clearly very much in Britain's interest to give every possible assistance to the American armed forces to enable them to reach the highest level of technical efficiency possible in as short a time as possible. Consequently, in his famous 'black box', Sir Henry Tizard carried drawings and detailed information on Britain's latest weapons and inventions. During the visit details were released on such things as the cavity magnetron which played such a crucial role in the development of radar, together with other top secret information on jet engines, chemical weapons, ship protection and anti-submarine devices. Nor was this all. Sir Henry Tizard was accompanied by Professor Cockcroft, one of Britain's leading physicists, who took the opportunity to exchange information on uranium research which at this stage was further advanced in Britain than in the United States.[33] Summing up the significance of the Tizard Mission the US Office of Scientific Research claimed that it was 'the most valuable cargo ever brought to the shores of the United States'.[34]

Given that both states saw positive advantages in scientific cooperation it was perhaps not surprising that the Tizard Mission was followed up by more permanent arrangements. During a visit to London by President Roosvelt's personal aide Harry Hopkins in January/February 1941, provisions were made to set up the British Central Scientific Office in Washington with a similar American body in London. The purpose of these offices was to coordinate the whole process of scientific exchange between the two states. According to one of the British official historians, 'from the Spring of 1941 the combination in science, research and development was close and unbroken to the end of the war'.[35]

Apart from secret scientific and technical collaboration, we now know that arrangements were also made in the intelligence field to work closer together during this period of 'constructive non-belligerency'.[36] After the informal and restricted pre-war cooperation between the navies of the two countries,[37] an attempt was made by the Special Intelligence Service (SIS) in June 1940 to extend collaboration by sending Colonel William Stephenson to New York to liaise with the American Intelligence agencies.[38] Prompted by Colonel Stephenson, President Roosevelt dispatched his special envoy, Colonel Donovan, on a visit to London in July 1940. Colonel Donovan had two main tasks: firstly, to assess Britain's determination and ability to continue the war; and secondly, to see if closer cooperation could be arranged between the US Navy Department and the Admiralty on intelligence. On his return he expressed his belief in Britain's resolve to stay in the war and recommended 'a full exchange of intelligence by direct liaison between the two naval intelligence departments'.[39] He also urged that the US consular reports should be made available to the British. His recommendations were 'favourably received' and from mid-August relations between the US Navy representatives in London with various sections of the British Naval Intelligence Directorate (NID) 'became very close'.[40] From September 1940 the President also agreed to British attachés in Washington receiving relevant information from US diplomatic and consular sources.

At the same time that Colonel Donovan was visiting Britain, further progress on intelligence cooperation was made during the 'Standardization of Arms' talks. The President and Prime Minister agreed to the pooling of information on supply and defence programmes and staff plans, 'however secret' the subjects were. In tune with this directive the Army representative on the US delegation revealed the progress his own Service was making on Japanese and Italian ciphers and 'formally proposed to the British Chiefs of Staff that the time had arrived for a free exchange of intelligence'.[41] Britain appears to have been a little slow to respond to this initiative at first but in February 1941 when two FBI officers were sent as pupils to the SIS London office the opportunity was used to advise the US on the important developments which were taking place on Axis ciphers at the Government Code and Cipher School (GC & CS) at Bletchley.[42]

The secret Staff Talks between January and March 1941 also helped to lay the foundations for a more formal intelligence relationship. The military missions created in both capitals were to include intelligence officers from all the Services.[43] For its part the British Joint Staff Mission in Washington was directed to 'maintain constant touch with the plans, operations, intelligence branches of the US Service Departments'.[44]

Important as these foundations were for the future of the joint war effort, the scale of cooperation reached and the value of the intelligence exchanged by December 1941 should not be over-exaggerated. According to the official history of intelligence operations, 'until the American entry into the war' the various activities between the intelligence communities 'added nothing of value to the stock of British intelligence except for the information derived from the exchange of Japanese Sigint between Washington and Whitehall'. It appears at this stage of the war at least, 'Washington still had little to offer'.[45]

At the same time that secret relationships were being established between the Services, scientists and intelligence organs during 1940 and 1941, other more open discussions were taking place about increased financial and material support for Britain's war effort. On 8 December 1940 Churchill sent a letter to the President dealing with the growing seriousness of the U-Boat threat and Britain's desperate need for financial help. Churchill saw it as 'the most important letter' he ever wrote.[46] Roosevelt was profoundly affected by the letter and in one of his 'fire-side chats' to the American people on 29 December he argued that the United States should become 'the arsenal of democracy'.[47] The President employed his famous garden-hose metaphor and launched the idea of lend-lease – of supplying Britain with the materials she needed immediately while postponing payment in kind until after the war ended. Not surprisingly, given the continuing isolationist feelings in the United States at the time, the debate which subsequently took place over the lend-lease bill created 'considerable uproar' which lasted for several months.[48] Once again, however, President Roosevelt portrayed it, not as an altruistic measure, but as an 'Act to Promote the Defense of the United States'. By March 1941, despite the opposition, the bill had passed through Congress with a majority of 317 to 71 in the House and 60 to 31 in the Senate. From Churchill's point of view the Act was of particular importance, not only in playing a crucial role in helping Britain to overcome the dollar-shortage which early wartime purchases in the US had caused, but also in contributing to the growth of the 'fraternal association' by which he put so much store.[49]

Despite lend-lease and the extension of US patrols beyond the 300-mile limit into the mid-Atlantic in April 1941, the United States was still not at war. President Roosevelt remained constrained in his attempts to further collaboration with Britain due partly to his own concern not to move too precipitately and partly to continuing opposition in Congress. As far as the latter was concerned, even after Hitler's attack on the Soviet Union in June and the President's pledge of aid to the USSR, Congress refused to allow those drafted under the Selective Security Act of 1939 to be kept in service for the duration of the existing emergency or to give Roosevelt the right to send them outside the western hemisphere. Even a measure designed to extend their service for eighteen months only passed Congress by a single vote.[50]

Against this background President Roosevelt met the British Prime Minister at Placentia Bay between 9–12 August. Despite the President's concern not to take any further dramatic steps towards belligerency the declaration of the Atlantic Charter highlighted in an important way 'the bonds of interest and principle' that united the two countries.[51] Apart from demonstrating solidarity and lifting British morale at a difficult time, the Conference also gave a further opportunity for the political leaders and Chiefs of Staff not only to get to know each other better but also to continue their discussions on future British strategy against Germany.

By the autumn of 1941, therefore, even before the US entered the war, the two countries had developed what Robert Sherwood refers to as 'a common-law alliance'.[52] There was no formal alliance as such but there was a plethora of public and secret arrangements linking the two states in an increasingly close partnership. In addition to lend-lease and thc Anglo-American Staff talks these arrangements took the form of an exchange of the latest scientific information; the cooperation of military and civilian specialists in both countries; relief for the British navy with the Atlantic patrols by the US fleet; US occupation of Greenland and Iceland; American repair facilities for damaged British warships and the training of RAF pilots and air crews in the United States.

Thus the three months prior to Pearl Harbour saw the United States on 'the verge of war' but with the President unwilling to make the fateful decision and commit the nation to all-out war. The *Greer, Kearny* and *Ruben James* incidents in September and October brought further revisions of the Neutrality Act whereby merchant ships were armed and allowed to sail into war zones. The US Navy was also now free to escort convoys to the British Isles. From President Roosevelt's point of view, however, everything 'short of war' had been done to assist Britain.[53] In the words of Robert Sherwood, 'The President of the United States was now the creature of circumstances which must be shaped not by his own will or his own ingenuity but by the unpredictable determination of his enemies.'[54] President Roosevelt was thus relieved of making the decision to commit the American nation to war by the Japanese attack on Pearl Harbour on 7 December and the German declaration of war four days later.

The Anglo-American war machine

The stimulation of British purchases in the United States, the rearmament undertaken following the National Defence Act of 2 July 1940, and the wide-ranging wartime experience and information provided by Britain, meant that the United States entered the war in late 1941, in some respects, reasonably well-prepared.[55] One of the first tasks, now that both states were in the same boat, was to transform the 'common-law alliance' into a proper marriage of closely interlocking efforts. This process began at the 'Arcadia' Conference in Washington in December 1941 when the two leaders and their military advisers met to consider the joint conduct of the war. At the meeting President Roosevelt and Prime Minister Churchill reaffirmed the priority, established at the earlier Staff talks, of defeating Germany first and enshrined the principle in a document known to the British as WWI and to the Americans as ABC–4/CSI.[56] Building on the foundations of the Military and Supply Missions set up in the period of undeclared war, arrangements were also made to establish a Combined Chiefs of Staff (COS) Committee and a number of Combined Boards. President Roosevelt and Prime Minister Churchill were to retain ultimate control but the Combined

Chiefs of Staff were to exercise a 'general jurisdiction over grand strategic policy in all areas' and the Combined Boards were to deal with the production and supply of the joint war effort as a whole.[57]

The Combined Chiefs of Staff Committee was designed to try to overcome 'the vexatious problem which introduces itself into all attempts to achieve unity of command in time of war': the problem of national responsibility.[58] The Combined COS Committee solved the difficulty by making British and American commanders accountable to a joint body while preserving the chain of responsibility intact. The principle of unity of command at the theatre level was also achieved on General Marshall's insistence by the appointment of a supreme commander of one nationality and deputies of the other.

The Combined Chiefs of Staff Committee and the attempts to achieve unity of command were only part, however, of a much larger integrated structure emanating largely from the 'Arcadia' Conference. Attempts to coordinate allied strategy required parallel attempts to coordinate production and supply. As one writer puts it, 'strategy determined production and supply determined strategy in an endless process of interaction'.[59] Following the Macready Plan[60] of 13 January 1942 a number of Combined Boards were established which included: the Combined Raw Materials Board; the Munitions Assignment Board; and the Anglo-American Shipping Adjustment Board. This was followed in June 1942 with 'the coping stone of the whole structure', when the Combined Production and Resources Board was set up.[61] The main purpose of these Boards was to bring together two or more departments of the British and American governments concerned with the joint war effort. In the words of the official historians, ' "the Boards" were a means of gearing together the two national administrations in order to deal more efficiently with matters of common interest'.[62]

To service the vast array of permanent committees, missions and Boards, which were rapidly being set up in the United States, large numbers of British officials crossed the Atlantic. From early 1942 onwards with the expansion of the war effort the numbers increased considerably, creating a sort of lesser Whitehall overseas. According to one commentator, 'it was as though the British government was functioning in duplicate on both sides of the Atlantic'.[63] One of the results of this was that the working and personal relationships achieved by British and American officials became increasingly close and informal. In many instances they even shared common telephone switchboards.

Such close personal ties were especially important in the overall structure of cooperation which developed. From the highest political level down through the Chiefs of Staff and field commanders to the work of innumerable committees a degree of friendship and intimacy characterized working relationships. The close partnership between the two leaders in particular was of crucial importance and set the tone and pattern for the whole joint war effort. Following the Washington Conference in January

1942 Churchill emphasized the closeness of the partnership when he cabled his Cabinet colleagues. 'We live here', he told them, 'as a big family in the greatest intimacy and informality. . . .'[64] Similarly at the highest military level the relationship between General George Marshall, the US Chief of Staff and Field Marshal Sir John Dill, the Chief British military representative in Washington until his death in November 1944, made an important contribution to the success of the Combined Chiefs of Staff Committee.[65] According to Henry Stimson it was their harmonious combination which made it possible for the Combined Chiefs to act 'not as a mere collecting point for individual rivalries between services and nations but as an executive committee for the prosecution of global war'.[66] Such personal ties were duplicated many times over on both the military and civilian sides, making the smooth and efficient working of the allied war effort possible. As such the Anglo-American war machine resembled a huge interlocking committee that never stopped meeting.[67]

Although the degree of cooperation achieved represented what one writer calls 'an integration of effort of truly astonishing proportions',[68] this should not be allowed to obscure the fact that important differences of interest at times produced bitter disputes, personal clashes and significant disagreements during the war. Neither should it be forgotten that as the war progressed the changing balance of strength between the two allies meant that Britain increasingly became the junior partner and the relationship appeared less 'special' than in the period of greater equality between 1941 and 1943. Christopher Thorne has ably summed up the need for a more balanced view of the wartime relationship in his study *Allies of a Kind*, in which he argues that 'the fact that the relationship between the UK and America . . . was at times a remarkably close one can be established without the need to wander off however well-meaningly into mythology'.[69] The truth of these remarks can be illustrated by considering various aspects of the combined war effort.

The war against Germany

The over-riding cohesiveness of the alliance together with important but secondary tensions was very much a feature of the allied operations against Germany. Both before and after American entry into the war, the priority of defeating Germany established at the Washington Staff talks in early 1940, was consistently pursued by both allies. There were, however, criticisms of this priority especially from those in US Naval circles who favoured a Pacific-first strategy. Even General Marshall himself on one occasion threatened to reverse the priority.[70] There were also serious disputes, even between those British and American war planners advocating the defeat of Germany first, over how the objective ought to be achieved.

The re-affirmation at 'Arcadia' in December 1941/January 1942 of the Germany-first principle involved the acceptance by both allies that a defensive war should be fought in the Pacific. The objective for 1942 was to be 'closing and tightening the ring around Germany, by sustaining the Russian front, arming and supporting Turkey, building up strength in the Middle East and gaining possession of the whole North African coast'.[71] The occupation of North Africa ('Super GYMNAST') in particular was accepted as the priority operation for 1942 while a large-scale land offensive against Germany was seen as unlikely before at least 1943.[72]

Despite this agreement, however, the period following the 'Arcadia' meeting saw the emergence of disputes between British and American military planners over the priorities established at the Conference. In April General Marshall and Harry Hopkins arrived in London with a memorandum advocating a more direct approach to the defeat of Germany through a major cross-channel attack ('ROUND-UP') in 1943 with perhaps a smaller preliminary assault ('SLEDGEHAMMER') in 1942.[73] In the Marshall plan the invasion of North Africa had no place because it would divert resources from the most important objective of striking at Germany directly as soon as possible. The two positions represented in the 'Arcadia' plan (WWI) and the Marshall memorandum reflected divergent views of strategy which were to cause friction in the Combined Chiefs of Staff meetings and in the major conferences at Casablanca, Washington, Quebec and Cairo during the next two years. WWI symbolized the British preference based on past experience and limited resources for a cautious peripheral strategy. The Marshall plan, however, highlighted the American interest in bringing their superior resources to bear in a concentrated direct effort against the enemy. In this debate the British Chiefs felt that American ideas were 'simply misconceived and impractical'.[74] The Americans on the other hand saw the British preference for North American operations as being due to political rather than military motives. Britain was seen by some to be more interested in protecting British interest in the Near East and Mediterranean than in defeating Germany.[75] The result was a certain exasperation and distrust which often dogged the discussions within the Combined COS Committee.

Despite the tension, however, which these differences caused, President Roosevelt's unwavering commitment to the Germany-first strategy and his willingness to overrule his own military chiefs kept the alliance together.[76] Indeed as a result of the President's support for the invasion of North Africa a combined Anglo-American team was set up in London to plan for 'Operation TORCH' which resulted in a much greater integration of operational military planning than had hitherto been achieved. The operation presented 'quite exceptional difficulties' which required a very high degree of cooperation between the military services of both countries.[77] Naval collaboration, air support, land operations and logistic services all had to be closely coordinated to achieve the successful landings. Thus the planning process and the conduct of the operation itself, which began on 8 November 1942, helped to create the kind of integrated team work so important in future combined operations, particularly for D-Day and the final assault on Germany in June 1944.

Successful as 'TORCH' was in laying the foundations for more efficient joint operations, disagreements between the allies continued to be a feature of strategic debate. Differences over landings in Sicily, Italy, Southern France and the Balkans at times disrupted the harmonious working relationship. Divergencies likewise occurred during the invasion of Europe, including the famous disagreement between the Supreme Allied Commander General Eisenhower and General Montgomery over whether to pursue a broad-front advance or a narrow thrust to the heart of Germany.[78] Indeed controversy over the balance between sectors on General Eisenhower's command at the 'Argonaut' Conference in January 1945 was described by some of those present as 'the most acrimonious dispute between the Combined Chiefs of Staff' during the entire war.[79]

Such clashes, however, on particular issues, important as they were, do not alter the fact that there remained on the whole a harmony of basic purpose between the two allies throughout the war against Germany. A close working relationship was achieved between naval forces of the two countries especially during the Battle of the Atlantic and between the air forces in the combined bomber offensive.[80] Particularly close cooperation was likewise developed between the military planning staffs and the air, sea and land forces involved in combined operations from 'TORCH' to the Normandy landings ('OVERLORD'). In the planning and execution of 'OVERLORD' in particular the full depth and variety of collaboration was demonstrated. The scale and complexity of the operations involved in the landings are clearly expressed in the account contained in the Official History:

> The numbers of men and quantities of material involved in the first phase, were impressive even for the Second World War. In the event, 185,000 men and 19,000 vehicles were carried across the Channel on D-Day and D + 1, in over 4,000 landing ships and craft, supported by some 1,300 merchant ships and ancillary vessels, and over 1,200 warships of all types, including seven battleships and twenty-three cruisers. Another 19,000 men were carried by air, by a force of 1,087 transport aircraft and 804 gliders – some 10,000 Allied aircraft supported the landings in various operations. . . . At the end of the first eleven days, 641,170 British, Canadian and Americans had been landed in North West France. The operation dwarfed all others hitherto undertaken – the invasion of North Africa and Sicily, the landings at Salerno and Anzio, the assaults on the Pacific islands. It was indeed the greatest conjunct operation in the history of war.[81]

The war against Japan

A much greater strain on the alliance came from the war that was conducted by the two countries against Japan.[82] In Europe, despite the gradual change in the balance of strength, both allies were able to make a major contribution to the combined effort. In the Pacific, South and South-East Asia, however, Britain's junior status was much more apparent and American predominance led to the natural desire to decide policies unilaterally. The strains which appeared, however, were not only due to the much greater contribution being made by the United States. They were also the product of different interests as well. For Britain the desire to defeat Germany was all-important and operations in the Far East were very much a secondary concern which should not be allowed to divert attention from the major task. To the United States, however, although 'Germany-first' carried the day, her interests in the Pacific and the humiliation of Pearl Harbour meant that the defeat of Japan was in practice a more demanding priority than it was to Britain. For Admiral King and the navy, as well as for many Republicans, it continued to the the first priority and frequent attempts (in many cases successful) were made to divert resources to the Pacific theatre. Indeed by the end of 1943 the 'Germany-first' principle had been modified to such an extent that 1,878,152 Americans were employed in the war against Japan while 1,810,356 were engaged in the fight against Germany.[83] Such was the concern in Britain over Washington's distribution of its forces that at the end of 1944 General Ismay wrote: 'I am afraid that our American friends – much as I like them – have only paid lip-service to the fundamental principle that Germany is public enemy No. 1 and they have already committed far too much a proportion of their available resources to the Pacific.'[84]

As in the Mediterranean there was also a great deal of residual suspicion in the United States about British post-war motives in the conduct of operations in South-East Asia. From the American point of view the main avenue of advance following Japanese successes was through northern Burma to re-open the route to China. The survival of China was seen as vital for the ultimate defeat of Japan. The British were seen to be much more interested in the reconquest of their colonial possessions. This could involve by-passing Burma or campaigning in Burma as a stepping-stone to South-East Asia.[85] As with the bitter controversy between Roosevelt and Churchill over India in 1942, the question of colonialism was at the heart of the dispute between the allies in South-East Asia. While the Americans looked north from Burma, the British looked south. Thus in the words of Robert Sherwood, 'in South-East Asia . . . the British and the Americans were fighting two wars for different purposes'.[86] These different interests were reflected in the bitter controversies which ranged at the major conferences in 1943 and 1944 and in the intervals between them.

The underlying divergence between the American emphasis on China and the British concern for Malaya and Singapore was epitomized by the affair of the 'Axiom' and Stilwell missions in early 1944.[87] In January, Lord Louis Mountbatten, Supreme Commander of the South-East Asian Command (SEAC) developed a new plan, 'Axiom', for operations in his command area. In line with previous British plans, 'Axiom' was designed to accelerate an advance to the China coast through operations against Sumatra and Malaya. From Mountbatten's point of view problems with Chiang K'ai-shek and the terrain made it difficult to establish overland communications with China through northern Burma in the foreseeable future. Such an overland route to China, however, had remained a basic premise of American policy since 1942 and work on such a route had pre-occupied Mountbatten's deputy, General Stilwell, since early 1943. Stilwell argued that Mountbatten's plan was deficient because it involved a frontal assault by way of Sumatra and required the construction of new air bases to support the operation. His alternative plan, however, to establish overland communications with China via northern Burma and Yunan, involved in contrast a flanking movement which would utilize existing air fields in India.[88] The clash of views led Mountbatten to send a mission in early 1944 to London and Washington to argue the case for 'Axiom' while Stilwell went over his Supreme Commander's head to send a group of his own to put his arguments to the Joint Chiefs in Washington. Stilwell's case, which was subsequently endorsed by the Joint Chiefs and by the President, was put forcefully by one of his political advisers, John Davies. In a memorandum to Harry Hopkins, Davies summed up the criticisms and suspicions of the British approach which were widely held in the United States at this time:

> S.E.A.C.'s plans for the future heavily discount the importance of China as an ally and the Chinese position on Japan's flank. . . . [They] reinforce the argument that Lord Louis' command is primarily concerned with the re-occupation, under British leadership, of colonial South-East Asia. The main American concern is, of course, to strike the Japanese where it hurts them most. This is not Sumatra and Malaya. It is in East China, Formosa, Manchuria and Japan itself. The quickest and most direct approach to this vital area is straight across Burma and South-East China.[89]

Significantly, by this stage of the war, although Churchill supported the 'Axiom' plan in the face of opposition from Roosevelt and the US Joint Chiefs, the directive which was sent to Mountbatten in June by the Combined Chiefs of Staff reflected to a large extent the American position.[90] Attempts continued to be made to reconcile the two positions but the realities of the predominant American position were increasingly reflected in the decisions which were made.

The 'Axiom' affair was symptomatic of the strain and suspicions which bedevilled Anglo-American relations in most of their operations against Japan. Although there were some positive aspects it was the troubled and unsettling features of the partnership that left a more noticeable mark still on the Far Eastern scene.[91] In his authoritative study of alliance relations in the war against Japan, Christopher Thorne reveals the extent of the rift. Not only were relations in this specific context 'extremely poor', he argues, but they 'placed a considerable strain upon the wartime alliance as a whole'.[92] In this sense, like Professor Kolko, he views the Anglo-American alliance as being 'an essentially European coalition'.[93] Thorne sees the Far East as an exception to the traditional generalized picture of close harmony between Britain and the United States. 'Neither militarily nor politically . . . did there exist as regards the Far East anything like the degree of collaboration between the two states that was achieved elsewhere.'[94] He argues that personal relationships also suffered. There was a 'lack of any spirit of cameraderie between British and American sections' and there was little of the 'mutual frankness and trust' so evident in military operations in Europe.[95]

Because of this Professor Thorne concludes, quite rightly it would seem, that the strains and difficulties 'amount to more than just a minor flaw in the Anglo-American war-time partnership'. He goes on to suggest that this requires something over and above a passing qualification to be made to that 'hands-across-the-sea' version of the entire relationship, whereby the 'whole course . . . from 1783 to the present day is deemed to consist of persistent even steady progress from mistrust to cordiality; a version which proclaims that, in terms of the twentieth century, the association of the two countries with one another has been solidly based . . . on a foundation of similar, even common policies.'[96] This is a qualification which undoubtedly needs to be kept in mind.

Atomic energy

Although the war against Japan provided one of the most difficult areas of Anglo-American wartime relations, the development of atomic energy which led to the surrender of Japan after the bombing of Hiroshima and Nagasaki on 6 and 9 August 1945 was the product, ironically perhaps, of what proved to be one of the most cooperative ventures of the alliance. Even here, however, there were similar problems to other areas of the wartime relationship especially in the early days of development. The great predominance of the United States in nuclear research and development once the American project got under way and the suspicion of Britain's post-war intentions caused difficulties which for a time led to a breakdown of Anglo-American cooperation.

The first steps towards collaboration in the atomic energy field were taken in the autumn of 1940 when Professor Cockcroft accompanied Sir Henry Tizard to the United States and, as already mentioned, 'the scientific secrets of the two countries were freely exchanged'.[97] During his visit Cockcroft found that work on atomic energy in the United States was several months behind that in Britain. The trauma of war and the publication of the Peierls-Frisch memorandum on the possible construction of 'super-bombs' had led to the setting up of the Maud Committee in Britain in April 1940.[98] The Maud Committee, described by Professor Gowing as 'one of the most effective scientific committees that ever existed',[99] spent fifteen months of intense work which culminated in the production of two reports in July 1941. Copies of these reports and the minutes of the Maud Committee were passed on to American scientists through the British Central Scientific Office (BCSO) which was set up after Tizard's visit.

The findings of the Maud Committee in particular, together with a report produced by Professors Pegram and Urey after a visit to the United Kingdom in October 1941,[100] had a dramatic impact in the United States. It was not long before Dr Vannevar Bush, Director of Roosevelt's new Office of Scientific Research and Development (OSRD) and his deputy Dr J.B. Conant, suggested to Dr Charles Darwin, head of BCSO, that a joint project should be established.[101] The British response, however, was rather ambiguous. Although the War Cabinet's Scientific Advisory Committee advocated 'close collaboration with the Canadian and United States Governments',[102] the American initiative was not firmly seized. No reply was forthcoming to Dr Darwin's enquiries until March 1942. There was even a two-month delay in the reply sent to Roosevelt following his letter to Churchill in October 1941 in which he himself suggested the need for closer collaboration. The general feeling in government circles in Britain at this time was that cooperation should be encouraged but that the projects should remain independent. The concern to protect Britain's own interest in this new and vital field was expressed by Lord Cherwell in a minute to Churchill at the end of August 1941.[103] In the debate about where the first separation process plant should be built, Cherwell felt strongly that if possible it should be erected in Britain. In his words:

> However much I may trust my neighbour, and depend on him, I am very much averse to putting myself completely at his mercy and would therefore not press the Americans to undertake this work: I would just continue exchanging information and get into production over here without raising the question of whether they should do it or not.[104]

At this stage then, when British nuclear research was in advance of that in the United States and when the Americans were pushing for a joint project, those concerned with atomic energy in Britain 'failed to seize the opportunity'.[105] They were willing to accept cooperation with American scientists but the independence of the British project was nevertheless considered to be an important interest.

While this secret debate was going on in Britain about the form collaboration with the United States might take, American research in the atomic energy field was gathering momentum. In November a Report of the Committee of the National Academy of Scientists confirmed the findings of the Maud Committee and an 'all-out' effort on the uranium bomb was initiated.[106] Not surprisingly perhaps, the Japanese attack on Pearl Harbour on 7 December considerably accelerated the American programme and within six months, given the greater resources of the United States, the US effort had already outstripped that of Britain. With such rapid American progress, the positions of the two allies had been reversed by mid-1942. American research had developed to such an extent that there were few attractions in a joint project with Britain. Visits by British scientists to the United States in early 1942 revealed the advances made.[107] Consequently the suggestions for a combined Anglo-American effort now began to come from the British side. In his Hyde Park conversations with Roosevelt in June 1942, Churchill urged that 'we should at once pool all our information, work together on equal terms, and share the results if any equally between us'.[108] When Sir John Anderson, the Cabinet Minister responsible for the British nuclear programme, wrote anxiously to Dr Bush in July about collaboration it was the latter who now demonstrated a lack of enthusiasm. Indeed despite the President's willingness to continue cooperation expressed at Hyde Park, Bush and Conant over the next twelve months demonstrated a reluctance to put this promise into effect.[109]

Another reason for the American unwillingness to consider wide-ranging collaboration with Britain was that the project in the United States was becoming more and more under the control of the military. As they achieved greater authority over the American project they began to question the complete exchange of information which had been taking place with Britain. As a result they suggested instead that information should only be given in areas where Britain could make use of it. It was this idea which was subsequently taken up by Dr Conant in a memorandum to the President in December.[110] In his memorandum, which Roosevelt accepted, Dr Conant advocated a much more restricted interchange of information.

The Conant memorandum, especially after the President had agreed at Hyde Park to a pooling of *all* information, came as a bombshell to the British. Attempts by Churchill to have the memorandum set aside at Casablanca in January 1943 and again at the Washington Conference in May 1943 led to sympathetic noises but unproductive action by the Americans.[111] Churchill also wrote repeatedly to Harry Hopkins about the matter during the period between the conferences with little result. While this was happening the flow of information between American and British scientists virtually ceased. Not surprisingly this breakdown in collaboration produced important strains in Anglo-American relations which continued until July.

Some progress towards improving the situation was made during the visit to Britain by Dr Bush and Mr Stimson, the US Secretary of War, in mid-July. In discussions it was revealed that one of the constraints in the United States on collaboration with Britain was a suspicion in Congress of Britain's post-war motives, especially in the commercial atomic energy field. The appointment of W.A. Akers, formerly Research Director of ICI, to the key post of Director of the British Nuclear Project ('Tube Alloys' as it was known) had helped to encourage this suspicion.[112] Although 'bewildered by the charge', the British immediately set about drafting an agreement to give the American authorities the necessary assurances about their post-war intentions.[113]

At the same time that the London talks were taking place, Roosevelt finally decided, on the advice of Harry Hopkins, to renew collaboration with the British.[114] He therefore asked Churchill to send his 'top man' to the United States to work out the arrangements for a new agreement. Sir John Anderson was duly sent and in August an agreement was reached with Bush, Conant and Stimson which the two leaders signed at the Quebec Conference on the 19 August.[115]

The Quebec Agreement ended an unhappy phase in Anglo-American atomic relations. According to the Articles of Agreement both parties agreed: never to use nuclear weapons against each other; nor to use them against other states without each other's consent; and not to pass on information to other countries without each other's consent. At the same time, to overcome American sensitivities on the matter Britain agreed that any post-war advantages of an industrial or commercial kind would be dealt with 'as between the United States and Great Britain on terms to be specified by the President of the United States to the Prime Minister of Great Britain'.[116] The Agreement also set up the machinery for renewed cooperation in the form of a Combined Policy Committee (CPC). In this committee there was to be a 'complete interchange of information and ideas on *all* sections of the project'.[117] Outside the committee, however, in the fields of scientific research and development there was to be a 'full and effective interchange of information and ideas between those in the two countries engaged in the *same sections* of the field'.[118] Thus a compromise was achieved between the views expressed in the Conant memorandum and the British desire for complete cooperation across the board.

Following the Quebec Agreement from mid-1943 onwards cooperation rapidly improved. Much of the credit for the smooth working relationship which soon developed must go to Professor Chadwick, as technical adviser to the British members of the CPC, and General Groves, the executive head of the American project.[119] According to Margaret Gowing, 'Chadwick fulfilled his exacting task superbly and one of his triumphs was the friendship which he established with Groves'.[120] Chadwick, ever conscious of the need for a close post-war relationship in the field of atomic energy between the two countries, also encouraged the exodus from Britain of as many scientists as the Americans would accept, to participate and gain experience from the work being undertaken. Overall there were fifty or so British scientists and engineers involved in the Manhattan project. Their combined contribution to the eventual development of the bomb in 1945 is difficult to estimate. Apart from the initial stimulus of the Maud Report, Groves himself often acknowledged that British scientists made an invaluable contribution. According to one American scientist involved, British help probably 'shortened by at least a year the time which would otherwise have been required'.[121]

Although British scientists made an important contribution there is no doubt also that they benefited enormously by being involved in the project. Involvement closely in the American work provided important knowledge about gaseous diffusion, electromagnetic separation and the methods of making bombs themselves which was to be important in the post-war period.

Concern in Britain about the need to continue cooperation after the war led to discussions on the subject between Churchill and Roosevelt at Hyde Park in September 1944. As a result of this meeting an *aide-mémoire* was initialled by the two leaders which identified Japan as a possible target when the bomb was 'finally available'.[122] Even more significantly it stated that '*full collaboration* between the United States and the British Government in developing tube alloys for military and commercial purposes should continue *after the defeat of Japan unless and until terminated by joint agreement*'.[123] Unfortunately for Britain the President was soon to die and the only American copy of the *aide-mémoire* was filed away by mistake in the papers of Roosevelt's naval aide, not to be found until some time later.[124] The only American to know of the President's intentions regarding post-war collaboration with Britain was Dr Bush.[125] However, perhaps because he was opposed to any commitment to Britain which would prejudice relations with the Soviet Union, he urged Roosevelt's successor, Harry Truman, to work for some form of post-war international control rather than develop bilateral relations with Britain.

Despite the close working partnership in the Manhattan projects from 1943 onwards the predominant American position, as in other areas of the war effort, increasingly had an impact on the atomic energy relationship. This was particularly seen in the reaction to the obligations set out in the Quebec Agreement. According to the agreement the consent of both parties was to be secured before the bomb was used. In fact when the bomb was completed Britain played virtually no part in the decision to use it against Hiroshima and Nagasaki. Japan was the target designated in the Hyde Park *aide-mémoire* but little discussion took place subsequently about the exact targets. Churchill, mindful of the limitations of Britain's position, did not wish to be too legalistic about the clause. Consequently when the United States asked for Britain's approval at a meeting of the CPC in April 1945 there was little or no debate. Instead, in July Churchill simply initialled a copy of the agreement reached at the CPC meeting between Stimson and the British representative, Field-Marshal Sir Henry Wilson, and on 6 August 1945 the first atomic bomb was dropped on the city of Hiroshima.[126]

Intelligence collaboration

Atomic energy was one of the fields in which the intelligence services of both countries worked closely together during the war. The driving force in both Britain and the United States to develop a uranium bomb as soon as possible was the fear that Germany might get there first. Consequently one of the main tasks of the British and American intelligence agencies, after high level contacts had been established with Colonel William Stephenson's arrival in New York in May 1940, was to find out about German research in the uranium field. As a result of joint intelligence operations it was discovered by 1943 that German research in fact had not developed as far as had been originally feared.

Apart from cooperation in the atomic energy field the intelligence agencies also worked closely together in a wide range of other operations, especially after the American entry into the war. Until recently the extent of this collaboration remained largely unknown. The publication of a number of works on ULTRA,[127] however, has revealed the depth and vital importance of these joint intelligence efforts. In the conduct of the war effort Sir William Stephenson himself has gone as far as to suggest that the 'history of the Second World War will now have to be revised in the light of the secret wars'.[128]

From what has been revealed it appears that the allied war effort was significantly affected by joint intelligence work in the sensitive fields of cryptology. In July/August 1939, following a Franco-British-Polish Conference of Cryptanalysts to discuss the German Enigma cipher machine, Britain received important information and a Polish-built Enigma machine.[129] As a result largely of this invaluable Polish help the GC & CS at Bletchley was able to make important progress towards deciphering German codes. Although some of the information derived from ULTRA was passed on to the United States before Pearl Harbour, as we noted earlier, the range and depth of cooperation in this field was somewhat limited in the period up to December 1941.[130] It seems likely, despite certain assertions to the contrary,[131] that Churchill only revealed the existence of ULTRA to Roosevelt at the Arcadia Conference in Washington between 22 December 1941 and 14 January 1942.[132] Even then, for a time after the American entry into the war, increased cooperation was only achieved 'slowly and in a haphazard and coincidental fashion'.[133] With the planning of 'TORCH', however, during 1942 a determined effort seems to have been made to introduce American officers to Britain's 'most guarded secret'. More effective collaboration was gradually achieved as more and more American advisers on ULTRA matters were trained in Britain and from 1943 onwards American commanders and staff officers were using ULTRA intelligence on a regular basis in the field. Resources were increasingly pooled as American specialists were sent to work alongside their British counterparts on intelligence and cryptanalysis at Bletchley. By 1944 the American involvement in ULTRA was 'virtually complete'.[134]

Relations in this, as in other areas of intelligence, did not always run smoothly. Personality clashes, departmental interests and national sensitivity over security on occasions created difficulties and friction between (and within) the intelligence agencies of both countries.[135] Serious as some of these problems were, however, it would be difficult to over-exaggerate the vital nature of this cooperation for the Allied war effort as a whole.[136] As Ronald Lewin has shown:

> The fact remains that after Americans first became fully involved in ULTRA they entered into an enormous inheritance which they did not squander. At every level, (from the Joint Chiefs of Staff down to the commanders in the field, the directors of the USAAF in its struggle over Germany, the naval units that shared in the battle of the Atlantic, the far-flung bomber commands of Chennault and LeMay), the whole of the American war effort came to be inter-locked with the British . . . drawing continuously and fruitfully on the unique source of ULTRA.[137]

This picture of the fundamental importance and at the same time irritating difficulties in the intelligence field, as mentioned earlier, mirrors to a large extent the other areas of the wartime alliance (with the exception of the war against Japan where the conflicts were more pronounced). The overall picture is one of a closely integrated war machine which at times was disrupted by strains which for the most part arose from the clash of divergent interests. There is little doubt, however, that if the term 'special relationship' has any meaning at all it refers to the Anglo-American partnership which developed both before and after the United States was precipitated into war. In terms of the range and depth of collaboration, the personal intimacy, the deep mutual trust and sharing of secrets, the relationship was remarkable, if not indeed unique. For Churchill, with his own Anglo-American background and deep commitment to the importance of the alliance, 'There never was a more serviceable war machine established among allies.'[138] General Marshall has also described the wartime relationship as 'the most complete unification of military effort ever achieved by two allied states'.[139] Reflecting these views other writers have concluded that 'the western alliance formed the closest and most far-reaching combination of sovereign states in war, on the basis of equality, that has yet been seen';[140] that it represented a 'vast network of informal relations without parallel in history';[141] and 'an intimate set of arrangements for the conduct of war which represented a fusion of national identities, if not sovereignties hitherto unprecedented'.[142]

There were differences and divergent secondary interests especially towards the end of the war which should not be forgotten, but nothing was ever allowed, in the last resort, to prejudice the achievement of the overriding common objective.

1 Discord and Collaboration 1945–1949*

Post-war difficulties and informal links 1945–1947

The history of Anglo-American relations in the defence field in the immediate post-war period in some, although not in all, respects corresponded with the basic pattern of relations of Anglo-American relations as a whole. Despite the difficulties and imperfections, the relationship during the war had been extraordinarily close. In the late 1940s some of this intimacy was to return as important informal links were developed and both countries worked closely in the development of the North Atlantic Treaty Organization. For the moment, however, in the two immediate post-war years, the relationship cooled as important differences arose.

The abrupt cancellation of lend-lease by President Truman in August 1945 and the subsequent haggling over the loan to Britain sent a shockwave through the new Labour government and produced a degree of animosity and mutual recriminations in both countries. Hostility and bitterness also arose over specific policy issues such as Palestine, while on the more general level suspicions existed in the United States of British Socialism. Many Americans found it difficult to understand the ingratitude of the British public in electing the 'colourless' Clement Attlee to replace a leader of the stature of Winston Churchill. The replacement of Churchill in itself was bound to weaken the alliance. Throughout the war, despite the difficulties, Churchill had always maintained the overwhelming importance of relations with the United States and emphasized the enduring ties between the English-speaking peoples.[1] It was not that the Attlee government did not recognize the importance of the American connection; they simply did not feel the same emotional and sentimental attachment to the American people which Churchill derived from the peculiar circumstances of the long and intimate wartime relationship and his own family ties.[2]

As the Anglo-American relationship in general became less special, so many of the links in the defence field were dissolved or simply dwindled away in the first two years after the war. In September 1945 President Truman announced the dissolution of most of the Combined Boards which had played such an important part in integrating the Allied war effort.

---

* The author is indebted to Arnold Wolfer's study, *Discord and Collaboration: Essays in International politics*, (Baltimore: The Johns Hopkins Press, 1967) for the title of this chapter.

Likewise the scale of military planning which had been so extensive during the war now virtually ceased, with the exception of those matters arising out of the occupation of Europe. After the close wartime partnership there was at this time 'no American commitment at all to come to the help of Britain' if she was attacked.[3] Even the prestigious Combined COS Committee which had been the symbol and nucleus of the joint war-machine in the initial post-war period performed only very limited functions.[4]

The Washington Agreements and the McMahon Act

The most important breakdown in defence cooperation at this time was in the field of atomic energy. The difficulties which arose were also to continue throughout the 1940s and early 1950s even when relations between the two countries had improved significantly in most other areas, including various areas of defence.

Despite the difficulties in 1942 and 1943 British scientists had made a significant contribution to the Manhattan Project and the eventual development of nuclear weapons which were used against Hiroshima and Nagasaki.[5] This contribution plus the terms of the Quebec Agreements of August 1943 and the Hyde Park *aide-mémoire* in September 1944 between President Roosevelt and Prime Minister Churchill led many in Britain to expect that the partnership in atomic matters would continue after the war ended. The Hyde Park *aide-mémoire* in particular had stated quite unequivocally that collaboration in the military and commercial fields 'should continue after the defeat of Japan unless and until terminated by joint agreement'.[6]

This expectation, however, was not fulfilled. Almost immediately after the war ended the flow of information on atomic energy began to dry up and eventually in August 1946 the McMahon Act was passed in the United States which prohibited the exchange of any atomic information between the United States and any other nation.[7]

The period from the end of the war until the passing of the McMahon Act was one of considerable uncertainty in the Anglo-American atomic relationship as decision-makers in both countries struggled with the implications of atomic power in the post-war world. With the Anglo-American agreements only known to a small group in the United States[8] and a new President in office there was a general consensus that some form of international control should be sought to try to harness the terrible destructive power of atomic energy for the good of mankind as a whole. Some advocated that the secret should be shared with the Russians to win their confidence and demonstrate American good will.[9] The most widely accepted view, however, was that knowledge about the bomb should remain 'a sacred trust' of the American people only to be given up to a properly constituted International Atomic Energy Agency.[10]

The idea of international control was also one shared by the Labour government in Britain. Indeed it was Prime Minister Attlee who wrote to Truman on 25 September 1945 suggesting discussions on the subject. In general, however, there was rather more scepticism in Britain about the prospects for achieving such control and the Chiefs of Staff in particular urged Attlee to press for the fulfilment of the wartime agreements on continued collaboration until an international agency was established.[11] Attlee's letter to Truman, however, went unanswered, largely due to the President's sensitivity over the effects atomic energy discussions between the United States, Britain and Canada might have on the Russians. The matter was, however, an urgent one for the British, and the Prime Minister telegraphed Washington asking for a meeting with the President. As a result it was agreed that the leaders of Britain, the United States and Canada would meet in the American capital on 9 November 1945.

Although suspicions about Soviet activities were growing at this time, especially after the defection of Gouzenko in Canada in September and his revelations of an extensive Soviet spy network,[12] the American, British and Canadian governments were intent on a conciliatory line at this time. The meeting in Washington therefore between Truman, Attlee and Mackenzie King, the Canadian Prime Minister, concentrated on approaches designed to achieve international control of atomic energy. Thus the Washington Declaration signed by the three leaders on 15 November offered to exchange 'fundamental scientific information and the interchange of scientists and scientific literature for peaceful ends with any nation that will fully reciprocate'.[13] Nevertheless at the same time discussions were taking place more privately on the question of Anglo-American collaboration between the advisers of the two governments. Despite the growing difficulties since the war ended, 'the principle of all-round collaboration' was finally agreed.[14] Significantly, however, because of the sensitivity of the issues involved in terms of the Washington Declaration on international control, it was decided not to produce a formal bilateral agreement which would have had to be submitted to the United States Senate. Instead a very brief informal document was signed by Truman and Attlee in a great hurry just before the conference closed. In fact such was the haste, as subsequent events were to show, that Truman seems not to have really understood the full implications or indeed the inherent inconsistencies in putting his signature to 'this flimsy piece of paper'.[15] While the Washington Declaration urged international control, the informal agreement confirmed once again 'full and effective cooperation in the field of atomic energy between the United States, the United Kingdom and Canada'.[16] A further memorandum was also produced on 16 November by Sir John Anderson and General Groves which directed the Combined Policy Committee, which had been the forum for cooperation during the war, to prepare a new document to replace previous agreements and understandings between Britain and the United States.[17]

Although Attlee returned home satisfied that the basis for future cooperation with the United States had been established, his hopes were soon to be dashed. The growing recognition of the inconsistencies of the Washington Agreements in the American administration, together with a widespread concern in Congress to retain a monopoly of the knowledge to produce nuclear weapons, led to the failure on the American side to implement the promise of full cooperation with Britain. Many in Congress were unaware of the secret undertakings to Britain but there were other American leaders, notably Secretary Byrnes and Dr Vannevar Bush who, it must be said, acted less honourably in their determination to terminate collaboration with Britain.[18] The result was that negotiations in the Combined Policy Committee produced little by way of agreement and by April 1946 Attlee was forced to write to Truman to intervene and break the deadlock which existed. Truman's reply, however, viewed charitably, reveals his lack of awareness of the significance of the document signed at the Washington Conference. According to the President the agreement referred only to cooperation 'in the field of basic scientific information and did not oblige the United States to provide Britain with engineering and operational assistance in building atomic energy plants'.[19] This reply caused deep resentment in Britain. To British government leaders and officials it seemed to be a denial of the phrase 'full and effective' cooperation agreed to in Washington and included in the Hyde Park *aide-mémoire*. In his reply to Truman on 6 June Attlee stressed the 'special relationship' in the field of atomic energy which had grown up during the war and urged the need for full information 'to which we believe we are entitled, both by the documents and by the history of our common efforts in the past'.[20]

By this stage, however, British protests were of no avail. Not only had Truman apparently made up his mind against continued collaboration with Britain but the McMahon Act was passing through Congress at this time. The Act, which eventually became law in August, virtually slammed the door against further exchanges of nuclear information between the two countries for a number of years to come.

The result of this breakdown in cooperation led the British to decide in favour of their own independent programme to produce nuclear weapons. Britain still viewed herself as a great power, as Foreign Secretary Bevin's statement to the House of Commons in May 1947 reveals.[21] As such it was inevitable that she should want to acquire the newest and most potent weapons. The decision was therefore made secretly by a small ad hoc group of Cabinet Ministers in January 1947 to go ahead and develop a bomb.[22] Significantly, Attlee explained the reasons for the decision many years later in terms of fear of American isolationism and the needs of British security.

We had to hold up our position vis-a-vis the Americans. We couldn't allow ourselves to be wholly in their hands, and their position wasn't awfully clear always. At that time we had to bear in mind that there was always the possibility of their withdrawing and becoming isolationist once again. The manufacture of a British bomb was therefore at this stage essential to our defence. You must remember that this was all prior to NATO. NATO has altered things. But at the time although we were doing our best to make the Americans understand the realities of the European situation – the world situation – we couldn't be sure we'd succeed. In the end we did. But we couldn't take risks with British security in the meantime. We had worked from the start for international control of the bomb. We wanted it completely under the United Nations. That was the best way. But it was obviously going to take a long time. Meanwhile we had to face the world as it was. We had to look to our defence – and to our industrial future. We could not agree that only America should have atomic energy.[23]

It is interesting to speculate whether Britain would have developed her own deterrent if the McMahon Act had not been passed. It may be that Britain would have been prepared to concentrate her research effort in the US in return for a supply of bombs. Events in the late 1940s, however, would seem to suggest that feelings of great power status as well as concern for British security interests would have required atomic bombs under British control and at least the potential to produce them in Britain even if there had been greater cooperation between the two states.[24]

Besides fear of US isolationism and concern for British security there seems to have been another important motivation behind the decision to go ahead with the bomb. 'Even after the McMahon Act was passed, the British were determined to renew the struggle for Anglo-American atomic cooperation.'[25] From Britain's point of view her own independent programme was a means by which the lost partnership could be revived. If Britain could show the United States that she was capable of manufacturing an atomic bomb on her own then it was felt that this might persuade them to re-open collaboration on the lines of the wartime partnership.

In the meantime there is little doubt that Britain suffered from the restrictions of the McMahon Act. The project cost more and took significantly longer without access to American technical expertise and experience. In one respect, however, the Act did have a beneficial effect. It made the British think for themselves and in this respect, according to one of the key figures in Britain's atomic programme, Christopher Hinton, 'it was the best thing that could possibly happen'.[26] This was perhaps going too far but it did mean that Britain was not constrained to copy American nuclear facilities which had been built 'hastily and therefore clumsily'.[27] Original work continued to be undertaken in Britain and many of the plants built were superior to those developed in the United

States. As such, Britain did have a contribution to make and as many hoped, this did in the longer term contribute to the revival of the partnership in the 1950s.[28]

Although the McMahon Act did lead to a significant breakdown in the atomic partnership and undoubtedly caused strains in Anglo-American relations, the difficulties should not be over-emphasized. It is true that in the first post-war years Britain and the United States 'kept their distance and were not inordinately fond of one another'.[29] Nevertheless they were 'still closer to each other than to any third power'.[30] The awareness of mutual self-interest meant that, even in the difficult field of atomic energy, cooperation was not wholly ended during this period. In May 1946 an agreement was reached between the two countries on an approximately equal division of uranium ore which up-dated the 1944 Declaration of Trust[31] and provided both countries with the uranium necessary for their independent atomic energy programmes. It is also interesting that one of the British officials involved in the negotiations with the Americans, Roger Makins, has subsequently maintained that 'the door to collaboration was *almost, though not quite*, hermetically barred by the passage of the McMahon Act'.[32] He points out that besides raw materials the machinery for collaboration in intelligence also 'continued without interruption'.[33] This was particularly important because 'the joint monitoring of atomic tests' which took place was not possible 'without acquiring much information about the weapons and their effects'.[34] Neither was this limited cooperation in atomic energy the only area of defence collaboration.

Residual defence links

In March 1946, as we have seen, Winston Churchill made his famous speech at Fulton, Missouri, warning of aggressive Soviet intentions and appealing for a renewal of the wartime alliance between Britain and the United States.[35] The speech caused some controversy in political circles in both Britain and America, coming as it did at a time when the Western governments, despite certain difficulties, were still struggling to prevent a total breakdown of the wartime partnership with the Soviet Union.[36] Irrespective of the criticisms of Churchill, however, beneath the surface some of the kinds of informal contacts which he urged amongst the military establishments of the two countries were beginning to take place. Growing difficulties over Germany and the Soviet failure to evacuate troops from Iran in March led to a growing awareness amongst those concerned with security that combined thinking ought to be undertaken.[37] As Walter Millis points out, as early as July 1946 the American Secretary of the Navy, James Forrestal, was informed that individual British political and military officials were seeking very close ties and informal diplomatic and military cooperation with the United States.[38] Ironically, therefore, just as Anglo-American relations were reaching one of their low points with the passing of the McMahon Act in August, there were signs that defence relations between the two countries, in some areas at least, were beginning to improve.

The 'Sequoia' Meeting

One of the most widely publicized initiatives at this time came from Field-Marshal Montgomery, the forthright British Chief of the Imperial General Staff (CIGS), who sought to follow up some previous 'low level discussions' in September 1946 when he visited Canada and the United States.[39] The purpose of Montgomery's mission was to hold discussions on the standardization of weapons, equipment and operational procedures. It appears, however, that he went further than this. Despite his instructions from Whitehall not to discuss his ideas for greater collaboration with the President, 'as no Ministers in Britain knew what was going on'[40] he somewhat characteristically proceeded to do just that. In his discussions with Truman, seeing he was on receptive ground, he urged discussions between the military staffs covering the whole field of defence. This, he points out, the President readily agreed to. Reporting this to London, Montgomery recalls that he received 'a second cold breeze', this time from the Prime Minister.[41] Attlee argued that he had no objection to further exchanges of information and methods of procedure but he warned that 'no specific commitments were to be entered into'.[42] Montgomery's initiative seems to have been a little premature, at least as far as the British government was concerned.

Concern in the United States also over what might appear to be a return to an alliance between Britain and the United States led to arrangements being made to hide the real purpose of Montgomery's meeting with the American Joint Chiefs of Staff. He was scheduled to meet them at 'a social gathering' on board the SS *Sequoia* cruising down the Potomac.[43] At this 'social gathering' agreement was reached that discussions should begin as soon as possible in Washington covering 'the whole strategic concept of the West in a Third World War, together with the best way of handling the business of standardization and combined action'.[44] According to Montgomery's account the American Joint Chiefs 'had been hoping and waiting for such an approach for some time'.[45] They were 'wondering when on earth the British would face realities and frankly broach the question of cooperation in all spheres of defence'.[46] The British CIGS saw his visit as being remarkably successful and important in the evolution of Anglo-American relations in the defence field because it established that 'the continuing functioning of the machinery of the Combined Chiefs was accepted without question by the President and the American Chiefs of Staff'.[47]

Significantly, on his subsequent visit to Moscow in January 1947, both Stalin and Marshal Vassilevsky asked him about the military talks with the United States and the continuing existence of the Combined Chiefs of Staff organization. Stalin apparently found it difficult to understand how talks on the conduct of war and training as well as plans on the standardization of weapons and training could be undertaken without a definite military alliance.[48]

It may be, as James Forrestal suggests, that the importance of Montgomery's visit should not be exaggerated.[49] Certainly Montgomery's view that there was widespread support in the American administration as well as in military circles for greater defence cooperation at this time tends to over-simplify the situation and ignore the criticisms of Britain and the restraints which made close ties difficult to achieve until mid-1948. Neither was the outcome of the Staff Talks in Washington very dramatic. In 1948 at a meeting of the Chiefs of Staff of the two countries, Lord Tedder was to complain of the separation which still existed in strategic planning.[50] Churchill apparently only secured a promise of joint discussions on the Strategic Air Plan from Truman as late as January 1952.[51] Nevertheless it is true that Montgomery's visit does symbolize the gradually developing system of defence links and informal contacts which were being re-established in the latter half of 1946. In December 1946, for example, discussions between the air forces of the two countries produced an agreement on the continuation of wartime collaboration in staff methods, tactics, equipment and research.[52] This was followed in January 1947 by a further agreement on the extension of cooperation in officer exchanges for training purposes and a visit by senior American air force officers to their counterparts in Britain.[53] Similar contacts were also established by the armies and navies of both countries. British officers were allowed to enter many research establishments in the United States and information exchanges on the non-nuclear level became much fewer.

Symptomatic of the renewed desire by the United States forces to collaborate with the British was the issuing of a significant Directive by the Coordinating Committee of the US War and Navy Departments in December 1946 by which:

> . . . all classified military information, including the United States order of battle, and all information about combined research and development projects to which the United Kingdom had contributed or was contributing and United States research and development projects, could be released to the United Kingdom.[54]

Although atomic energy was omitted from the Directive, it did nevertheless cover a very wide range of other military information including 'intelligence, technical and scientific information on weapons and methods of manufacture and non-technical information about the United States forces'.[55] This information was released subject to the condition that Britain would not pass on the information to third countries without specific approval from the United States.[56]

At the same time that contact between the Services was developing, secret cooperation in important areas of research continued. One such field was that of chemical and biological warfare where 'programmes remained so closely in step as to be virtually integrated'.[57] This is an area which has not received the same publicity as atomic energy but where the 'special relationship' was to continue unabated throughout the post-war period.

As Richard Rosecrance has pointed out, 'the deductions to be drawn from the somewhat checkered career of Anglo-American relations in the first two years after the war are far from straightforward.[58] There were certainly stresses and strains in the alliance and on the American side in particular there was a conscious attempt in the immediate post-war period to dissolve many of the close wartime links between the two countries. Despite the scepticism on both sides of the Atlantic over future relations with the Soviet Union there remained an unwillingness to enter into any formal joint defence commitments which might further prejudice those already difficult relations.[59] Nevertheless, despite the sensitivity expressed at the political level, informal military contacts were gradually being re-established. No concrete agreements were signed or formal alliance created but there is no doubt that during 1946 and early 1947 the foundations for such an alliance were being laid.[60] As 1946 wore on the military leaders in both countries began to think in terms of an operative Anglo-American accord in any future military crisis. If war came each side saw the other as being its most important ally. As such the two years after the war saw the proliferation of informal working arrangements and understandings as air forces, armies, navies, defence departments and foreign offices discussed the common problems facing them. By 1947, as one American officer puts it, there was a considerable amount of 'healthy hanky-panky' taking place through a variety of Anglo-American channels.[61]

The Cold War Alliance 1947–49

During 1946 suspicions between the Western Powers and Russia grew, even though as yet it had not erupted into the Cold War. Disagreements built up over reparations, the future of Germany, over Poland and Eastern Europe in general and over Iran and Turkey. As relations with the Soviet Union deteriorated mutual interests brought the United States and Britain closer together after the initial post-war cooling of relations. The fusion of the British and American zones in Germany in December 1946 was followed in March 1947 by the Truman Doctrine and the dramatic American acceptance of British commitments in Greece and Turkey. Shortly afterwards the launching of the Marshall Plan in June 1947 saw Britain playing a leading role initiating and orchestrating the response of the European states as increasingly the British Foreign Secretary, Ernest Bevin, worked to bind the United States and Europe closer together. With the Soviet rejection of Marshall aid, the Cominform Declaration of October 1947 and the break-up of the Council of Foreign Ministers meeting in December 1947, the Cold War had arrived. As the level of hostility heightened so Anglo-American military collaboration grew even closer.

Initially discussions took place over particular areas vital to Western interests, especially the Middle East. The Pentagon Talks of August 1947 were taken a stage further by the Washington Conference which lasted from October 16 to November 7 of the same year.[62] In these talks the strategic importance of the area to the West and the need to achieve a common approach to the problems of the region were discussed. Towards the end of 1947, however, Ernest Bevin, was beginning to think in terms of more ambitious and comprehensive security arrangements. In the summer of 1947 he had refused to allow the British Chiefs of Staff to specifically name Russia as the potential enemy for their military planning.[63] By December, however, his disillusionment with the Soviet Union was finally complete. From then on his major preoccupation became the organization of the Western European states into a defensive alliance closely linked with the United States. On 13 January 1948 he informed the United States of his interest in establishing some form of union in Western Europe, backed by the Americans and the Dominions.[64] In March, following the Communist coup in Czechoslovakia and with the Soviet Union applying pressure to Norway, Bevin presented the United States Secretary of State, George Marshall, with his specific proposals for a Western European Union together with a joint plan of Atlantic security and a Mediterranean system of security.[65] Although the American leaders were not as yet prepared to enter into formal commitments they nevertheless encouraged the British and the other Western European states to believe that their joint effort would present the United States with a suitable basis for extending some form of political support and material assistance.[66] What form this support would take was not clear, however, until late 1948.

On the 17 March 1948 the Brussels Treaty was signed by Britain, France, Belgium, the Netherlands and Luxembourg, committing the member states to meet armed attack in Europe 'with all the military and other aid and assistance in their power'. From Bevin's point of view the Brussels Treaty was the prototype of the Atlantic alliance and a preliminary step to a wider association which would include the United States.[67] A major step towards the achievement of this goal was taken on 11 June with the passing of the Vandenberg resolution. The resolution provided for 'the association of the United States, by constitutional process, with such regional and other collective arrangements as are based on continuous and effective self-help and mutual aid, and as effect its national security'. With the eruption of the Berlin blockade in late June the Vandenberg resolution was followed by a meeting of the US Joint Chiefs between August 20–22 at Newport, Rhode Island, at which they made 'far-reaching plans' for the defence of Britain and Western Europe.[68] The first of these plans provided for 'strategic and command relationships in Western Europe in which Britain was envisaged as taking the leading role'. This was to be reflected shortly afterwards by Field-Marshal Montgomery's appointment as Chairman of the Commanders-in-Chief Committee and the creation by the Brussels Powers of a Western European Defence Organization. The second Joint Chiefs of Staff plan set out the main lines of American action in the event of war. An American would be appointed 'Supreme Allied Commander-in-Chief' and the plan outlined the contribution the United States would make to European defence. As such American military planning was based on the assumption that the United States and Western Europe would be allies and that they would jointly resist aggression from the east.[69]

Such plans, however, still did not commit the United States to a formal treaty. The ideal for the United States remained greater integration between the European states in the defence field, as in other fields, with Britain taking a leading role and the American government providing military assistance from outside.[70] The British, however, were less interested in close European defence integration and more concerned that the United States should be part of an Atlantic pact. Movement towards a more formal commitment did not come until after the American election and even in mid-November the Secretary of State, James Forrestal, was asking the European states whether an implicit military relationship would be sufficient with substantial military shipments from the United States.[71] Was it necessary, he asked, to sign a pact to support the Western European powers in the event of hostilities?[72] It was only after the British Chiefs of Staff argued that an implicit military relationship would be totally inadequate that the American administration agreed in January 1949 to proceed to a security treaty which would include not only the Brussels Powers and the United States but also Canada, Denmark, Portugal, Norway, Italy and Iceland. Ernest Bevin had finally achieved his objective and on 4 April 1949 the North Atlantic Treaty was signed.

An important impetus to the creation of the Atlantic Alliance came with the Soviet blockade of Berlin in June 1948. Besides its contribution to the multilateral defence pact in which Britain and the United States were brought together as the two most important members of the new alliance, the blockade also provided the occasion for a more immediate operational bilateral partnership. From June 1948 until May 1949, when the blockade was lifted, the air forces of the two countries collaborated closely in a joint airlift to the beleaguered city. In October 1948 a Combined Airlift Task Force was set up to provide more effective synchronization of the combined effort. Before long, the intimacy and the degree of inter-allied cooperation was in some respects as great as that achieved during the wartime partnership and, as Bevin was to claim, the achievements, in the ordinary conditions of peace could be compared with some of the highest exploits of the war.[73] In the period of the blockade over 200,000 flights were made and over 1½ million tons of supplies were carried by the two air forces.

The Berlin blockade, however, had another and, in the longer term, even greater impact on the bilateral defence relationship. The intensity of the crisis led to the arrival at three RAF stations in East Anglia in July of sixty American B29 Superfortresses.[74] By September the number had risen to ninety B29s at seven RAF stations. The reasons for the arrival of the aircraft in Britain, at least initially, were political rather than military. They were a token of US interest in the defence of Europe. Their symbolic effect was emphasized by the fact that although the B29 was the American delivery vehicle for atomic weapons the B29s in Britain were not modified until 1949/50 to carry nuclear bombs. From then on, however, until the late 1950s Britain became one of the principal bases for an American strategic attack on the Soviet Union and as such it became inevitable that she would be in the front line of any future war with the Soviet Union.

Given the importance of this presence it is rather surprising that no formal agreements were signed at this time covering the use of the bases, in particular the circumstances under which nuclear weapons could be delivered by US aircraft flying from British soil. As the British Secretary of State for Air revealed to the House of Commons on 28 July 1948, the American units were not visiting Britain under a formal treaty but 'under informal and longstanding arrangements between the two air-forces for visits of goodwill and training purposes'.[75] The initial request to station three groups of heavy bombers in Britain came from the United States and was seen by the Americans as being advantageous to their interests. As James Forrestal, the US Secretary of Defence, recorded in his Diaries at the time:

> We have the opportunity *now* of sending these planes, and once they are sent they would become something of an accepted fixture, whereas a deterioration of the situation in Europe might lead to a condition of mind under which the British would be compelled to reverse their present attitude.[76]

The Americans were also surprised at the casual way in which their planes were received in Britain. The American Ambassador in Britain, Douglas, was even instructed by Washington to ask Bevin whether in fact the British government had fully explored and considered the effects on public opinion of the arrival of American aircraft in Britain.[77] In June 1949 the Commander of the American Air Forces in Britain himself highlighted the unusual nature of the arrangements at a press conference when he explained that, 'Never before in history has one first-class power gone into another first-class power's country without any agreement. We were just told to come over and "we shall be pleased to have you".'[78]

Mr Bevin in particular welcomed the presence of US bombers in Britain as helping to bind the United States closer to Western European defence. In 1949, However, when the Americans made a request to take over some airfields in Oxfordshire, he recognized the need to work out an agreement to safeguard the British government on two points.[79] Firstly, on Britain's right to terminate the arrangement, and secondly, on the position if the United States ever wanted to conduct operations from the airfields before Britain was at war. The matter was discussed in 1950 and an informal agreement was reached in the form of a letter to the US ambassador.[80] The 'Ambassador's Agreement', as it was called, however, only assured Britain of the right to terminate the arrangements regarding the US presence in Britain. It did not include consultation on the operational use of US bombers. It was only in October 1951 that, before leaving office, Prime Minister Attlee reached an agreement with President Truman on the use of American aircraft from British bases.[81] This was subsequently confirmed in a joint statement issued on 9 January 1952 during Churchill's first visit to Washington as the new Prime Minister. Even then these 'Attlee-Churchill Understandings', as they became known, were rather vague and open-ended. Referring to these understandings, Harold Macmillan told the House of Commons on 12 December 1957 that 'the use of bases in an emergency was accepted to be a matter for joint decision by the two Governments in the light of the circumstances prevailing at the time'.[82]

Atomic Energy Apart

The growing intimacy of Anglo-American relations in the late 1940s symbolized by these important informal arrangements relating to American air bases in Britain was not, however, characteristic of all areas of the defence relationship. Just as atomic energy was one of the most important areas of difference in the immediate post-war years so now, despite the growing intensity of the Cold War, attempts to re-open cooperation continued to cause difficulties and strains in the partnership. Although in line with other aspects of the relationship agreements were reached in atomic energy matters, they were rather limited and proved to be disappointing, particularly to the British. Indeed they were the source of some irritation in relations between the two states. In this sense Margaret Gowing is right when she argues that atomic energy remained something apart from all the other strands that were weaving a new and stronger 'special relationship' at this time.[83]

At the end of 1947, as the international atmosphere darkened, the prospects of renewed collaboration appeared quite good. With the initiative coming from the United States to re-open talks the situation appeared hopeful to the British. American officials, including Carroll Wilson, the General Manager of the United States Atomic Energy Commission (USAEC), were hinting that it would not be long before 'the log-jam might break'.[84] American concern to re-open talks, however, at this time seems to have derived from mixed motives. For some key American political figures like Dean Acheson there was a feeling that Britain had been rather harshly treated by the United States after the wartime agreements had promised to continue collaboration in the post-war period. There were others, however, who were less interested in fair play for Britain. When the USAEC revealed the nature of the wartime agreements to the Joint Congressional Committee in May 1947 two American Senators, Vandenberg and Hickenlooper, found some of the provisions, especially the one relating to a British veto on the American use of the bomb in the Quebec Agreement to be 'astounding' and 'unthinkable'.[85] For them talks were needed to remove these 'intolerable' restrictions on the use of American power. At the same time there were other American officials who were particularly concerned that the 1946 Agreement with Britain on the equal allocation of uranium was leaving the US short as it attempted to expand its nuclear programme. Britain had more than she required and therefore had to be persuaded to relinquish some of her supplies to the United States. Although in the negotiations which took place Britain apparently only saw 'the warmer, less calculating side of the Americans',[86] on the whole, as the United States official atomic energy historians point out, calculations of the national interests involved were uppermost in the minds of the American authorities.

> They had apparently agreed that they would strive to abrogate the wartime agreements, to acquire British ore stocks, to get a much greater share of Congo production, to restrict the storage of raw materials in Britain to a minimum and to obtain British and Canadian support for ore negotiations with South Africa. In return the United States would give *some* information.[87]

Talks began at a meeting of the Combined Policy Committee on 10 December 1947 and an arrangement known as the *modus vivendi* was agreed at a meeting of the same committee on 7 January 1948.[88] The document was not signed but both sides agreed to adhere to its terms. As such it did not have to be referred to Congress and it did not come within Article 102 of the UN Charter. According to the new agreements cooperation and the exchange of information were to take place in nine specific areas which were not, however, related to military weapons. In exchange the United States was to receive a much larger share of uranium ore, taking the total supplies from the Congo for 1948 and 1949. Britain's power of veto over the American use of atomic weapons contained in Clause 2 of the Quebec Agreement was also removed as was Clause 4 which placed restrictions on British industrial exploitation of atomic energy.[89]

The package deal was received in Britain initially with some satisfaction. According to one British official it would 'wipe out the misunderstanding and bitterness of the past and put our relationship on a solid basis'.[90] In fact these hopes of a fresh start to the atomic partnership were not fulfilled. Although some useful information was received, on the whole the *modus vivendi* did not live up to expectations. Some Americans seem to have been taken by surprise in the summer of 1948 by the news that Britain was going ahead with its own atomic weapons programme[91] and increasingly as the year wore on the British failed to receive the kind of information they felt entitled to under the agreement. Just as in 1945, there was a feeling in Britain that the Americans were not honouring their agreements and atomic energy once again became the source of friction in Anglo-American relations as arguments over the *modus vivendi* took place.

Assessments of the *modus vivendi* have varied greatly in their conclusions. For Margaret Gowing, the official British historian of the period, there were serious flaws in the agreement,[92] particularly Britain's surrender of the veto on the American use of the atomic bomb. Professor Gowing recognizes that Britain might not have been able to enforce a veto but she argues that Clause 2 was of supreme importance because 'it gave Britain a contingent right to consultation before action was taken that might lead to her own annihilation'.[93] This together with a number of other weaknesses leads her to suggest that 'in the long history of strange atomic energy agreements, the *modus vivendi* emerges as the strangest of them all'.[94] To Roger Makins (now Lord Sherfield), however, who was one of the British officials involved in the negotiations, the agreements were, despite their limitations, of great value to Britain.[95] According to him the right of veto was not a realistic one anyway, and the agreements did at least re-open cooperation with the United States which had virtually ceased with the McMahon Act. In this respect Lord Sherfield is right. The *modus vivendi* did, in some respects, break the 'log-jam' and at the same time it did provide Britain with some very useful information 'at a critical time'.[96] However, although Professor Gowing seems to be a little harsh on the agreements they did nevertheless have weaknesses, as she points out. Just as British interests later would seem to have been better served had a more precise agreement on the use of American bases in Britain been secured, so British negotiators might have pressed usefully for the right of consultation over the use of American atomic power in general.

However the *modus vivendi* is viewed, there is little doubt that the agreements were the source of continuing problems in Anglo-American relations in the late 1940s. On the American side one of the major reasons for the reluctance to supply certain information was the concern in military circles especially over the vulnerability of the British nuclear programme to Soviet attack. During 1949 approaches were made to the British to consider giving up their attempts to develop nuclear weapons in exchange for the 'fullest atomic cooperation including a supply of bombs to Britain "on call"'.[97] The British, however, rejected criticisms of the vulnerability of their atomic plants and, at this stage, were not prepared to discuss any suggestion which made them wholly dependent on the United States and which interfered with the independence of their programme.

Another explanation of the American reticence to provide information at this time was the disagreement which still existed in political circles in the US over cooperation with Britain. On 14 July 1949 the famous Blair House meeting took place at which the Administration discussed the position with leading members of the Joint Congressional Committee. At the meeting the President, Dean Acheson and General Eisenhower all put forward the case for increased collaboration which was even supported by Senator McMahon. Once again, however, Senators Vandenberg and Hickenlooper expressed their opposition. Senator Vandenberg in particular argued that the US were already generously providing economic aid and he deplored the way the United States were always being asked to 'bail out Britain'.[98]

Faced with the strength of this opposition the Administration was obliged to take a cautious line in further formal negotiations which opened with Britain between September and November 1949. These negotiations were necessary from the American point of view because the ore arrangements agreed to in 1948 were scheduled to run out at the end of 1949. Once again, however, agreement on the wider issues of cooperation eluded the delegates. Despite the news of the Russian atomic explosion and the proclamation of the People's Republic of China in September, American insistence on concentrating the atomic programme of the West in North America and Britain's concern to maintain the ability to produce her own nuclear weapons divided the two sides. At the meeting of the Combined Policy Committee at the end of November, significantly, Britain modified her position somewhat and went as far as to suggest an integration of the production and storage of atomic weapons.[99] Britain would continue research into all aspects of atomic energy but she would hand over all weapons production to the United States in exchange for a stock of bombs under her own control and a full exchange of information.[100] Although such integration was further than Britain had hitherto been prepared to go and was in line with trends in NATO the proposals on this occasion proved unacceptable to the United States.[101] Once more the only area of limited agreement was in the field of uranium, where supplies continued to be allocated on a year-to-year basis. The arrest on the 2 February 1950 of Klaus Fuchs, the naturalized British atomic spy, and the emergence of Senator McCarthy in the United States, finally ended for the time being the possibility of any progress towards cooperation in atomic energy between the two countries. Even without these events, however, the divisions which existed were likely to preclude any dramatic breakthrough in the negotiations.[102]

Atomic energy was then, by the end of 1949, the one main exception to the 'special relationship' which was being re-established in Anglo-American relations in general and specifically in the defence field. In the period since 1945 the relationship had gone through two main phases. An initial phase of coolness at the end of the war and then with the emergence of Soviet intransigence and expansion, a second phase in which there had been an increasing attempt to re-establish close ties in the political, economic and military fields. Relations in the atomic field, although at times giving hope of a wide degree of cooperation, never achieved the kind of intimacy characteristic of other areas. Apart from atomic energy, in other respects the defence relationship mirrored the general pattern with the informal defence links of 1946/7 providing a portent of the closer partnership to follow and the attempts to maximize the mutual defence effort in 1948/9 providing one of the most important and distinctive manifestations of the gradual renewal of a more 'special relationship' between the two countries.

2 Collaboration and Discord 1950–1956

The pattern of progress towards greater intimacy in Anglo-American defence relations, apart from atomic energy, continued in the early 1950s. As the period developed, however, a cyclical relapse occurred as important political-military differences began to emerge. These differences culminated in 1956 with the serious rupture at Suez which shook the alliance between the two countries to its very foundations. During the period leading up to Suez atomic energy once again was to remain the big exception to the general pattern of events. Ironically, despite the continuing difficulties over nuclear matters in the early part of the period, as friction began to appear in other areas of the relationship, important agreements were reached in atomic cooperation which helped to lay the foundations for a genuine renewal of the wartime partnership later in the decade.

Security agreements, Korea and NATO

Despite the establishment of NATO in April 1949 various bilateral defence links between Britain and the United States continued and were further extended in the early 1950s. Following the December 1946 Directive by the Coordinating Committee of the US War and Navy Departments a further series of security agreements were signed between 1948 and 1950 which collectively became known as the *Burns–Templer Agreements*.[1] In all there were seven documents, including an Agreement on Security Classifications by the Combined Chiefs of Staff in August 1948; an Agreement setting up a United States–United Kingdom Military Information Board in October 1949; and a series of five Agreements arrived at in Washington between 20 and 27 January 1950. According to the most important of the 1950 agreements:

> The United States and United Kingdom are agreed that it is in the interests of both countries that there should be a full and frank interchange *to the greatest practicable degree* of all classified information and intelligence, except in a limited number of already declared fields, it being understood that either Government may subsequently declare any newly-developed fields or projects as excepted upon due notification to the other Government.[2]

Significantly, under this agreement important information was provided to Britain over the whole field of guided missiles, 'where co-operation had hitherto been bad'.[3]

These agreements also provided the basis for numerous Memoranda of Understanding (MoUs) from 1950 onwards whereby technical information on conventional weapons systems and other military subjects was passed both ways across the Atlantic.[4] Thus under the Burns–Templer Agreements both Britain and the United States were able to benefit from the latest military ideas and inventions of the other. There were inevitably loopholes in the agreements deriving from the fact that the exchange of secrets had to be undertaken 'within the limitations of national policy'. However, there is no doubt that they provided an important basis in the years to come for the exchange of a wide range of military information beneficial to the interests of both states. The agreements also provided a precedent for other similar kinds of agreement in the future.

A much more dramatic manifestation of the close ties between the two countries came in the operational field with the outbreak of the Korean War in June 1950. Although no attempt was made to recreate the integrated wartime machinery, the continuation of the Combined Chiefs of Staff Committee provided a focus for joint discussions on cooperation between the two allies. The United States provided the bulk of the UN effort to stem the North Korean invasion but with the exception of Turkey, Britain provided by far the largest non-American contribution to the war through the Commonwealth Brigade and British naval units in the Far East. Indeed, despite the fact that Britain's interests were not perceived to be involved to the same extent as those of the United States, Prime Minister Attlee was concerned to make a major effort in support of his closest ally.

In many respects from Britain's point of view the partnership in arms which developed in the Korean War was of more importance in political than in purely military terms. Throughout the war Britain's primary concern (as with other American military adventures in Asia in the future)[5] was to advise caution on the part of the United States administration not to get dragged into a major war with China in the Far East which would divert its attention from the defence of Europe. At the same time Attlee was concerned to demonstrate Britain's willingness to come to the aid of the United States. It was hoped that Britain's concern to shoulder her share of the war effort and to support the United States in the Far East would reinforce the Truman government's determination to provide the necessary support for Western European defence in the future. Thus the Labour government was prepared to undertake a massive rearmament programme, initially of £3400 million and later £4700 million over three years, without a formal promise of American aid at a time when the British economy was still in a delicate state.[6] The political position of the Labour government was also in jeopardy due, in part, to such a large-scale defence effort. To his great credit, however, Attlee put national interests first.[7] As one British Cabinet Minister put it, during this period 'none of us was taking the alliance for granted'.[8] It was generally believed that Korea might be a feint by the Soviet Union to throw the West off-guard prior to a Soviet probe into Western Europe. As Churchill put it in a broadcast on 26 August: 'My eyes are not fixed on Korea . . . the supreme peril is Europe. We must try to close the hideous gap on the European front.'[9] If Soviet eyes were fixed on Western Europe Britain and her European allies would need all the help they could get. In this sense the British contribution in Korea was a tribute to the continuing belief in British political circles of the importance of the Anglo-American alliance and the need for American help in European defence.[10]

At a series of discussions between political and military officials of both countries in Washington in July and October 1950 and indeed at the famous meeting between Attlee and Truman in December, the link between Korea and the need to strengthen European defence arrangements was a constant theme.[11] The North Atlantic Treaty did not in itself explicitly provide for the creation of an integrated defence organization. It called only for the establishment of a Council empowered 'to set up subsidiary bodies as may be necessary'. The possibility of a more direct and immediate Soviet threat which the Korean War suggested led to the recognition in Washington and London that the time had come to establish an integrated defence structure in Europe with a unified command. The defence organization envisaged, however, was to be one fashioned around the Anglo-American alliance and resting on Anglo-American power. As Manderson-Jones has pointed out:

> . . . the pre-eminence of the Anglo-American alliance was most clearly reflected in the Anglo-American directorate of NATO, which in structure and organization was an all too obvious expression of the hard facts of Anglo-American co-operation constituting the mainstay of Western security. NATO's Standing Group, for instance, amounted to little more than a revival of the World War Two Combined Chiefs of Staff Committee, now with the addition of France, while SHAPE, which in the event of war would automatically assume full responsibility for all military operations in the European theatre, was in most respects the reincarnation of SHAEF. Not only in structure but in appointments too with General Eisenhower as SACEUR and Lord Ismay as Secretary General of NATO and Vice-Chairman of its Council.[12]

The willingness of the United States to cooperate so closely with Britain at the multilateral as well as bilateral level, on a formal as well as informal basis, signified the recognition by the American government that despite the disparity in power, the partnership with Britain was of particular value. Hubert Humphrey saw Britain as the 'keystone of our

North Atlantic system'[13] and in similar vein President Truman acknowledged in the meeting with Prime Minister Attlee at the end of 1950 that the Anglo-American partnership was 'the mainspring of Atlantic Defence'.[14] One highly respected American journalist, Joseph Alsop, even went as far as to suggest in the *Washington Post* at the time that if the Anglo-American alliance should be dissolved, 'every military plan in the Pentagon would have to be torn up'.[15]

That Britain should be considered as 'the one and only powerful ally' by the United States at this time should be no real surprise.[16] Despite the relative decline in her power Britain was still by far the strongest state in Western Europe. Her arms production exceeded that of the other European partners combined and, despite the vulnerability of her economy, it still occupied a unique position amongst Western European economies in general. Industrial production was running at 30 per cent of non-Communist Europe as a whole and was vastly superior to France and Germany in the early 1950s. According to an American survey written in August 1951, Britain alone of the Western European states had the resources which entitled her to be viewed as an independent military power.[17]

Britain's special importance to the United States in the defence field was emphasized by the vast amount of equipment and defence support aid received by the British as a result of the Military Defence Assistance Act of 1949 and the Mutual Security Act of 1951. Deliveries of military hardware covered a wide spectrum and included aircraft and artillery as well as electronic and engineering equipment. Of particular importance were the seventy B29s received by Britain from March 1950 onwards to help plug an important gap in the defence programme until her own bombers began to enter service in the mid-1950s. Just as important as the strategic bombers was the financial assistance given by the United States. Between 1951 and 1956 Britain received in the region of £400 million worth of defence aid and over £300 million of off-shore procurement which was not only of great assistance in the major rearmament undertaken by the Attlee government but also played no small part in enabling Britain to continue performing her considerable global responsibilities in the early 1950s.

Growing strains in the alliance

The picture so far presented of the Anglo-American partnership reaching a post-war peak in the Korean War, providing the mainspring of Atlantic defence, and characterized by a 'plethora of informal agreements' is only a partial one, however. The primacy of the anti-communist alliance remained a constant feature of Anglo-American relations but alongside the cooperation in both the Far East and Europe important differences over security issues increasingly emerged which created important strains in the partnership.

One cause of dispute arose in 1951 over the signing of the ANZUS Treaty between the United States, Australia and New Zealand. For perhaps political as well as strategic reasons the two Commonwealth countries recognized that they would have to look in future to the United States rather than Britain for defence. For the United States the arrangement was merely a formalization of the role they had played during and after the war, and represented part of a wider system of alliances which the American government was attempting to establish to contain the spread of communism. From the point of view of Britain, however, to be excluded from an alliance between her major ally and two countries with whom she had traditionally had such close relations, especially in terms of security, was rather upsetting. Britain welcomed the Treaty but, as the Foreign Secretary at the time, Herbert Morrison, admitted in somewhat restrained terms, 'it would not have been unwelcome to us if we had been included in the proposed pact'.[18]

Despite the irritation over ANZUS there were other important divergences of interest as well. During the joint discussions about Korea much the same kind of arguments about the relative importance of Europe and the Far East which had caused problems between 1941 and 1945 arose once again, causing difficulties in Anglo-American relations. For geographical, political and strategic reasons the victory of the communist forces in China and the threat of Soviet advances in the Far East posed a serious threat to the United States which required a major response. The spread of communism was also a source of serious worry to the British leaders but they did not view the danger in quite the same light. They remained more doubtful than the American government about the solidarity of the Sino–Soviet Alliance and the prospects of a 'domino' effect in the Far East. With the different perspectives of the two states, important difficulties arose during the Korean War over what to do about Chinese involvement in the war as well as over the recognition of China and the issue of Formosa.[19] While pressure came from some American circles to widen the war, as the situation deteriorated the British counselled moderation and tended to look for ways to achieve a cease-fire. Thus when news reached London that American generals were pushing for the use of atomic weapons Attlee flew to Washington to add his weight to those opposing such an escalation of the war. From Britain's point of view everything had to be done to prevent the United States from becoming sucked into a major war in Asia which would only deflect the American administration from its recent commitment to Western European defence, which the Labour Foreign Secretary Bevin had worked so hard to achieve.

The concern to prevent American over-involvement in Asia, which might be deterimental to British security interests, became in some respects an even greater source of dissension with the changes of government in both countries. It might have been expected that the return of the Churchill government in October 1951 and the election of President Eisenhower in November 1952 would have resulted in much closer ties between the two countries as wartime friendships were renewed at the top. This was not, however, wholly to be the case. Indeed relations, especially in the Far East and Middle East, became particularly difficult as the personal antipathy of Sir Anthony Eden, the British Foreign Secretary and John Foster Dulles, the American Secretary of State, contributed to the widening of already divergent interests.[20]

Apart from residual difficulties over the Korean War and the China problem, the source of greatest dispute in Asia focused on Indo-China. The deterioration of the French position during 1953 led to a serious debate in the United States about the value of direct intervention and the need to establish a regional defence organization in South-East Asia to meet the perceived spread of communism. Although sympathizing with those such as Admiral Radford, the US Chief of Staff, and Vice-President Nixon, who advocated intervention to save the French position, Dulles favoured a more ambiguous policy of threats which left open the prospect of intervention to make the communist forces more amenable to negotiation. Dulles's attempt to establish a firm unified Anglo-American commitment along these lines, however, was rejected by the British. To Churchill and Eden, the Secretary of State's proposals were likely to lead to confrontation with China and the Soviet Union. Instead Eden favoured a more diplomatic solution at the conference table. With Stalin dead, the British government saw the best prospects of achieving a compromise agreement in Indo-China through the Geneva Conference (which had been called initially to deal with the lingering problem of Korea and more generally in easing tension with the Soviet Union). The difference in approach and the friction which it caused was highlighted by Eden's refusal to allow Sir Roger Makins, the British Ambassador in Washington, to attend the preliminary conference on a South-East Asian collective defence organization held on 18 April 1954.[21] Britain was later to become a member of SEATO when it was set up in May 1954 but in April the Foreign Secretary was concerned not to prejudice the success of the talks on Indo-China scheduled to take place in Geneva.

The problems were to remain even after the Geneva Conference had produced a negotiated compromise agreement. Dulles portrayed what Harold Macmillan has described as 'elephantine obstinacy' and refused to sign the agreements.[22] Instead the American Secretary of State declared that the US would 'take note of them'.

While Britain was attempting to secure a negotiated settlement to the Indo-China problem and thereby prevent American involvement in another Asian war, difficulties were also occurring over specifically European defence issues. In September 1950 the United States made an appeal for German rearmament to help counter the vast superiority of Soviet conventional military strength in Eastern Europe. In so doing they made it clear that if the European members of NATO refused to go along with their proposal the United States might not take part in an integrated European Command. For the French this created a particularly difficult dilemma. Continued American involvement in the defence of Europe was at this time as important to the French government as it was to the British. At the same time, however, vivid memories of the past made them shrink from the prospects of the creation of a new German national army. The French responded on 25 October 1950 with the Pleven Plan which advocated the setting up of a European Defence Community (EDC). The plan envisaged the creation of a European Army, into which national contingents would be integrated at the level of the smallest possible unit.

The strength of the plan from the French point of view was that there would be no German army as such, but German battalions distributed amongst European brigades. The plan also appealed to the European integrationists, especially in France, because it proposed that the new army would be under a European Minister of Defence and responsible to a European Assembly. It was also envisaged that there would be a European Defence Council and a European defence budget. As such the EDC proposal was in line with plans for a European Coal and Steel Community put forward in May 1950 and the aspirations of those such as Monnet and Schuman for even wider political integration which were supported by the United States.

Ingenious as the Pleven Plan was, neither the Labour government at the time nor the Conservative government which came to power in Britain in October 1951, felt able to join the proposed EDC. Churchill had himself suggested the creation of a European army in August 1950, but, with the reality of joining such a force, Churchill's Conservative government, like its predecessor, was prepared to associate itself with the EDC but was not willing to become a member.[23] To governments of both left and right, Britain continued to have global responsibilities which precluded absorption into a purely European military or political community.

Despite American support for the EDC and belief that Britain's future lay in some form of European union, there was little pressure in the early 1950s for Britain to join. The central importance of resisting the spread of communism meant that the American government was prepared to accept Britain's independent position. Eden reports in his memoirs that on a visit to Rome at the end of November 1951 for a North Atlantic Council meeting he was actually discouraged from joining the EDC by General Eisenhower, who at this time was SACEUR. Eisenhower told Eden that an offer by Britain to join at that time would in his opinion be 'a mistake'. 'He thought we should do all in our power to encourage the European Army, but, if we were to offer to enter it at this stage, we should further complicate the budgetary and other technical arrangements and would delay rather than hasten a final solution'. Eisenhower's view was that both

Britain and the United States 'could be more effective supporting the European Army within the Atlantic Organization'.[24]

In line with this approach, when concern was expressed in Europe and especially in France over Britain's lack of enthusiasm for the EDC, an Anglo-American agreement was reached to provide a joint declaration of support for the Community. According to this undertaking, which accompanied the signing of the EDC Treaty in May 1952, it was agreed that:

> If any action from whatever quarter threatens the integrity or unity of the Community, the two governments will regard this as a threat to their own security. They will act in accordance with Article 4 of the North Atlantic Treaty.[25]

As the process of ratification of the treaty lingered on, however, between 1952 and 1954 a change began to take place in Anglo-American relations. Dulles increasingly urged Britain to take a more positive role in securing a solution to the problem of European defence. At the Bermuda Conference in December 1953 he even hinted at the possibility that the United States Congress might not continue its firm support for NATO if the situation continued to drag on.[26] Dulles followed this up at a press conference later in the month by his famous warning of the possibility of an 'agonizing reappraisal' of American foreign policy if the EDC should fail.[27] In a meeting with Eden the next day Dulles seemed to blame Britain for the problems which had arisen. Because of this he suggested that the United States and Britain were approaching 'a parting of the ways with regard to American policy'.[28] If things went wrong, he pointed out, 'the United States might swing over to a policy of Western hemispheric defence, with an emphasis on the Far East. This might not be immediately apparent, but once the trend started it would be difficult to stop.'[29]

Whether or not Dulles was bluffing is difficult to say. Certainly there were those in the United States who would have welcomed a change of emphasis away from Europe to the Far East. Such a possibility had always been of concern to British leaders both during the war and afterwards. Consequently with the announcement that the French National Assembly had rejected the EDC on 30 August 1954 Eden was bound to take the threat seriously. In order to preserve the alliance structure, which had become the cornerstone of British security policy, the Foreign Secretary responded with what H. G. Nicholas has described as 'the most adroit diplomatic operation of his career'.[30] Others see Eden's reaction as a belated attempt to save the situation which he had helped create by failing to take a lead earlier. However Eden's diplomacy is viewed, it achieved its objective. Between 11 and 17 September 1954 Eden toured the European capitals attempting to sell a salvage plan which was finally accepted at the London Conference (28 September to 3 October 1954) and the Paris

Conference (20 to 22 October 1954). According to the agreements signed in Paris the Federal Republic of Germany would be granted full sovereignty simultaneously with its accession to NATO and the Western European Union (WEU). The WEU itself was created by an agreement to extend the Brussels Treaty Organization to include the Federal Republic as well as Italy. The WEU was also to determine the maximum defence contribution to NATO which, in the case of the Federal Republic of Germany, was limited to twelve divisions.[31] Thereby the United States got the rearmament of Germany which they saw as being important to counteract Soviet conventional strength and France received safeguards on resurgent militarism in Germany. At the same time, to propitiate the French further, the British government made an historic pledge to maintain a permanent presence on the mainland of Europe of four divisions or the equivalent strength and the Second Tactical Air Force.

As such Britain was promising to go much further than she had hitherto been prepared to go in relation to the EDC. Ernest Bevin's policy had been to go into Europe as far as, but no further than, the United States. Sir Anthony Eden was now proposing to go further into Europe than the United States ever would, in order to retain that American commitment which was seen by both Labour and Conservative governments as being so vital to British and European security. The central aim of policy remained the same but the changed circumstances required a significant change of course in British policy. In a memorandum to the Prime Minister before the Nine Power Conference in London in September 1954 which had been called to discuss the EDC crisis, the Foreign Secretary highlighted the need for change in Britain's traditional position in this way:

> I realize that this would be an unprecedented commitment for the United Kingdom, but the hard fact is that it is impossible to organize an effective defence system in Western Europe, which in turn is essential for the security of the United Kingdom, without a major British contribution. This situation will persist for many years to come. By recognizing this fact and giving the new commitment we may succeed in bringing the Germans and French together *and keeping the Americans in Europe.*[32]

Eden's proposals were generally welcomed in the United States and thereby achieved the Foreign Secretary's major objective of preventing the threatened radical change in American strategic policy.

The new arrangements contained in the Paris Agreements had only been achieved after further strains in the relationship. The difficulties over Korea, Indo-China, the EDC (and also the Quemoy–Matsu Crisis), however, tended to be periodic and they were not characteristic of every aspect of the relationship in defence-related matters. In the fields of atomic energy and strategic planning in particular, relations progressively improved as the period wore on.

Atomic energy and strategic planning

To begin with, the difficulties which had characterized the late 1940s continued into the early 1950s. There was an amendment to the McMahon Act in the United States in October 1951 but it was limited to specific areas which would be of benefit to the American nuclear programme and 'was of very little help to the British'.[33] Under the new amendment it became possible to export fissile material from, or to, the United States provided that, in the President's view, 'the common defence and security' would not be adversely affected. As long as there was unanimous agreement in the USAEC, specific arrangements could be made involving the communication to another nation of restricted information on refining, purification and treatment of source material, reactor development, production of fissile material and research and development on all these areas. There was, however, to be no communication of restricted information on the design and fabrication of atomic weapons.

Problems also existed over the reluctance of the American authorities to act positively to a British request to use American facilities to conduct her first atomic test. A request was made to the American Chiefs of Staff in the summer of 1950 for the use of their facilities but no reply was received until October. When the reply was at last forthcoming it informed the British Chiefs of Staff, 'in somewhat curt terms', that the British request could not at present be considered.[34] A further request was made in the spring of 1951 which was again rejected. Faced with this refusal by the United States to help her ally in this field Britain decided instead to hold the test at Monte Bello after getting the necessary permission from Australia. Once again the British were rather bitter that although permission had been given to the US to base its strategic bombers in Britain, the Americans were not prepared to reciprocate in the case of test facilities. Eventually in 1951 the US did put forward proposals which would have enabled the British to have conducted their test in the United States but by this stage it was generally felt in Britain that Australia would be more advantageous from a political point of view. Mr Shinwell, the Minister of Defence at the time, argued in favour of the test taking place in Australia because it would show that Britain was 'not merely a satellite of the United States'.[35] British officials also felt that there was a danger that if the test took place in the US, the Americans could at any moment 'turn off the tap and leave us helpless'.[36] Largely for these reasons the incoming Conservative government eventually made the decision in favour of Monte Bello.

At the same time that these problems were taking place over test facilities, further difficulties were encountered in discussions over the use of nuclear weapons. Besides the attempt to secure agreement about the use of American strategic bombers operating from British bases, planners in Britain from the beginning of 1949 had also been trying in vain to get information about the American Strategic Air Plan as a whole. Even after Clement Attlee's visit to Washington in December 1950 to caution President Truman on the use of nuclear weapons in Korea, the British Chiefs of Staff remained concerned about the consequence of Britain's lack of knowledge about nuclear weapons if war broke out. The Chief of the Air Staff in particular urged that it was a matter of 'vital importance and extreme urgency that the United States should agree to an immediate joint study of the strategic use of the bomb, and to a disclosure to Britain of plans for its use'.[37] The existing situation he saw as being 'quite intolerable'. The Foreign Secretary at the time, Herbert Morrison, made much the same point in September 1951 when he met Dean Acheson, the American Secretary of State, to talk about the Strategic Air Plan.[38]

For all the pressure from London, however, little had been achieved in terms of discussions about the plan when the Conservatives returned to power in October 1951. The situation changed significantly, however, with Churchill's visit to Washington in January 1952 when, for the first time, there was a willingness to begin talks on the plan. Churchill was apparently told as much about the Strategic Air Plan as the Secretary of State, Dean Acheson, himself knew and he was given a personal briefing by the American Air Force. In some respects therefore, the January 1952 Washington visit was important in the evolution of Anglo-American military relations in that it produced 'a far better and more sympathetic feeling' towards Britain in the United States.[39] On the basis of his new and more favourable climate the American Secretary of Defence went further and authorized joint discussions on the strategic and tactical aspects of the Air Plan and by the end of 1952 the British COS apparently had received 'on a highly personal basis a great deal of information about the Plan'.[40]

It was this knowledge in large part which enabled the British Chiefs of Staff to undertake a major reappraisal of strategic doctrine in 1952 which seems to have had a significant influence on American and subsequently NATO strategic thinking. The Prime Minister returned from Washington deeply impressed by the awesome effects of the thermonuclear weapons which the Americans were working on. He immediately asked the British COS to review British strategy in the light of these new technological developments. The Chiefs met at a conference held at Greenwich in the early summer of 1952 and produced a Global Strategy Paper which has been described as 'the most influential British defence paper of the post-war period'.[41] The paper pointed out that the main aim of the West remained one of preventing Russia and China from achieving their objectives by 'infiltrating and disintegrating the free world, and to prevent war'. The British Chiefs emphasized, however, that new technology meant that there was now no defence against atomic attack and this meant the need to emphasize deterrence. They suggested that 'the primary deterrent must be Russian knowledge that any aggression would involve immediate and crushing atomic retaliation'.[42] To achieve this the allies had to possess not only atomic weapons and the means of delivery but also the capability at least to hold a Soviet advance in Western Europe with conventional forces.

According to the document the British part in Western strategy was fourfold:

> . . . to exercise influence on Cold War policy, to meet NATO obligations, to prepare for war in case the deterrent failed and to play a part, albeit a small one, in the main deterrent, the air offensive. This fourfold problem must be solved without ruining the economy.[43]

For both economic and strategic reasons the main implications of the paper was that although conventional forces were still important for overseas Cold War commitments and indeed in Europe, greater stress should be placed on nuclear deterrence. It was recognized that the main Western striking force rested with the American Strategic Air Command (SAC) but it was nevertheless felt that Britain still had an important part to play in this field. The Chiefs of Staff believed strongly that the task could not be left entirely to the Americans. In an argument later to be used widely by proponents of an independent British deterrent in the mid-1950s the COS maintained:

> We feel that to have no share in what is recognised as the main deterrent in the Cold War and the only Allied offensive in a world war, would seriously weaken British influence on United States policy and planning in the Cold War and in war would mean that the United Kingdom would have no claim to any share in policy or planning of the offensive.[44]

It was also felt that there were targets of primary strategic interest to Britain which the United States with a limited stockpile of nuclear weapons could not be relied upon to deal with adequately.

The Global Strategy Paper with its relative emphasis on nuclear deterrence came at a time when NATO, on American urging, had adopted the Lisbon goals with the emphasis on conventional rearmament. As such the Paper was in direct conflict with NATO planning and with American pressure for German rearmament and the formation of the European Defence Community. In July 1952 Sir John Slessor, the British Chief of Air Staff, went to Washington to discuss the Paper with the Americans. The initial response was predictably rather hostile. This was partly because of the political implications for German rearmament and her integration into NATO, and partly because of the impact on the proposed EDC, all of which it was felt would be undermined by the adoption of such a strategy. Opposition also arose because the American Chiefs of Staff believed that the proposals were more the product of economic than strategic reasoning. They were seen as being 'simply a rationalization of a British intent to renege on their NATO force commitments'.[45]

Despite these initial American criticisms and reservations about Britain's 'new assessment', the longer term response proved to be more favourable. In many respects the British Paper anticipated and perhaps helped to bring about changes which the American government itself introduced with the 1953 'New Look'.[46] It may be true that at the doctrinal level the Dullesian 'massive retaliation' strategy put relatively greater emphasis on nuclear deterrence than the Global Strategy Paper but there is little doubt that the re-assessment of strategy in 1952 in Britain and 1953/4 in the United States was based on very much the same kind of reasoning.

As both allies adopted a similar strategic doctrine their views – not surprisingly, given their predominance within NATO – also became increasingly reflected in alliance strategic planning. In sharp contrast to the emphasis on conventional rearmament represented by the 1952 Lisbon goals, the December 1954 NATO Council adopted, on Dulles's recommendation, a tactical nuclear doctrine which placed much greater stress on the role of nuclear weapons in deterring Soviet aggression and indeed in stopping Soviet forces if deterrence failed.

Despite the improvements in cooperation in strategic planning and the evolving similarities in strategic thinking, it is true that Churchill was no more successful in 1952 and 1953 than his predecessors in achieving greater technical cooperation in atomic energy with the United States. Before he went to Washington in January 1952 the Prime Minister seems to have believed that it would be relatively easy for him to renew collaboration with the United States. The Prime Minister was very proud of the close wartime cooperation in atomic matters and he was particularly critical of the way the Labour government had apparently thrown away the post-war benefits promised in his Hyde Park *aide-mémoire* with Roosevelt. Thus he hoped during his visit to be able to 'arrange to be allocated a reasonable share of what they have made so largely on our initiative and substantial scientific contribution'.[47] If the Prime Minister was 'living in the past on this issue',[48] as his special adviser, Lord Cherwell, believed, the discussions with Truman in January 1952 must have rapidly brought about the realization of the extent to which the relationship in atomic energy had changed since his last period in office. He soon recognized that there was no chance of a change in legislation given the mood in the United States. He therefore changed his position somewhat and attempted to get the Americans to allow 'the maximum cooperation' within the limits set by the McMahon Act.[49] Even this, however, failed to improve the flow of information and apart from some improvements in intelligence cooperation the remnants of the 1948 *modus vivendi* continued to govern cooperation during the following year.

The success of Britain's first atomic test at Monte Bello on 3 October 1952 led to new hopes that closer cooperation with the United States might result. No American observers were invited to the test to demonstrate that the programme had thus far been an entirely British affair. Having recognized that Britain was capable of conducting such a test alone, the Prime Minister, in particular, believed that the American authorities would finally realize that there was no purpose to be gained by wasting resources by the duplication of effort. Speaking in the House of Commons on 23 October 1952 Churchill explained the significance of the test:

> We have conducted the operation ourselves and I do not doubt that it will lead to a much closer American interchange of information than has hitherto taken place . . . . There are a very large number of important people in the United States concerned with this matter who have been most anxious for a long time that Britain should be kept better informed. This event will greatly facilitate and support the task which these gentlemen have set themselves.[50]

One of those in the United States who felt that Britain had been rather unfairly treated after the war in the field of atomic energy cooperation was General Eisenhower.[51] Consequently, with his election to the Presidency in November 1952, the prospects from the British point of view of a general improvement in collaboration in the one area of the relationship which had proved most difficult since 1945 seemed much brighter. Within a short period after the American election Churchill was pressing for a 'restoration of the nuclear relationship which had existed when they were comrades in arms'.[52] Armed with a promise obtained from American officials in October 1952 to exchange data on the effects of nuclear weapons, together with a photographed copy of the original Hyde Park *aide-mémoire*, Churchill met the new President at Bermuda in December 1953. At the meeting Eisenhower promised to ask the next session of Congress to make changes in the existing atomic energy legislation which would permit a greater sharing of information and equipment with Britain. Promises of 'a new era' in collaboration on nuclear matters had been forthcoming on a number of occasions in the past, only to be dashed by the failure or inability of American governments to live up to their word. On this occasion, however, the optimism in British circles was to be justified. President Eisenhower sent a message to Congress on 17 February 1954 requesting amendments to the McMahon Act. By this time the mood had changed in the United States and the opposition to increased cooperation with Britain which had been so strong in the first eight years or so after the war had declined in intensity.

The result of the President's request was the Atomic Energy Act of 1954 which allowed the sharing of data on the external characteristics of nuclear weapons in terms of their size, weight, shape, yield and effects.[53] The Act did not, however, go so far as to permit cooperation on the design and fabrication of the nuclear components themselves.

The American administration, especially Dulles, viewed the new legislation as being particularly important for NATO as a whole. In December 1954 the NATO Council accepted a tactical nuclear strategy and the Atomic Energy Act enabled the United States to make information available to her allies on the training of forces with tactical nuclear weapons. The Act also resulted, however, in Britain receiving 'preferred treatment' and as such laid the foundations for the full blossoming of nuclear cooperation in the late 1950s.

As a consequence of the 1954 legislation two agreements were signed on 15 June 1955.[54] One provided for the exchange of information on civil uses of atomic energy, which included the transfer of fissile materials and equipment. The other, in the defence field, provided for the exchange of information on the military aspects of atomic energy concerned with: (a) the development of defence plans; (b) the training of personnel in the employment of and defence against atomic weapons; and (c) the evaluation of the capabilities of potential enemies in the employment of atomic weapons. In many respects these agreements, particularly the one governing military information, signalled a small but significant step forward in cooperation between the two countries and led to further requests from Britain for increased collaboration. Although the major breakthrough did not come until 1958, the 1955 Agreements did at least provide an improved atmosphere which contributed to greater intimacy between the scientific communities of each country.[55]

In June 1956, for example, an important agreement was signed which had long-term consequences for Britain and the 'special relationship'. Under this agreement the United States agreed to provide Britain with vital information on the nuclear submarine *Nautilus*.[56] It was largely this agreement which provided data on nuclear ship propulsion reactors and thereby contributed to Britain's capability to produce nuclear submarines which put her in a unique position to accept the offer of Polaris missiles at Nassau in December 1962.[57] Despite the fact that the missiles were also eventually offered to France, Britain was the only European state at the time capable of developing a nuclear submarine from which to fire Polaris.

Arrangements were also established in October 1956, at the time when difficulties were coming to a climax over Suez, which allowed British and American nuclear scientists to cooperate in research on the control of thermonuclear reactions.[58] The United States had conducted its first thermonuclear test in November 1952 but Britain's independent research in this field meant that, by the mid-fifties, she had something to offer the

US. By 1956 the British thermonuclear programme was well under way. As a result of a series of research decisions taken in 1952, the final decision to produce thermonuclear weapons was taken in 1954 and in May 1957 Britain was in a position to undertake her first test in this field at Christmas Island in the Pacific. Once again Britain's competence and independent expertise in this field encouraged the United States to accept cooperation as the British had originally hoped it would.

Suez and the ruptured alliance

Despite the earlier difficulties, therefore, the period from 1953 to 1956 saw an improvement in the fields of nuclear cooperation and strategic planning. Significant as this new intimacy was in the field of information exchange, however, it was not representative of Anglo-American relations as a whole or indeed of political–military relations in general between the two countries. It represented an important qualification, but the general picture of frequently strained relations remained the characteristic feature of the early and middle fifties.

Apart from the difficulties in the Far East, SouthEast Asia and Europe the area which brought the alliance to breaking point was the Middle East. As in other areas the poor personal relations between Dulles and Eden played their part. Even more than this, however, the difficulties which arose were the result of a clash of interests, in which Britain was prepared to act without her major ally's knowledge or approval because of the importance of the issues at stake, and the United States was prepared to bring about the failure of its junior partner's policies with which it disapproved.[59]

For Britain the Middle East, and particularly Egypt, had been vital areas in strategic thinking for nearly a century. In the post-war period, as the Cold War developed and its own power declined, the government hoped to secure American assistance, together with moderate Arab support, for a common front against communism. Such a plan, however, ignored the rise of Arab, and especially Egyptian, nationalism. It also neglected the continuing suspicions of British imperialism in the United States and overrated the extent to which the American government would be prepared to make an explicit and sustained commitment in support of the British position in the Middle East. Thus the British attempt to establish a Middle East Defence Organization (MEDO) in 1951 and to retain a military presence in Egypt in the period up to 1954 foundered on both Arab objections and lack of enthusiastic American support. Even with the Baghdad Pact (formed in April 1955) which the United States had done so much to initiate, fear of alienating radical Arab opinion which opposed the Pact, prevented the American government from joining or indeed even openly endorsing it. With some justification British leaders felt bitter at having to face the brunt of Arab criticism alone.[60]

The differences between the two allies over Middle Eastern affairs finally came to a head, however, with the Suez crisis between July and November 1956. The detailed story of the misunderstandings in Anglo-American relations and the sheer folly of the leading figures in both countries has been told many times and need not detain us here.[61] Suffice it to say that the Anglo-French invasion of the Canal without informing Washington brought an orchestrated series of political and economic manoeuvres by the American government against its two allies designed to halt the operation. Of these pressures, economic sanctions in particular proved to be decisive. Britain was brought to the edge of bankruptcy, with the offer of help from the United States only if the military campaign was called off. Nor were political and economic pressures the only ones used. A degree of military obstruction was also apparently employed. According to one source, during the operation:

> American submarines suddenly were detected all over the ocean. Finally the Commander of the British Mediterranean Fleet had to ask his Sixth Fleet counterpart to bring them to the surface. There was a distinct possibility that the British might inadvertently destroy an American submarine. There seemed little doubt that the Sixth Fleet had orders to obstruct the operation by all peaceful means.[62]

In most respects Suez represented the post-war nadir in Anglo-American relations particularly in the political-military relations sphere. Despite the continuation and indeed improvement in certain areas of cooperation, especially atomic energy, defence-related issues in the Far East, Indochina and Europe had been the sources of intermittent friction in the alliance from 1950 onwards. Suez represented the culmination of these difficulties and demonstrated the limits and fragility of the 'special relationship' which both countries had carefully rebuilt in the late 1940s and early 1950s. Both Dulles and Eden seemed to have regarded the clash of interests involved as being at least for the moment more important than the health of the Anglo-American alliance.[63]

3 The Preferential Relationship 1957–1962

Despite the trauma of the Suez crisis, both Britain and the United States moved very quickly in the latter part of the 1950s to repair the alliance. A realization of the harmful effects of the clash over Suez together with a deterioration in the relations with the Soviet Union helped to bring the allies closer together again.[1] Significantly the symbols of the renewed determination to work together were particularly evident in the defence field. The progress made in 1954 and 1955 in the atomic energy field was maintained and in 1958 the McMahon Act was finally repealed, returning Britain to the kind of wide-ranging collaboration with the United States which she had enjoyed during the war and which she had worked so hard to re-establish after 1946. After the earlier problems, atomic energy was now not only in line with the other aspects of the alliance but provided the most important manifestation of the return to a close partnership.

Collaboration was also extended in other areas of defence relations, including the vital delivery systems for nuclear weapons. After a number of important agreements it was in this field that another crisis occurred in 1962 over the Skybolt missile which, although not quite as severe as Suez, nevertheless seriously threatened the fabric of the alliance for a time. Just as Suez proved to be a milestone in the return to collaboration, however, so the Skybolt crisis resulted in a far-reaching agreement at the Nassau Conference in December 1962 which greatly reinforced, and indeed extended further, the special defence relationship between the two countries.

The Bermuda and Washington Conferences

After Suez, although Winston Churchill was no longer in office, he wrote a personal letter to President Eisenhower, unknown to the Foreign Office or the Secretariat at 10 Downing Street, appealing for a restoration of close relations between the two countries. This rather moving letter is perhaps worth quoting in full because, as Harold Macmillan himself has noted, it was probably of 'material assistance' in helping to re-establish close links with the United States.[2]

> There is not much left for me to do in this world and I have neither the wish nor the strength to involve myself in the present political stress

and turmoil. But I do believe, with unfaltering conviction, that the theme of the Anglo-American alliance is more important today than at any time since the war. You and I had some part in raising it to the plane on which it has stood. Whatever the arguments adduced here and in the United States for or against Anthony's action in Egypt, it will now be an act of folly, on which our whole civilization may founder, to let events in the Middle East come between us.

There seems to be a growing misunderstanding and frustration on both sides of the Atlantic. If they be allowed to develop, the skies will darken and it is the Soviet Union that will ride the storm. We should leave it to the historians to argue the rights and wrongs of all that has happened during the past years. What we must face is that at present these events have left a situation in the Middle East in which spite, envy and malice prevail on the one hand and our friends are beset by bewilderment and uncertainty for the future. The Soviet Union is attempting to move into this dangerous vacuum, for you must have no doubt that a triumph for Nasser would be an even greater triumph for them.

The very survival of all that we believe in may depend on our setting our minds to forestalling them. If we do not take immediate action in harmony, it is no exaggeration to say that we must expect to see the Middle East and the North African coastline under Soviet control and Western Europe placed at the mercy of the Russians. If at this juncture we fail in our responsibility to act positively and fearlessly we shall no longer be worthy of the leadership with which we are entrusted.

I write this letter because I know where your heart lies. You are now the only one who can influence events both in UNO and the free world to ensure that the great essentials are not lost in bickerings and pettiness among the nations. Yours is indeed a heavy responsibility and there is no greater believer in your capacity to bear it or well-wisher in your task than your old friend

Winston S. Churchill[3]

President Eisenhower expressed his agreement with these sentiments for a rapid return to a close partnership between the two countries in a long personal reply to Churchill.[4] He was also aware that the initial step had to be taken by the United States. One of the first illustrations of the desire to repair fences came in the defence field with the American proposals in January 1957 to deploy a number of IRBMs in Britain. The weapons and specialized equipment were to cost Britain nothing and British personnel were to man the sites as soon as they were trained. From the British point of view the American offer was very welcome because it provided outward proof of restored relations which the new Prime Minister, Harold Macmillan, had made the corner-stone of his foreign policy. More than this, however, Macmillan saw that the provision of IRBMs 'would give us a rocket deterrent long before we could hope to produce one ourselves; moreover it would provide full training for our own men in these new and sophisticated armaments'.[5] At a time when the Conservative government was in the process of adopting its own 'New Look' in defence with greater emphasis on nuclear deterrence this was an important consideration.

The details of the arrangements to provide the IRBMs were worked out at the Bermuda meeting between President Eisenhower and Prime Minister Macmillan between 21–4 March 1957.[6] At the meeting, which Eisenhower later described 'as the most successful international conference that I had attended since the close of World War II',[7] Britain was given sixty Thor missiles. The missiles were to be deployed under a 'two-key system' in East Anglia with the missiles and warheads provided by the United States and the supporting facilities by Britain.

Having taken this first step towards a restoration of close links, further collaboration followed swiftly. In late October 1957, two weeks after the launching of the Soviet Sputnik, Macmillan went to Washington to attempt to achieve a further breakthrough in an even more important area of the relationship: that of atomic energy. By this time the atmosphere between London and Washington had improved to such an extent that participants at the talks compared the degree of intimacy with that achieved at Cairo and Casablanca.[8] At the meeting two technical committees were rapidly set up: one under Sir Richard Powell, Permanent Secretary in the Ministry of Defence, to consider collaboration on weapons systems; the other under Admiral Lewis Strauss, the Chairman of the US Atomic Energy Commission and Sir Edmund Plowden of the Foreign Office, to consider nuclear collaboration.[9] On the latter question the President, and even John Foster Dulles himself, had by this time become convinced that the McMahon Act was 'obsolete'.[10] Macmillan reports that Eisenhower even went so far as to describe the Act as 'one of the most deplorable incidents in American history, of which he personally felt ashamed'.[11] In line with this view, the 'Declaration of Common Purpose' which was issued at the end of the Washington Conference included not only a general agreement on greater cooperation between the two countries but also a commitment by the President to 'request the Congress to amend the Atomic Energy Act of 1954 *as may be necessary and desirable to permit close and fruitful collaboration* of scientists and engineers of Great Britain, the United States and other friendly countries'.[12]

Unlike some of the earlier promises made by American governments in this field the President's request led to legislation which enabled both states to sign the *Agreement for Cooperation on Uses of Atomic Energy for Mutual Defence Purposes* on 3 July 1958.[13] Under this Act, which is without doubt one of the most important peacetime agreements ever arrived at between the two countries, Britain was able to receive information from the United States on the design and production of nuclear warheads as well as fissile material. Significantly also, Britain was the only state to benefit from the agreement. Under its terms the transfer of information and materials was permitted solely to those countries which had made 'substantial progress' in the development of nuclear weapons and where it would improve the existing atomic weapon design, development and fabrication capacity of the recipient country. The intention to provide Britain alone with 'special' or preferential treatment was implicit in the report of the JAEC which defined 'substantial progress' in a way which could only apply to the United Kingdom. The report argued that

> .... the cooperating nation must have achieved considerably more than just a mere theoretical knowledge of atomic weapon design or testing of a limited number of atomic weapons. It is intended that the cooperating nation must have achieved a capability of its own of fabricating a variety of atomic weapons and constructed and operated the necessary facilities including weapons research and development laboratories, weapons manufacturing facilities, a weapons testing station and trained personnel to operate each of these facilities.[14]

The significance of the agreement, apart from the fact that it discriminated in favour of Britain, was that it provided a continuing basis for wide-ranging nuclear collaboration between the two countries especially in the field of the design and production of nuclear warheads which has continued through to the present day.[15] As a result of the agreement Britain was able to design and produce smaller, more sophisticated warheads of her own which were needed firstly for the ill-fated Blue Streak missile and later for the American Polaris missile. In this field as a result of American assistance Britain has been able to retain an important lead over all the other nuclear medium powers.

As with previous agreements the intimacy which the repeal of the McMahon Act recreated also encouraged further intimacy in nuclear relationships. In May 1959, for example, an amendment to the 1958 Atomic Energy Act was signed which contained a provision enabling Britain to buy from the United States component parts of nuclear weapons and weapons systems. It also made it possible to exchange British plutonium for American enriched uranium.[16] As a result of the 1958 Act and its subsequent amendment Britain was able to purchase a marine nuclear propulsion plant from the US for the first British nuclear submarine, the *Dreadnought*.

Out of the meetings at Bermuda in March and at Washington in October therefore, a series of agreements were signed which recreated a solid partnership in the defence field between Britain and the United States. Given the seriousness of the split at Suez, the degree of intimacy and cooperation achieved in little more than twelve months seems remarkable. This is particularly the case when it is remembered that Britain was adopting a strategy which emphasized nuclear weapons at a time when both the United States and to a certain extent NATO were beginning to move away from the concept of 'massive retaliation'.[17] It is perhaps interesting to ask how such a rapid rapprochement (with the American President's willingness to support the British deterrent) can be explained. No doubt a degree of sentiment and the close personal ties between the leaders played their part.[18] The frankness and mutual trust between Eisenhower and Macmillan which stemmed from their Second World War days together, led them both to give the Anglo-American alliance the highest priority after the Suez débâcle. There was more to it than this, however. Not only was the Soviet Union apparently adopting a more confident and aggressive line in relations with the West, with the leadership struggle resolved, but her military strength was also rapidly expanding. To match what seemed to be the emergence of a 'bomber gap' and to deter possible Soviet moves in Europe the United States felt that it required an up-dating of its capacity to strike at the Soviet homeland. Britain had been prepared to act as the main base of the American Strategic Air Command (SAC) from 1948 onwards and now for a time she was the only European state prepared to provide launch-sites for American Intermediate Range Ballistic Missiles. Inevitably the common defence planning, training and equipping of the forces under the 'two-key system' involved, could only take place if British commanders knew more about the use of these missiles and had some access to American intelligence estimates of Soviet capability.

The launching of Sputnik in October 1957 undoubtedly provided a new urgency and concern to strengthen Western defences as a whole and in particular to increase scientific and technological cooperation with America's most advanced partner in the alliance. Britain obviously had the capability and determination to continue in the nuclear business and increasingly President Eisenhower recognized the need to avoid unnecessary duplication and wastage in the military field.

Nor was the cooperation likely to be a one-way process for the United States. The British thermonuclear test at Christmas Island in the Pacific in May 1957 had been very successful and American officials were 'subsequently amazed to learn the full extent of British knowledge and expertise'.[19] In some areas, as Aubrey Jones, the Minister of Supply, told the House of Commons in 1959, British scientists and engineers were further advanced and had information which was of considerable value to their American counterparts.[20]

Thus the darkening international atmosphere, the apparently rapid increase in Soviet military capability and British expertise in certain fields made a renewal of the alliance with Britain valuable from the American point of view. As far as Britain was concerned the cooperation achieved as a result of the Bermuda and Washington meetings was not only of obvious benefit but it also signalled the success of the policies pursued by both Labour and Conservative governments since the McMahon Act of

1946.[21] The patient process of continuing with her own deterrent in the hope that eventually full-scale cooperation would be resumed had finally paid off. Without her own independent atomic programme it seems highly unlikely that Britain would have received the kind of preferential treatment she did on nuclear matters and the same rapport between governments would not have been achieved.

In many respects the 1958 Agreement and the related agreements which followed brought atomic collaboration to the very heart of the 'special relationship'. The decision to renew cooperation, however, also had an important effect on the bilateral alliance in general as well as on other areas of the relationship in the defence field. As Andrew Pierre puts it, 'the very act of nuclear-sharing . . . created an environment in which American trust in the British government deepened so that American officials discussed a wider range of military and political topics *more frankly with their British counterparts than with officials of other* friendly nations'.[22]

This trust was particularly evident in the relationship between the armed forces of the two countries. Relations between the Services had, in general, been good throughout the post-war period despite the ups and downs of political relationships. By the latter part of the 1950s informal ties were especially close between the RAF and USAF. This was partly the result of similar experiences which both had gone through in establishing themselves as the 'newest' of the Services and partly due to their close working relationship in the Second World War. This close partnership had further been enhanced by the establishment of American air bases after 1948. As Strategic Air Command (SAC) had established a nuclear bombing capacity in the 1940s it also provided a model for the RAF when the British attempted to develop a V-Bomber force in the 1950s. Indeed the RAF received every encouragement from the US Air Force to develop a strategic nuclear bomber force. Such was the intimacy between the two Services that they even helped each other in inter-service disputes and clashes in Whitehall and Washington over budgetary allocations.[23]

From the US Air Force's point of view the relatively small British V-Bomber force was seen as a supplement rather than an unnecessary duplication of resources. General Powers, the Commander of SAC, in particular, argued that Britain's bombers made an important, indeed essential, contribution to the Western deterrent as a whole. In the General's words, 'Having regard to Britain's closer proximity we rely on her V-Bombers to provide an important part of the first wave of the allied retaliatory force.'[24] For Britain to play her part in this 'retaliatory force', close liaison with SAC was obviously necessary and according to one senior RAF officer 'a complete interchange of views on nuclear strategy, nuclear weapons, bombing tactics and equipment' began in the late 1950s which 'continued right up to the demise of Bomber Command in 1968'.[25]

The same period also saw the growing integration for operational purposes of British and American nuclear striking forces, together with the establishment of joint targeting procedures through direct links between Bomber Command Headquarters in Britain and the Headquarters of SAC at Omaha, Nebraska.

The Anglo-American strategic debate

Discussions about the role of nuclear weapons were not confined to the air forces of each country or even to the respective Services. The middle and late 1950s saw the development of a 'wider market for strategic ideas' in both countries.[26] Increasingly civilians on each side of the Atlantic began to involve themselves in the debate about nuclear strategy which was becoming an important issue at this time. Faced with much the same kind of problems individuals like Alistair Buchan, Denis Healey, Richard Crossman, P. M. S. Blackett, Anthony Buzzard and John Strachey in Britain and Bernard Brodie, Albert Wohlstetter, Henry Kissinger, Thomas Schelling and Herman Kahn in the United States, turned their minds to the complexities of deterrence and notions of limited war. For most of these 'critics' the declaratory strategy of the West based upon the Dullesian doctrine of 'massive retaliation' was rapidly losing its credibility as the Soviet Union developed the capability to strike not only Western Europe with nuclear weapons but also the United States itself. The strategic literature in both countries began to emphasize the need for a graduated deterrence policy with increased flexibility to avoid the stark choice of nuclear surrender or suicide offered by a strategy based on 'massive retaliation'.

How far American thinkers and writers influenced their British counterparts or vice versa in this 'golden age' of strategic thought is difficult, if not impossible, to establish. Certainly the volume of literature in the United States was much greater than in Britain, its quality was often better and American writers achieved much greater publicity for their works. It is nevertheless true that 'critics on both sides of the Atlantic benefited from personal contacts with each other and from the rapidly mounting literature on nuclear strategy being written by the defence intellectuals of the Anglo-Saxon world'.[27] British writers undoubtedly played their part. They made an early and important contribution to the debate which has often tended to go unrecognized.[28]

The Lebanon and Jordan landings

Apart from the Anglo-Saxon strategic debate and the close collaboration established at the nuclear level, shortly after Suez, cooperation was re-established in the operational sphere. Not only did the armed forces of the two states work together closely to meet a perceived threat to their interests and those of their friends, but they did so in the geographical area where the alliance had come so close to collapse in November 1956.

After forestalling the Anglo-French invasion of the Suez canal President Eisenhower asked Congress on 5 January 1957 to authorize economic and military aid to states in the Middle East that requested it, 'against overt armed aggression from any nation controlled by international communism'. To some observers the Eisenhower Doctrine, as it became known, represented a rather cynical attempt by the US to replace British influence which had suffered such a humiliating blow at Suez largely as a result of American policies.[29] To others, however, the American initiative was more an indication that the Eisenhower administration was having second thoughts about its role at Suez and now recognized the need to fill the rather dangerous power vacuum which they had helped to create.[30] Whichever is true, and it may well be that both motivations played a part in the formulation of the doctrine, the United States seems to have been genuinely prepared to work closely with Britain from August 1957 onwards. This was to include joint military action in July 1958, when a coup in Iraq brought an appeal from Lebanon and Jordan for Western assistance. Both President Chamoun of Lebanon and King Husain of Jordan feared attempts to overthrow their governments and looked to Britain and the United States for military help to retain their positions.

Following the visit to Washington on 16 July by Selwyn Lloyd, the British Foreign Secretary, and Sir William Dickson, the Chief of the Defence Staff, arrangements were made to land US Marines in the Lebanon and British Paratroops in Jordan. The operations undertaken to provide support for two important pro-Western regimes were characterized by a high degree of coordination in both planning and execution. As Robert Murphy confirms, 'The British navy provided support in the Mediterranean and made facilities in Cyprus available to us while the United States gave logistic support by flying supplies into Jordan for the British contingent there.'[31] The provision of Globemasters by the United States was particularly important to the operation in Jordan. The British lines of communication were vulnerable and the use of the large American transport aircraft to fly in supplies from Cyprus to Amman contributed in no small part to the success of the operation.

Overall the operations were a further clear demonstration of the renewal of Anglo-American cooperation. In November, President Eisenhower emphasized this point when he wrote to Prime Minister Macmillan about the landings. In his letter the President pointed out that both countries could 'take special satisfaction in the complete understanding and splendid cooperation which was evident between our two governments in these undertakings'.[32]

The 'Metallic Warrior' and the continuing saga of US bases

Despite the wide-ranging cooperation which had been re-established by the late 1950s various problems did however arise from time to time causing a certain amount of friction in the alliance. Apart from a certain amount of anti-Americanism in Britain after Suez, one of the biggest worries continued to centre on the use of American bases in Britain. Two incidents in particular occurred in February 1958 and July 1960 respectively which raised the question once again about the precise conditions governing the use of these bases. Apart from the 'Attlee/Churchill Understandings' the arrangements under which American aircraft operated from Britain were as vague in the late 1950s as they were in 1951 and 1952. The situation was complicated somewhat by the further agreement announced in February 1958 to base American Thor missiles in Britain under a 'two-key system'. Shortly after the publication of the agreement on 27 February, the British and American governments were rather embarrassed by a speech made by an American Air Force colonel. In his speech the officer, Colonel Zinc, claimed to have 'in his hands full operational control of rockets and rocket bases in Britain'.[33] The speech caused a rumpus in Britain and in his memoirs Harold Macmillan describes the incident in the following terms:

> There was a great 'flap' this morning over an extraordinary statement by a certain Colonel Zinc – an American 'Eagle Colonel' of the Air Force who claims to be about to take over operational command of the rockets and rocket bases in England. As this is in direct contradiction (a) to the terms of the agreement published last Monday (b) What we told Parliament on Monday and in the debate yesterday, Colonel Zinc has put his foot in it on a grand scale.[34]

Events were eventually smoothed over but it appears that the temporary difficulties caused by this 'metallic warrior' did not represent just an isolated incident. Although he does not elaborate Macmillan goes as far as to suggest that the Anglo-American alliance was 'constantly being put in jeopardy by the folly of American officers in all ranks'.[35]

The Prime Minister no doubt had the 'Colonel Zinc incident' in mind when he went to Washington on 7 June 1958. In his discussions with the American President, Macmillan once again brought up the question of US bases in Britain and the use of bombs and warheads which were under joint control. As a result both heads of state apparently initialled an agreement at the end of the talks which replaced 'the loose arrangement made by Attlee and confirmed by Churchill'.[36]

The RB 47 incident

Despite this agreement, however, another problem arose in July 1960 which highlighted the deficiencies which continued to exist over the use of American bases. On 1 July an American RB 47 aircraft set out from a British base at Brize Norton and disappeared shortly afterwards during an electro-magnetic survey flight across the Arctic Ocean. The mystery of the aircraft's disappearance occurred at a time of deteriorating East–West relations. The U2 affair and the failure of the Paris Summit in May, together with problems in the Congo and lack of progress in disarmament negotiations, had resulted in growing tension between the super-powers. Ten days after the RB 47 was lost the Soviet authorities announced that the plane had been shot down over Russian territorial waters. This was followed by a strong warning to the British government of the dangerous consequences which might follow 'the provocative acts of the American Air Force operating from British territory'.[37] The Western powers later claimed that the whole affair was staged by the Khruschev administration deliberately to provoke an incident. According to the official US reply on 13 July the RB 47 was not flying over Russian territory when it was chased and shot down by a Soviet fighter. In the interim between the Soviet warning and the American reply, however, the incident did create quite a storm in the House of Commons. Once again, for a short time the whole question of American aircraft flying from bases in Britain became a political issue. The Prime Minister records that the problems raised by the RB 47 incident caused him 'to look carefully again at the *precise terms* of the agreements for the American bases in order to ensure that they were watertight'.[38] The result was a further careful re-examination of the Bases Agreement by the two governments.[39]

'The bolt out of the sky'

Although the continuing difficulties over US bases in Britain caused periodic problems they were little more than an irritant in Anglo-American relations. The main trend within the alliance during the final years of the Eisenhower administration was one of growing intimacy, as we have already seen. In this close partnership Britain undoubtedly received more than she gave but her own contribution was far from negligible. She provided the benefit of her independent research in the nuclear field, bases for US aircraft and missiles, facilities at Christmas Island in the Pacific for American hydrogen bomb tests and inventions in the more conventional areas of defence, including the steam catapult, the angled deck and improved landing aids for aircraft carriers. Britain also provided invaluable diplomatic support for the United States at a very difficult time in the Cold War.

In return the United States provided assistance for 'her most reliable ally' across the whole spectrum of the defence field. Of all the different collaborative arrangements American help for the British nuclear deterrent was by far the most important. Quite apart from the information on atomic energy from 1958 onwards, the United States also contributed to the British delivery system throughout the 1950s.[40] American B29s had filled the gap until the V-Bomber force was ready and from 1955 Rolls Royce had been given access to details about the liquid-fuelled engine of the Atlas missile developed by the North American Aviation Company. This information was to be used in the development of the British Blue Streak missile which was designed to be the main vehicle for the delivery of Britain's strategic nuclear weapons in the 1960s as the V-Bomber force became increasingly vulnerable.

By the end of 1959, however, the future of Blue Streak was seriously in doubt. Quite apart from the rapidly escalating costs, due largely to some pioneering work done in Britain,[41] the missile was increasingly criticized on strategic grounds. The main problem arose from the fact that the missile was liquid-fuelled and as such took between ten and fifteen minutes to prepare. The limited warning time available and the rapid improvement in the accuracy of missiles produced by the two super-powers at this time meant that Blue Streak itself was becoming vulnerable to a Soviet pre-emptive strike. The growing obsolescence of the rocket even before it was operationally deployed led to a decision by the Defence Committee of the Cabinet to abandon it as a military system on 24 February 1960.[42] No formal announcement was made, however, until an understanding could be reached with the United States on a replacement.

The matter was discussed during the British Prime Minister's visit to Washington from 21–27 March and Macmillan managed to secure 'a valuable exchange of notes about Skybolt and Polaris'.[43] As the Royal Navy had no real desire for Polaris at this time[44] and the RAF were intent on preserving the life of their V-Bomber force, the burden of military advice given to the government was in favour of the sophisticated air-launched ballistic missile, Skybolt. On the basis of the notes exchanged between the two governments therefore at Camp David, the British Cabinet took the formal decision to cancel Blue Streak and to purchase Skybolt from the United States. The House of Commons was duly informed of the decision on 13 April.[45]

Although the preferred system at this time was Skybolt it seems that the Polaris system remained an option for the future. President Eisenhower was unwilling to make a definite arrangement on providing Polaris because of negotiations which were in progress at this time on whether NATO should be equipped with the missile. Nevertheless according to Macmillan 'it was *certain* that we could obtain Polaris, although at a heavy cost, in one form or another when we might need it'.[46] This commitment was to be of particular importance later when the crisis over Skybolt came to a head.

In the meantime, however, the British Minister of Defence, Harold Watkinson, went to the United States in May 1960 to finalize the formal agreement on Skybolt. At the same time that this agreement was being concluded a second arrangement was negotiated to set up an American submarine base at Holy Loch in Scotland. This arrangement had been agreed in principle at Camp David and was seen by the British Prime Minister as being 'more or less in return for Skybolt'.[47] Watkinson, however, kept the two deals separate. In the Cabinet discussions which followed his trip an attempt was made to tie the Holy Loch agreement to a definite commitment by the United States to provide Polaris when Britain wanted them. The Prime Minister, however, no doubt conscious of the relationship between Skybolt and Holy Loch established at Camp David, persuaded his colleagues to accept the broad assurances which Eisenhower was willing to give in the form of a 'gentlemen's agreement'.[48]

From Britain's point of view the Skybolt agreement reached in June was particularly advantageous. Robert McNamara revealed in 1963 that the United States undertook 'to bear the entire cost of the development of the missile'.[49] All Britain had to pay for were the missiles themselves and she was allowed to buy up to one hundred of these. The main problem, however, was that at this stage the missile was still at an early stage of development and there was no absolute certainty that it would ever enter service. In fact doubts about the missile were expressed right from the beginning by high-ranking American officials including the Secretary of Defence, Thomas Gates himself, and his deputy, James Douglas.[50] Gates was not convinced that Skybolt was necessary given the progress with the Minuteman and Polaris missiles which were also being developed at this time and he was pessimistic about the extreme costs likely to be incurred in overcoming the technical difficulties of an incredibly complex and hitherto untried experiment in ballistic systems.[51]

With a change of government in the United States in 1961 the project was continued but increasingly the new management techniques of Robert McNamara provided quantitative evidence that Skybolt was likely to have serious flaws in terms of cost effectiveness. Throughout 1962 the prospects for the missile worsened as Minuteman neared production and Polaris was fully up to the expectations of the defence planners. Skybolt on the other hand had failed four successive tests and had the lowest accuracy, reliability and yield of any of the American strategic missile systems,[52] and was also the most expensive.

On the basis of an evaluation of these technical limitations McNamara finally came to the conclusion in November 1962 that the air-launched ballistic missile was unsuitable and unnecessary for American defence strategy and ought to be scrapped. What the Secretary of Defence seems to have largely ignored, however, was the political repercussions which such a decision would have on Anglo-American relations. 1962 had been a bad year for the British Prime Minister, Harold Macmillan. The introduction of a pay-pause, the unpopular application to join the European Economic Community, electoral defeats, the sacking of a third of the Cabinet, together with criticisms over the British role in the Cuban crisis, had significantly tarnished the 'Super-Mac' image. In these circumstances the success of the independent deterrent, which the Macmillan government had put special emphasis on, was seen as crucial. The decision to cancel Skybolt, therefore, upon which the future of the British nuclear force depended, had profound implications for the Prime Minister himself and for the British government as a whole.

Robert McNamara, however, seems to have lacked the necessary political acumen to understand the impact of his 'technical' decision on the British. Consequently when the Secretary of Defence came to London on 11 December to see Thorneycroft, the British Minister of Defence, to explain the uncertainty about the future of Skybolt, the stage was set for a major clash between the allies.

Despite the rather poor handling of the situation by the United States authorities, responsibility for the crisis which developed should not merely be placed on the shoulders of McNamara and his Department. It must be remembered that in October the United States had been on the brink of nuclear war with the Soviet Union over the Cuban Missile crisis and as such the leading political figures had 'just been through the GREAT problem of their lives'.[53] After the trauma of the confrontation it was difficult to deal with many of the lesser issues, including Skybolt. As Sorenson observes, 'after Cuba, it seemed a small problem. All problems did!'[54] The missile crisis was also followed almost immediately by the Sino-Indian border conflict which further deflected the attention of the key decision-makers in the United States away from the rather minor difficulties over a weapons system.

Apart from these 'extenuating circumstances', Britain's contribution to the crisis should not be ignored. 'British Ministers have constantly argued that before November they were never told that Skybolt was in any kind of trouble and the American cancellation thus came as a bolt out of the sky!'[55] Such a claim in fact would seem to be less than fair. Shortly after the Skybolt agreement was signed, as we have seen, Thomas Gates not only expressed doubts about the missile's future within American political circles but actually advised his opposite number in Britain on 'at least two occasions' not to exclude the possibility that the missile might fail.[56] Britain was warned not to go 'too far overboard for it'. It is true that both the Douglas company who were producing Skybolt and the USAF remained optimistic throughout about its final development. Neither did McNamara give any indication to the British Defence Minister, Harold Watkinson, that there were any problems with the missile when he visited the United States in May 1962. Indeed Britain was asked to indicate exactly how many missiles they required. At the same time, however, the British government must have been aware of the problems affecting the development of Skybolt. Quite apart from the warnings of Thomas Gates, the Ministry of Defence were receiving reports from two RAF Officers who had been assigned to Douglas solely for the purpose of keeping the government informed of Skybolt's progress.[57] Doubts were even expressed about the project by President Kennedy himself in January 1962 when he went out of his way to inform a visiting British Minister, Julian Amery, of the increasing uncertainty about the project. When Amery almost 'fell off his chair in shock' the President felt obliged to reassure him that the United States remained 'anxious to make it work'.[58] Nevertheless Amery must have been aware at least of the possibility of cancellation and the doubts about the project among American officials.

The information received by Britain from the United States was undoubtedly ambiguous and this continued right up until November 1962. There would seem, however, to be no justification for the claim that the decision to scrap the missile came as a complete surprise to the British government. Indeed the chairman of the British military defence staff in Washington from 1959 to Autumn 1962, Air Chief Marshal Sir George Mills, took the unusual step after the crisis had been resolved of writing to the *Daily Telegraph* to deny that Britain had been 'let down' by the US. He pointed out in his letter:

> We have been warned constantly from the beginning that the continuation of the project was not 100 per cent certain and that the Americans would have to scrap it if it did not meet their requirements. In fact I cannot recall any conversations between senior American and British people when Skybolt was discussed and this straightforward warning was not given.[59]

Indeed it may well be that the British deliberately provoked the crisis situation themselves for domestic political reasons and to put Britain in a strong bargaining position with the Americans. The cancellation of Skybolt without an offer of a suitable alternative would undoubtedly have harmed the political reputations of both Macmillan and Thorneycroft and caused problems for British security interests. There were those in important positions within the American administration such as George Ball, Walt Rostow, Bob Bowie and Henry Owen, who saw the opportunity which the cancellation of Skybolt presented to end the preferential treatment given to Britain and thus re-assess American policies towards Europe. In order to prevent this and retain the special defence relationship some State Department officials certainly believed that the British Minister of Defence 'deliberately provoked a crisis atmosphere'.[60] According to one of these officials 'the thing was whipped up into a crisis on purpose by Thorneycroft and Macmillan. Thorneycroft didn't want to have the issue discussed at lower levels.'[61] According to this interpretation Thorneycroft sought the intervention of President Kennedy because he was known to value his relationship with Harold Macmillan. The 'inference of bad faith' by the Americans would then be used by the British to secure a favourable outcome in any negotiations between the two leaders.

If the British were as Machiavellian as this, and they may well have been, the need to be so may have stemmed from their belief that the United States was deliberately trying to force Britain out of the nuclear club. These suspicions were enhanced by the famous statements made by Robert McNamara at the NATO ministerial meeting in Athens in the spring of 1962 and at Ann Arbor in June of the same year. On the latter occasion, the Secretary of Defence described limited nuclear capabilities operating independently as being 'dangerous, expensive, prone to obsolescence and lacking in credibility as a deterrent'.[62] Shortly afterwards McNamara claimed that he had not been referring to the British. This disclaimer, however, did little to dispel the impression in London that his Ann Arbor speech was directed as much at Britain as France.

This view, held by many members of the British government, was further reinforced by the meeting between Thorneycroft and McNamara on 11 December 1962 in London. The atmosphere at the meeting was apparently 'disconcertingly cool'.[63] Indeed one commentator described it as 'one of the bluntest talks ever within the Anglo-American alliance'.[64] The American Secretary of Defence began by charting the technical shortcomings of Skybolt. Thorneycroft, however, was much more interested in the political implications of any cancellation of the missile and he challenged McNamara on the issue of whether he wished to deprive Britain of her deterrent. 'If this was not his intention would he be prepared to say so publicly and help Britain maintain it?'[65] McNamara, however, was only empowered to make two offers, neither of which was satisfactory from the British viewpoint. Firstly, the US were prepared to hand over to Britain all the development work on Skybolt without charge plus a further $30 million 'to counter any charge of American bad faith'.[66] Alternatively, they would provide Britain with the Hound Dog missile instead of Skybolt. By this stage in the negotiations, however, remembering the promise made by President Eisenhower at Camp David, Polaris was the only missile Britain was prepared to accept. The issue was therefore left to be resolved at the forthcoming meeting at Nassau between Kennedy and Macmillan.

By early December 1962 the news of the imminent cancellation of Skybolt had reached the public in Britain, causing a swell of anti-American feeling. At the same time Dean Acheson, the former US Secretary of State, made his famous speech at West Point in which he commented that Great Britain had lost an empire and had not yet found a new role.[67] The remark, which was only a minor part of a wide-ranging talk on the Atlantic Alliance, struck a sensitive nerve in Britain and 'inflamed political passions out of all proportion to the importance of the speech'.[68] In consequence by the time Macmillan and Kennedy met at Nassau 'the atmosphere between London and Washington had become electric' and the cancellation of Skybolt was seen by the British as the main item for discussion.[69]

In this atmosphere the Skybolt story has been described as

> a crisis compounded of drama and deceit, of uncertainty and distrust, of muddled perceptions and disappointed expectations, of high political stakes both won and lost, of miscalculation and misjudgement, at times carefully concealed from the public eye, at times skilfully exposed for the public's benefit.[70]

Although perhaps not as traumatic as Suez the effects were not dissimilar. The crisis not only disrupted the Anglo-American alliance but brought it once again almost to breaking point.

The Nassau Meeting 18–21 December

The meeting at Nassau, described by David Nunnerley as 'one of the great confrontations in the history of Anglo-American relations',[71] opened with a brief discussion on the Congo, India and the Test-Ban Treaty. It was not long, however, before the Skybolt issue assumed the centre of the stage. In a masterly opening speech the Prime Minister provided a *tour de force* of the great benefits which the close partnership between Britain and the United States had brought in the past. He reflected on the intimate collaboration of the wartime period and the great contribution Britain had made to the development of atomic energy. He reminded the Americans of the way in which the relationship had been restored after the Suez débâcle when relations had been particularly strained. Macmillan then went on to review the background to the Skybolt agreement, emphasizing not only the relationship between Skybolt and the Holy Loch base but also the understanding over the provision of Polaris if Britain desired it in the future. 'President Eisenhower had assured me', he pointed out, 'that if necessary, we might rely on obtaining Polaris.'[72]

President Kennedy, however, was under pressure from within his own delegation not to provide Polaris. In his reply, therefore, he emphasized the political problems which such an offer would create by upsetting various European countries, especially France, at a time when the negotiations over Britain's application to join the Common Market were reaching a crucial stage. He also explained that discussions were taking place in the United States about the need for some form of multilateral force to solve the problems of nuclear sharing in NATO. Once again the provision of Polaris bilaterally to Britain would prejudice the success of such a force. In the light of this the American President suggested a proposal worked out with the British Ambassador, Sir David Ormsby-Gore, during their flight together from the United States. According to this proposal the Americans would abandon Skybolt for their own use but they would split the future development costs evenly with the British. From the point of view of the Prime Minister, however, Kennedy had already compromised Skybolt with his criticisms of the missile on television in the United States a few days earlier. In rejecting the offer Macmillan replied that 'a British marriage with Skybolt was not exactly a shot-gun wedding but the virginity of the lady was regarded as doubtful'.[73]

Macmillan then proceeded to refute the view that Polaris would complicate Britain's application to join the Common Market or upset the French. He pointed out that he had met de Gaulle at Rambouillet shortly before Nassau and that the General had been sympathetic about Britain's deterrent. It was agriculture, he argued, which created the problem, not Polaris or the close ties between Britain and the United States.

By this stage of the conference the discussions were becoming 'protracted and fiercely contested'.[74] The Americans made two further offers to break the deadlock. One included the provision of the Hound Dog missile which McNamara had offered Thorneycroft at their earlier meeting and the other involved postponing settlement of the issue while a joint study group considered alternative weapons systems. Both, however, were firmly rejected by the British as being unsuitable. Macmillan argues in his memoirs that in the discussions which followed he had 'to pull out all the stops – adjourn, reconsider, refuse one draft and demand another . . .'.[75] At one point he suggested, in classic diplomatic style, that if agreement could not be reached he would prefer not to patch up a compromise. 'Let us agree to part as friends,' he argued. 'If there must be a parting let it be done with honour and dignity.'[76] Britain would not welch on her agreements. Then switching the attack, he went on to ask the President if he wished to be responsible for the fall of the government on the issue? He warned that if this happened there would be a wave of anti-American feeling in Britain and even the possibility that an anti-American faction might assume the leadership of the Tory Party in an attempt to cling on to power.

In the end Macmillan's eloquent and emotional arguments paid off. Kennedy had not contemplated the drastic break in relations which the British Prime Minister seemed to be envisaging. He greatly valued the close relationship he had built up with Macmillan which was of even greater significance as a result of his 'inability to establish a close rapport with his other allies'.[77] The President therefore sought a compromise agreement which would preserve Britain's independent deterrent and at the same time would not openly contradict the multilateral ideals of his government.

The result was the 'Statement on Nuclear Defence Systems' which has been described without too much exaggeration as an agreement 'drafted in masterly ambiguity'.[78] One of the American officials present claimed it was 'the worst drafted language anyone had ever seen'.[79] This was not altogether surprising because the document was put together in a matter of a few hours without the benefit of specialist advisers. Largely as a result of this haste the statement was riddled with somewhat muddled terminology which was later to cause significant differences of interpretation.

According to the statement the United States would make available to Britain Polaris missiles without their warheads 'on a continuing basis'.[80] This much was clear. The main problem, however, arose over whether the British forces including Polaris were to be assigned to a *multinational* or *multilateral* force. Paragraph Six provided for the allocations from the US Strategic Forces, from the UK Bomber Command and from tactical forces held in Europe, to be made available to a 'NATO nuclear force and targeted in accordance with NATO nuclear plans'. This would in essence be a *multinational* force. Paragraph Eight also assigned the British Polaris submarines to the same force. The same paragraph, however, also went on to commit the Polaris force to a NATO *multilateral* nuclear force. This multilateral approach was again adopted in Paragraph Seven in which both governments agreed that the purpose of providing Polaris missiles 'must be the development of a multilateral NATO nuclear force in the closest consultation with other NATO allies'.

The 'extraordinary ambiguity' of the agreement was further reflected in the contradiction between multilaterialism and independence. According to Paragraph Eight Britain's Polaris fleet would be 'used for the purposes of international defence of the Western Alliance in all circumstances' except 'when Her Majesty's Government may decide that supreme national interests are at stake'. But as Andrew Pierre quite rightly points out, it is very difficult indeed to imagine 'Britain considering the use of nuclear weapons in circumstances other than those involving the supreme national interests'.[81] In effect, therefore, although the British force was ostensibly committed to the proposed multilateral force, in practice, Macmillan had secured the independence as well as the continuation of the British deterrent which he considered so necessary.

In his memoirs, Macmillan admits that at Nassau 'the arguments were more violently contested than in any previous meeting' he had attended with the Americans. He describes it as 'an exhaustive experience'.[82] Even after the agreement had been signed differences of interpretations were to continue not only over multilaterism but also over the financial aspects of the deal. In the haste to conclude the agreement not only was terminology muddled but the question of development costs was overlooked. The British thereafter assumed that they would not be asked to contribute to the R & D costs but would only be required to pay for the missiles they purchased. They were therefore surprised a little later when it was revealed that the Pentagon were in fact expecting Britain to share some of the research and development costs on a pro-rata basis. As Britain was planning to build five nuclear submarines compared with the forty-one planned by the US, this would have worked out at about 12 per cent extra.

This request from the United States authorities was badly received in Britain. The American Defence Secretary was seen as being 'very grasping' and in rejecting the Pentagon demands the Prime Minister appealed directly to the President to intervene on the issue.[83] Once again a compromise deal was arrived at whereby Britain would add an extra 5 per cent to the retail cost of the missiles bought. Thus 'if we bought fifty million pounds of missiles, we would pay fifty-two and a half million pounds'.[84] Macmillan described the outcome as being 'not a bad bargain'.[85] In fact this was something of an understatement. Britain was to receive the latest American missiles under the Polaris Sales Agreement, which was signed in April 1963 on what can only be described as 'extraordinarily favourable and inexpensive terms'.[86]

The Cuban Missile crisis

The problems over Skybolt leading up to the confrontation at Nassau took place at a time when the United States and the West were faced with what was probably the greatest threat of nuclear war in the post-war period: the Cuban Missile crisis. To some observers the crisis not only produced a major confrontation between East and West but it had a profound effect on Anglo-American relations as well. According to John Mander, 'if any one day saw the death of Britain's "special relationship" with America it was Tuesday, 23 October 1962 . . . who can doubt that the Skybolt affair, Nassau and Mr Acheson's speech were influenced by it?'[87]

The main reasoning behind this assertion is that while the world teetered on the brink of nuclear holocaust all the major decisions affecting the safety of the West were made by the United States. Despite her nuclear forces, Britain, it is argued, remained 'a hapless bystander' unable to influence the vital decisions being made in Washington which might bring about her nuclear devastation.[88] Many contemporary British observers apparently believed that 'the Americans not only failed to consult us, but have treated us with contempt'.[89] Anthony Howard in the *New Statesman* argued on 26 October 1962 that 'The British government could hardly have had its dependent status more brutally spelled out to it than it has this week'.[90]

In fact we now know that this view was an over-simplification. The 'delicacies of crisis management' at the time concealed the extent to which Britain was consulted. It has been argued by the Prime Minister that by the regular telephone calls from President Kennedy and the presence of Ormsby-Gore in Washington Britain was actually 'intimately involved in the decisions taken'.[91] Kennedy apparently told Macmillan on the eve of his crucial broadcast to the American people on 22 October:

> . . . we shall have to act more closely together. I have found it absolutely essential, in the interest of security and speed, to make my first decision on my own responsibility, but from now on I expect that we can and should be in the closest touch. . . .[92]

During the crisis Britain was responsible for the decision not to call a NATO 'alert' and also, through the British Ambassador Sir David Orsmby-Gore, for the decision to shorten the 'interception line' from 800 miles to 500 miles to give the Russians more time to contemplate the repercussions of their actions. Certainly the British Prime Minister had no doubts that he played an important role in the crisis. 'We in Admiralty House', he argues, 'felt as if we were in battle headquarters.'[93]

While it would be wrong, however, to under-estimate Britain's role in the crisis it would also be wrong to exaggerate the degree to which Macmillan was able to influence the decisions made in Washington. Britain's views on the NATO 'alert' and the 'interception line' made an important contribution but in the last resort all of the major decisions were made, as they had to be, by the President of the United States and his select body of advisers. Cuba did not destroy the 'special relationship'. Indeed in some ways it demonstrated its vitality. What it did do, however, was to reflect the major imbalance in power terms between Britain and the United States and the limitations on the influence of the smaller partner when the United States was locked in a super-power confrontation with the Soviet Union.

Thus, although the early 1960s brought the two countries to what was the highest point in defence collaboration in the post-war period, the growing disparity in power and increasing American preoccupation with its relationship with the Soviet Union, provided important pointers for the future of the Anglo-American alliance in general and to a certain extent for the defence relationship between the two countries.

4 The 'Close Relationship' 1963–1969

The amendments to the McMahon Act in the late 1950s and the Nassau Agreement in the early 1960s represented in many respects the highest point in post-war collaboration between the two states in defence matters. From 1963 onwards relations in general were not bad: indeed cooperation in many different areas of policy, including defence, continued to be very close. Nevertheless relations, especially at the highest levels, have since then rarely if ever recaptured the kind of warmth and intimacy which led to agreements such as those between 1958 and 1963. Increasingly, divergences of national interests, preoccupations with domestic problems and a growing disparity in power tended to produce a cooling of relations between the two countries, which were reflected to a certain extent in a number of irritating difficulties.

The MLF/ANF debate

The gradual erosion of the 'special' defence links began almost immediately after the Nassau Agreement. Indeed the Agreement itself contained within it (as we have already seen)[1] the seeds of future difficulties between the two countries. Apart from the dispute over financial questions, the source of greatest concern and disagreement centred on the question of the creation of a Multilateral Force (MLF).

After the difficulties in NATO in the late 1950s, especially with France, over the question of nuclear control, the United States had long sought a technique to try to involve the European states in nuclear matters without relinquishing ultimate control over her strategic forces. For a powerful coterie of officials in the State Department led by George Ball, the MLF represented the most suitable arrangement to resolve this problem.[2] With what one writer describes as 'messianic zeal' they advocated initially the establishment of a force consisting of Polaris submarines which would be jointly owned and operated under the control of SACEUR.[3] It was also envisaged that the force would be manned by crews of mixed nationality. A later American proposal substituted twenty-five surface ships, instead of the submarines. Each would be armed with eight A-3 Polaris missiles with a range of 2500 miles. Such a force, it was suggested, would be financed by the participating countries with no nation contributing more than 40 per cent of the total.

The essentially bilateral arrangement agreed at Nassau had been something of a setback for this group of MLF enthusiasts with their concern to provide a wider American-European understanding.[4] Nevertheless the acceptance by Britain of a commitment (albeit of an ambiguous kind) to a multilateral force led to a vigorous campaign by the State Department in the following two years to establish such a force. In their dealings with the British, who remained sceptical of the efficiency of the project, American officials apparently adopted a tough approach. Andrew Pierre, who was on the staff of the American Embassy in London at the time dealing with the MLF, has revealed that a variety of arm-twisting tactics were employed to try to achieve British acceptance of the particular proposals put forward by the State Department.[5] The Americans apparently even threatened to proceed with the setting up of the force without Britain if need be.[6]

Significantly all this appears to have taken place without the knowledge of President Kennedy. The President himself saw the MLF merely as an exploratory idea and one which he became increasingly sceptical of. According to Harold Wilson, the leader of the Opposition at the time, the President told him in April 1963 'that he had never really been keen on the MLF' and 'was not pushing it but he thought the Europeans wanted it'.[7] He was apparently taken aback when he heard from the British Prime Minister of the day, Sir Alec Douglas-Home, of the kind of pressure which was coming from his own bureaucracy.[8]

Shortly afterwards, however, the President was assassinated and the MLF was duly presented to his successor Lyndon Johnson, 'in such a manner as to elicit a strong commitment to forcing quicker action on the plan than President Kennedy had ever intended'.[9] The new President also seems to have had some doubts about the MLF but such was the strength of the State Department commitment that in the early period of his Presidency at least he was prepared to go along with what was portrayed as a continuation of policy.

British reaction to US proposals was decidedly unenthusiastic, especially in the Ministry of Defence. Criticisms centred on the vagueness of the system of control envisaged and doubts were expressed about the necessity as well as the practicality of the force. There were also economic objections. Britain would be expected to pay about 10 per cent of the total costs which it was estimated would work out at about £150 million spread over ten years. For the individual Services this might mean a diversion of resources away from planned weapons systems which they considered more necessary to perform their roles. It is perhaps not surprising therefore that the MLF had no backers amongst the military hierarchy in Britain. It was opposed not only by the Minister of Defence at the time, Peter Thorneycroft, but also by the Chief of the Defence Staff, Lord Mountbatten and the Chief Scientific Officer, Sir Solly Zuckerman.[10]

Despite their reservations, however, the Foreign Office, having been subjected to 'unusually heavy pressure'[11] from the State Department, gradually came round to supporting the concept. Concern not to harm Anglo-American relations and a reluctance to be isolated from a European nuclear force which would include Germany seem to have been the key determinants in their 'conversion'. The split between the Foreign Office and the Ministry of Defence, together with the continuing pressure from the United States, led to the search in Britain for an alternative scheme to the MLF. There was an obvious need to respond to US proposals but at the same time sceptism of the MLF dictated that a new approach be devised which would be more in line with British interests.

'The Thorneycroft Proposals'

The British response took the form of 'the Thorneycroft proposals' which were first presented to the NATO ministerial meeting held in Paris in December 1963 and subsequently submitted in detail in July 1964 to a working group set up to consider the MLF.[12] These proposals advocated a multilateral force of aircraft and missiles which had an interdiction role in European defence. The plan envisaged a force consisting of British Canberras, American and West German F104 Star-Fighters, the Pershing surface to surface missile in service with US and German forces, the projected British TSR2 and the American FIII, plus the British V-Bombers redirected away from their strategic role to a new NATO interdiction role. Units of the force (although not individual aircraft) would be mixed-manned and it would be jointly financed. It was envisaged that overall command of the force would rest with the NATO Supreme Commander (SACEUR).

From the British point of view the great advantage of 'the Thorneycroft proposals', compared with the MLF, was that the force would be made up of existing weapons or at least ones which it was hoped would soon be coming into service. This would avoid the cost of producing a wholly new surface fleet. The proposals also had other advantages. Significantly, no mention was made of Britain's proposed Polaris submarine force and thus any weakening of the commitment to an 'independent' deterrent, so dear to the hearts of Conservative leaders, was avoided. It was also noticeable that Britain would be likely to play a disproportionately larger part in such a force compared with the envisaged 10 per cent contributions to the MLF. A further advantage, especially from the point of view of the RAF, was that acceptance of such a force would involve a firm commitment by the government to the development of the sophisticated TSR2 aircraft, the future of which was increasingly in doubt.

Reaction to 'the Thorneycroft proposals' in Washington was cool. Although initially some angry American officials saw them as an attempt to block the MLF,[13] the Johnson administration did, nevertheless, eventually agree to consider the proposals in detail. They were, however, to be considered 'as a complement, rather than an alternative, to the MLF'.[14] In the meantime, despite the continuing reluctance to commit herself to the MLF, Britain agreed to send thirty Royal Naval officers and seamen to participate in a mixed-manning experiment which took place on the American destroyer *Admiral Claude V. Ricketts*. The Conservative government also continued to play an active role in the MLF working group discussions which were taking place in NATO.

During 1964, however, very little progress was made on the issue. Apart from the scepticism of the British government about the project, it was an election year and not surprisingly the Conservative leaders were reluctant to make important decisions of this kind until the general election was over. The issue was particularly sensitive because although the Labour opposition was no more favourably disposed towards the MLF than the government, the whole debate about the force had important implications for the future of the British deterrent on which major differences of opinion between the parties existed.

The Conservatives and the 'independent' deterrent

As the election campaign got under-way in Britain the Conservative Party put great stress on the need to retain an 'independent' nuclear deterrent. On becoming Prime Minister, Sir Alec Douglas-Home had emphasized the importance of nuclear weapons as a 'ticket of admission' to top-table discussions about the great 'life and death' issues of international relations.[15] Great stress was placed, with some justification, on the important role which Britain was able to play in the Nuclear Test Ban Conference and especially British initiatives which had contributed to the partial Test Ban Treaty of 1963.

Government leaders also argued that another reason why Britain needed her own nuclear force was to retain a degree of independence from the United States. Somewhat ironically perhaps, speaking in the House of Commons on 30 January 1963, just after the Nassau Conference, Harold Macmillan emphasized that nuclear forces provided Britain with an ability to act on her own in the future if her interests diverged from those of her allies.[16] Implicit in Macmillan's argument was the need for an insurance policy should British and American interests be at odds as they were at Suez. Macmillan suggested that

> . . . this perhaps is the most vital argument of all, there may be conditions, there must be areas, in which the interests of some countries may seem to them more vital than they seem to others. It is right and salutary that a British government, whatever may be the particular

> conditions of a particular dispute, should be in a position to make their own decision without fear of nuclear blackmail . . . I would hope that Britain will be able, for as long as possible, to maintain her position free from threat, and should be able, should the necessity arise, to make her independent decisions on issues vital to her life.[17]

The elaboration of this argument during the 1964 election campaign, however, caused certain misgivings within the Tory Party and even amongst members of the Conservative Cabinet itself. Some Conservatives realized that Britain's deterrent was not as credible or as independent as official party policy constantly stressed. They also regretted that the government's policy was based 'on an assumption of mistrust of the United States'.[18] It was difficult for them to envisage any situation arising in which Britain would use her nuclear weapons without American consent. In turn they found it hard to understand how Britain could ask the United States to make available her missile technology while simultaneously threatening to use the very same missiles independently.[19]

Labour's alternative defence policy

The Labour opposition also recognized the weaknesses of the Tory official line. They saw clearly that the government's attempt to emphasize the importance of the 'independent deterrent' had significant implications for traditional post-war Tory policy of pursuing intimate relations with the United States. Although there had long been misgivings in certain quarters of the Labour Party about the US, the front bench saw an opportunity which was too good to miss. Here was a chance of appearing to be the party most closely aligned with the United States by arguing for the abandonment of nuclear weapons (a call much loved by the Labour Left) and relying instead on closer relations with the Americans.[20]

In presenting their alternative policy the Labour Party emphasized the need to build up conventional forces rather than nuclear forces. In so doing they consciously put themselves much more in line with American defence policy than the government. Robert McNamara's criticisms of independent deterrents and his stress on the need for European powers to provide the conventional forces for his 'flexible response strategy' had brought a certain divergence of opinion between the two governments from 1962 onwards. To the British government, as to other European governments, 'flexible response' created a greater range of options and thereby raised doubts about the availability of American strategic forces. Some form of 'massive retaliation' was seen as being a more effective deterrent. These differences in strategic policy were taken up by the Labour Party. They recognized that President Kennedy could be a very useful electoral ally.[21] Consequently, by promising to re-negotiate the

Nassau Agreement (with the implication that the deterrent might be abandoned) and at the same time promising to build up conventional forces, the opposition party were quite deliberately offering a defence policy which was far closer to the ideal envisaged by the American government. In so doing Labour were portraying themselves as being the party more likely to work in close harmony with the United States: indeed the party capable of forming a new kind of 'special relationship' in defence.

One of the most explicit statements of the party's concern to work closely with the Americans on security matters was made by Gordon Walker in an article he wrote for *Foreign Affairs* in April 1964.[22] In his article the shadow Foreign Secretary maintained:

> We do not wish to cancel it [the Nassau Agreement]. We want to negotiate a far-reaching new arrangement with Washington. The opening of talks to this end would be one of the first acts of a Labour government.
>
> We would want to have a real share with the United States in shaping nuclear policy and strategy and we accept, both as a fact and as something desirable, that the last decision must be in the hands of the President. *But we want to participate fully, intimately and without limit in the formulation of the ideas, policy and strategy that together make up the doctrine upon which any particular decision of the President must depend*. We would want to share in the decisions about the deployment and targeting of nuclear weapons and in future production plans. We would also seek to conclude agreements under which we could execute enough specialist work to benefit from the industrial fall-out that comes from production of nuclear weapons.
>
> This would be to ask a lot from America. But in exchange we would recognize and support the ultimate nuclear monopoly of the United States in the west.[23]

Gordon Walker had made much the same point in a speech to the House of Commons in November 1963. Labour, he argued, wanted to achieve 'intimate participation' in the evolution of the strategic thinking and contingency planning which would 'lie beneath an American decision to use its strategic nuclear force'.[24] A Labour government would also try, he suggested, 'to reach a point at which the President's decision – because those are the decisions that matter in the world – can only be made on the basis of an agreed, continuously worked out and elaborated nuclear strategy and doctrine'.[25]

Despite the support this policy received in both the British press and in Washington itself, it was not without its own weaknesses. It was one thing to advocate greater intimacy in the American defence decision-making process, it was quite another to spell out precisely how this might be achieved. To which forums was Gordon Walker seeking entry? It was already the case, as Andrew Pierre has pointed out, that there was a wide spectrum of arrangements in existence 'designed to give Britain that sense of participation' which the Shadow Foreign Secretary was arguing for.[26] These included:

1. The Joint Strategic Planning System at the headquarters of the US Strategic Air Command at Omaha, Nebraska, where British officers participated in targeting decisions.
2. A wide range of informal bilateral arrangements between various ministries of the two governments.
3. Various 'understandings' between the two countries including one which could be traced back to the Quebec Agreement of 1943, that the two heads of state would consult each other, if possible, before firing nuclear weapons.

It is true that Britain had no role in the Pentagon's weapons research and development decision-making process, or in the military planning of the Joint Chiefs. But then such involvement by one sovereign state in another's defence planning in areas as sensitive as these would have been very remarkable.

Another problem implicit in Labour's proposed position was the absence of any attempt to coordinate their foreign and defence policies. If the United States was to be the custodian of all the nuclear power of the Western alliance then it followed that the foreign policies of the European states would need to be closely aligned with American policy; 'for it is difficult to see how military power could be integrated without a parallel coordination of foreign policy'.[27] One of Labour's traditional post-war criticisms of Tory governments, however, had been that Britain had become too dominated by the United States and that what was needed was a much more independent foreign policy. Thus on the one hand Labour leaders were advocating a much more intimate role in defence planning with the United States. On the other hand there remained a strong sentiment within certain sectors of the party in favour of becoming less identified as an American satellite. It was not only the Tory Party therefore which had a dilemma over 'independence' and the 'special relationship'!

There was a further difficulty in the Labour position which centred on the (deliberate) ambiguity of statements made during the election campaign about the re-negotiation of the Nassau Agreement and the future of the deterrent. Very little attempt was made to spell out exactly what was meant by 're-negotiate' or to indicate what course of action would follow if 're-negotiation' failed to achieve Labour's desired objectives. One of the main reasons for this fuzziness was obviously that the leaders of the party were concerned to retain the support of those who were both for and against the deterrent. They wished to provide themselves with a broad enough base to justify any future policy.

The ambiguity of Labour's policy was seen clearly in the contradictory statements which were made by members of the Shadow Cabinet. Gordon Walker, for example, in his *Foreign Affairs* article in April 1964, argued that Britain should not 'seek to make or possess nuclear weapons of her own'.[28] Labour's Defence spokesman, Denis Healey, on the other hand, took a different line. He suggested that although Polaris would not be purchased to sustain Britain's 'independent deterrent' they might have utility in an alliance context. As he pointed out:

> We do not believe that it is a necessary or sensible use of our resources to spend more money on retaining an independent nuclear capacity. We have repeatedly said we have no interest in the Polaris programme as a contribution to an independent British deterrent. *Whether it is of any value as part of an alliance effort we cannot make up our minds until we negotiate the question with the United States.*[29]

Harold Wilson himself was also very cagey about the policies of a future Labour government. Despite his vigorous attacks on the illusions of the government's independent nuclear role and his criticisms of the Nassau Agreement, he, like Denis Healey, was very careful to keep his options open on the nuclear question.[30]

The difficulties of interpreting Labour's position (which is perhaps in itself a tribute to Harold Wilson's smokescreen) can be clearly seen from the differing analyses presented in the press at the time. In late 1963 both the *New Statesman*[31] and the *Observer*[32] suggested that Labour was unlikely to scrap the bomb despite the statements made to the contrary by some opposition spokesman. By April 1964, however, *The Times* in an Election Paper was confidently predicting that a future Labour government 'would abandon plans to establish a fleet of missile carrying submarines and would therefore not maintain an independent nuclear striking force after the V-Bomber ceased to be effective'.[33] Then as the election drew closer a consensus amongst political observers began to emerge that the differences between the two parties on defence were in fact more apparent than real. It now increasingly appeared likely that Labour would retain nuclear weapons after all. *The Economist* in particular noted that:

> In a very English way, without anybody saying anything, the argument about Britain's nuclear status looks as if it is being softly, fuzzily and rather satisfactorily compromised. . . . If one goes beneath the surface of public remarks, it begins to look entirely possible that things are changing. . . . One's guess nowadays is that if the Labour party came to power next month it might well decide to go ahead and build Polaris submarines (if they could not be converted into hunter killers) and then

try to solve the problem *by putting the submarines under some sort of joint allied command.*[34]

Just before the election even *The Times* reversed its original prediction and now recognized that it was unlikely that the re-negotiation of the Nassau Agreement would lead to a dramatic reversal of policy.[35] Like *The Economist*, it suggested that instead of abandoning the nuclear force a Labour government would probably commit the Polaris submarines to some form of allied force as an alternative to the MLF.

The Labour government and the MLF/ANF debate

With the election of a Labour government in October 1964, the most immediate problem to be resolved in the field of foreign and defence policy was that of the MLF. The Americans made it very plain to the new government that they expected the British to join the proposed multilateral force. In his account of the early days of his administration Harold Wilson recounts the pressure for a swift decision from across the Atlantic:

> We knew that President Johnson was pressing the MLF with even more fervour than President Kennedy, though his enthusiasm was the result of fanatical pressures from his top officials, particularly Mr George Ball, the Under-Secretary of State, and Mr Walt Rostow.[36]

Such was the American impatience for a decision that they set the British a 'deadline' of December 1964 for concluding an agreement on the issue. The new government therefore, which had been out of power for thirteen years, was being pressed to make a major policy decision on a particularly complex security issue less than two months after assuming office.

If this in itself was not an indication of the changing nature of Anglo-American relations, the choice of December 1964 was of even greater significance. The sole reason for this date seems to have been that the American government felt that the MLF had to be ratified by the *Bundestag* before the German elections which were scheduled to take place in 1965. The Americans were particularly concerned to avoid undue political controversy in the Federal Republic. Thus, as Alastair Buchan has pointed out, 'the American pressure on Britain stemmed from Washington's practice of giving the demands of German internal politics priority over Britain'.[37] This view is further endorsed by Andrew Pierre who has argued that 'underlying the American attitude was a tendency to pay too much attention to the nuclear neurosis of Germany and not enough to those of Britain, or in effect to take Britain for granted'.[38]

Although the significance of this one issue, as far as the 'special relationship' was concerned, should not be exaggerated, nevertheless it was indicative of the evolution of American–European relations by the mid-1960s. West Germany was emerging as an important economic as well as political force within the EEC while Britain laboured outside the Community with growing economic difficulties. The geographical position and conventional military strength of the Federal Republic was also recognized by the United States as being of vital importance in the defence of Europe. This was especially so with the growing French criticisms of the alliance and periodic attempts by Britain to reduce BAOR to ease her balance of payments problems. Thus at a time of steadily increasing Soviet conventional superiority, the *Bundeswehr* represented an important and relatively stable component of Western defensive strategy. In consequence a new, very close, some would say 'special', relationship was being formed between Bonn and Washington which, as it developed, to a certain extent helped to erode the exclusiveness of the Anglo-American relationship in Europe.

The period of November–December 1964 was an early stage in this process. The British Prime Minister was given a clear indication of the American determination to secure agreement over the MLF issue in a series of meetings with US officials which took place before his visit to Washington on 6 December. The American Ambassador in London, David Bruce, the British Ambassador in Washington, Lord Harlech, and Harvard Professor Richard Neustadt, on a visit to Britain, all made it plain to Harold Wilson that the success of his forthcoming talks 'would depend on the acceptance of the MLF'.[39] The choice of Professor Richard Neustadt as an emissary to convey such a message was, in itself, significant. President Kennedy had apparently been concerned about the problems which had occurred at the Nassau Conference and had set up a high-level inquiry under Professor Neustadt to see what had gone wrong. The President had been presented with the report just before his assassination.[40] Neustadt was now sent to London on 25 November to make sure that the Washington talks were fully prepared on both sides and, on a basis that would prevent the kind of misunderstanding which many American officials believed had occurred in December 1962.[41]

Professor Neustadt was not the only visitor to London in this period. George Ball, still one of the most passionate supporters of the multilateral force, also arrived in Britain to convey much the same kind of message about the MLF and the forthcoming Anglo-American talks. Harold Wilson recalls Ball's forceful advice in his memoirs:

> He made it clear that there could be no question of going back on the MLF, that the American government would expect us to support it and that unless I was going to be in a position to say so, it would be better if I cancelled my trip.[42]

The Labour Party in opposition had been as critical of the MLF as the

Conservatives. Now in office Labour leaders retained their earlier scepticism. The new government therefore found itself with the difficult task of trying to prevent the multilateral force from being set up in such a way as not to alienate her major ally.

The solution was found at the government's first major review of defence policy held at Chequers on the weekend of 20–22 November 1964. At the meeting, which included all the leading Labour Ministers and their Permanent Secretaries together with the Chiefs of Staff and their advisers, an alternative plan to the MLF was devised. Instead of the rather vague suggestion of greater participation in US strategic planning which they had put forward while in Opposition, a new proposal was devised for an Atlantic Nuclear Force (ANF). According to Wilson's statement to the House of Commons on 16 December,[43] the ANF would consist of:

1. The British V-Bomber force (with the exception of aircraft earmarked for deployment outside the NATO area);
2. The British Polaris submarine;
3. An equal number (or more) of American submarines;
4. Any French forces which they might like to subscribe;
5. 'Some kind of a mixed-manned and jointly owned element in which the existing non-nuclear powers could take part.'

The control of the ANF would be entrusted to some form of single authority 'linked to NATO' and containing representatives of all countries taking part. According to the British Prime Minister the United States, Britain and France, if she participated, would have a veto over the use of all elements of the force. He went even further to argue that 'Any other country participating would also have a veto if it wanted, though collectively they could, if they so desired, exercise their veto as a single group.'[44] All member countries would thus have a veto over the release of any of the nuclear components of the force.

This ingenious proposal represented an attempt by the British government to retain its planned Polaris forces while at the same time fulfilling the election pledge of re-negotiating the Nassau Agreement. On coming to office the Labour government apparently discovered that work on the Polaris agreement had 'passed the point of no return'.[45] As a justification for retaining the forces it was suggested that the out-going Conservative government had 'sewn up the contracts for the manufacture of the submarines' so effectively that the compensation costs in case of cancellation 'would have equalled the total costs of the vessels'.[46] By committing the force to the ANF, however, Wilson was able to present the proposal to the party's left wing as being an alteration of arrangements agreed to at Nassau and a renunciation of the 'independent nuclear deterrent'.

According to the plan Britain's nuclear forces were to remain part of the ANF 'for as long as NATO lasted as an effective organization'. One cannot avoid the impression, however, that this was something of a smokescreen to hide what many would see as a reversal of policy. Control would still remain in the hands of the British government.[47] As the Prime Minister was careful to point out, the Polaris submarines would remain 'a nationally owned and manned contingent'.[48] In his statement to the House of Commons Mr Wilson assured members that 'there will not be any system of locks which interferes with our right of communication with a submarine or our right to withdraw the submarine'.[49] It seems also that there was very little difference in practice between the clause which allowed for the withdrawal of the Polaris force when 'supreme national interests' were at stake, agreed to at Nassau, and the new proposal which permitted the withdrawal of the British contribution to the ANF if the alliance broke down. In both cases Britain presumably would decide when that situation had been reached. It was only likely to be in those kinds of circumstances that use of the force would be contemplated.

Apart from retaining the deterrent and appearing to have fulfilled its election manifesto, the ANF plan had other advantages as well for the Labour government. One important advantage was its relative cheapness compared with the MLF. Like the 'Thorneycroft proposals', it was based on the use of existing forces. For a government which had faced serious financial difficulties just after taking office this was obviously an important consideration. Apart from the economic savings, the ANF also had certain political advantages for Britain. With the commitment of Polaris submarines, V-Bombers and possibly the TSR2, Britain would be a major contributor to the new force. She would therefore be able to play a proportionately greater role in the formulation of policy than that envisaged under the MLF. Further political benefits would derive from demonstrating to the US not only Britain's interest in mixed-manning but also her concern to help improve consultations on nuclear strategy within the alliance. The ANF in particular would give Germany the kind of improved status in nuclear matters which the State Department had been seeking for some time.

Harold Wilson presented the ANF idea to President Johnson at their meeting in Washington between 7–9 December. Given the run-up to the conference the British delegation must have been surprised by the President's response. Instead of the dire consequences of failing to accept the MLF which had been warned, Lyndon Johnson expressed his willingness to give serious consideration to the ANF proposals. The reasons for this apparent change in the American position appear to lie in the detailed preparations which the President himself undertook for the talks. President Johnson had 'never been personally very far committed to the mixed-manned fleet' but had relied on certain key advisers in the State Department.[50] When he immersed himself deeply in the subject, however, before the December meeting, he discovered 'a lack of Congressional support for the MLF, grave misgivings within the administration and among the attentive public, the open hostility of the French, the division of opinion in Bonn, the lack of enthusiasm in a number of other European capitals, and the increasing opposition of the Soviet Union'.[51] As a result of this discovery an NSC memorandum was produced in which the President ordered State Department officials to stop pressurizing America's allies on the MLF issue. Instead Johnson indicated that the US would be prepared to negotiate on alternative proposals with her NATO colleagues. As part of this new approach the British Prime Minister was given the task of trying to forge some form of agreement with the West Germans.

The December meeting therefore proved to be something of an anti-climax as far as the MLF issue was concerned. Instead of the serious clash in relations which had been promised, the talks turned out very much better than the British could have hoped for. There is no doubt either that the ANF proposals played an important part in helping to defuse the controversy. The question arises, however, over whether the ANF was regarded by the British simply as a device designed solely to scuttle the MLF or whether it represented a serious alternative proposal?

There was a great deal of discussion in the press at the time which suggested that perhaps the former was true. Reflecting this view one contemporary wit pointed out that 'this was the first time in history that one non-existent fleet sank another non-existent fleet'. The *Daily Telegraph* at the time also reprinted a cartoon from the *Christian Science Monitor* which showed a ship named 'the multilateral force' having been torpedoed by a submarine.[52] The submarine which was labelled the ANF had the Prime Minister standing in the conning tower. Harold Wilson refers to this cartoon in his memoirs and he concludes with obvious satisfaction that the MLF 'was never to surface again'.[53]

There can be no doubt that the British were relieved that the pressure for the MLF had ceased. Nor can there be any doubt that ANF was designed to achieve this purpose. Nevertheless the British proposals had been seriously thought out. There is a certain amount of evidence to support the view that Britain would have been prepared to reach an agreement based on some kind of ANF/MLF proposal if the United States had insisted on it.[54] Given the preceding events the British delegation can hardly have been confident about reversing American policy when they went to Washington for the December talks. They were not to know that the President had changed his mind about the multilateral force. Thus the ANF was not merely a tactical instrument, it represented a genuine attempt to provide an alternative solution to a difficult problem not only in Anglo-American relations but in the Western alliance as a whole.

Labour and the 'dependent' deterrent

The defence debate in the House of Commons which followed the

Washington talks brought Conservative accusations that Labour's nuclear policy involved the surrender of the 'independent deterrent' which they considered so important. In his reply the Prime Minister set out to destroy the myth about the 'independence' of Britain's nuclear forces 'once and for all'.[55] In his speech Mr Wilson made it plain that in many important respects the Polaris programme would remain dependent on the United States. He offered to give opposition leaders 'chapter and verse' about certain fundamental components which Britain was going to manufacture but 'which were not covered in the contracts and for which it was necessary to turn to America for help'.[56] He went on to say:

> The question is whether, after 1968, we shall be in a position to supply all the fissile materials required to maintain the effectiveness of our warheads, having regard to the half-life of these materials and so on. . . .[57]

Mr Wilson was in no doubt that Britain would not be in such a position. Although he declined to specify the materials which the Americans would have to supply, most informed observers believe he was referring particularly to tritium, a radioactive material used in thermonuclear warheads; especially in the kind of advanced compact warheads used for Polaris missiles.

Britain's dependence on the US was not only confined to the question of materials. The Prime Minister went on to point out that because of the 1963 Test Ban Agreement, Britain's warheads had not been tested in the atmosphere. This meant that Britain would either have to depend on untested warheads with all of the uncertainties which that would entail or, which was more satisfactory, depend on information from the United States from their own earlier tests.[58]

To round off his argument against his Conservative critics, Wilson raised the question of the possible circumstances when the deterrent would be used independently of the United States. Finally, he said,

> We want to know what sort of war they were going to have the deterrent for. Obviously not some nuclear Suez. We acquit them of that. Obviously not as a contribution to a trigger mechanism to bring the American bomb into action when the American government did not want to do it. The argument we have had is that one day we may get some lunatic American President who, when the crunch came, was prepared to retire to Fortress America and to leave Europe to its fate. We have now answered that point, because we have made it clear that this (the British nuclear force) is committed to NATO as long as the alliance lasts. So I put it to the leader of the Opposition – what are they voting about tonight? It is not a nuclear Suez. It is not the trigger for the American strategic deterrent. We are left with one possibility – that the leader of the Opposition is talking about the embarking on a go-it-alone war with the Soviet Union when the rest of the alliance does

not wish to do so. Is that it? Our credibility depends on this – it depends on the credibility of the Government. I want the leader of the Opposition to tell us, as a former Prime Minister, as the head of the alternative Government, knowing that a go-it-alone war would mean a certain amount of posthumous revenge against the Soviet Union and total annihilation of all human life in Britain, whether he would be prepared to press that button in that kind of war. If he is not prepared to answer that . . . this has proved that their argument is a charade.[59]

Although the Prime Minister dismissed the insurance function of nuclear weapons rather too easily, he seems to have made his point in the debate. The British deterrent would continue to depend in a number of important ways on the United States. Having disposed of the independence argument to his own satisfaction and having shown how dependent in fact Britain was on the US, Wilson emphasized the contribution of the deterrent to the alliance. The Labour leader talked of the government's intention to 'internationalize' or to 'collectivize' the nuclear force. As the Prime Minister told the House of Commons in May 1966:

We intend to collectivize our nuclear position whether in the Atlantic, Pacific or anywhere else. . . . We do not intend to preserve the myth of the independent deterrent . . . it would be part of a collective security agreement with no pretence at independent national status.[60]

The 'close relationship'

This attempt by the new government to emphasize the difference between its own policies and those of its predecessor was reflected not only in the change of labels attached to the nuclear deterrent but also in the description of Anglo-American relations in general. The Prime Minister went out of his way during his period in office to place much less stress on the term 'special relationship'. Wilson no doubt was conscious of the traditional suspicion of the United States in sections of the Labour Party and he must also have been aware of the powerful opposition in the US to a continuation of the preferential treatment, especially in the military field, which had characterized relations in the past decade. Harold Wilson probably had these two audiences in mind during his visit to Washington in December 1964 when he suggested an alternative description of the bilateral alliance. In his speech at the White House, the Prime Minister argued against the continuing use of the term 'special relationship' because of its links with the nostalgia of Britain's imperial age. He told his audience:

We regard our relationship with you not as a *special* relationship but as a *close* relationship, governed by the only things that matter, unity of

> purpose and unity in our objectives. We don't come to you at any time on the basis of our past grandeur or any faded thought of what that grandeur was. . . . We have, and we always will have, a close relationship.[61]

Wilson's use of the term 'close relationship' might be thought with hindsight to symbolize a recognition by the Prime Minister and the British government at this time that the bonds of Anglo-American relations were beginning to loosen. Such an interpretation, however, would not seem to match the realities of the moment (especially in defence matters). The change in the description of the relationship, like that of the deterrent, was more verbal than substantive. It represented a concession to political sensitivities in the Labour Party and across the Atlantic. For the British government and for Wilson in particular the retention of the whole spectrum of intimate relations with the US remained an important, indeed vital, policy objective.[62]

In the defence field the continuation, with minor modifications, of the Polaris programme naturally meant the retention of very close links in that particular field. The Polaris Sales Agreement included all of the technical data covering the installation, operation and maintenance of the missiles. Under the agreement Britain was able to purchase 'the launching system, components of the inertial navigation system, the fire-control system, some of the communications equipment, and even the high stress steel for the submarine hulls'.[63]

As Andrew Pierre put it, 'the construction of the submarines was to be truly an "Anglo-American" enterprise'.[64] The test-firing of the missiles was held off Cape Kennedy and close working contacts were established between the British Polaris Executive Staff (PES) and the US Special Projects Office (SPO). The PES had been set up shortly after the Nassau Agreement by the Admiralty Board and not unnaturally it was modelled very closely on the American equivalent, the SPO. The Chief Polaris Executive in Britain, Rear-Admiral Mackenzie, and his staff of nearly five hundred, adopted many of the same kinds of management techniques to maintain strict time and financial control that had been developed for the US Polaris programme.

It was not long either before these kinds of management skills were being adopted in other areas of British defence planning, thus helping to bind the two defence establishments even closer together. In the 1965 White Paper Denis Healey went out of his way to emphasize the debt owed to the US when he outlined the new systems of cost-benefit analysis now being used which were 'based to a considerable extent on techniques, well-publicized in Washington. . . .'[65]

By the mid-1960s Denis Healey himself exemplified the close liaison between the defence establishments of the two countries with 'the admirable working relationship'[66] which he had managed to build up with his counterpart Robert McNamara. Mr Healey apparently saw the American Secretary of Defence as very much 'a man after his own heart'[67] and from their first official meeting in December 1964 they worked closely, trying in particular to cut costs in the defence field by greater cooperation. Attempts were made to set up a system of pooling research and development work and various off-set agreements were negotiated to enable Britain to purchase the latest defence equipment from the United States. After the Plowden Report in December 1965 especially, greater attention was placed on British purchases of American aircraft, such as the FIII.[68] In return the US promised to buy arms from Britain to ease the financial burden on the Treasury.

Similarly, when problems arose in the summer of 1966 over off-set costs between Britain and West Germany for the maintenance of BAOR, the US government agreed to meet the emergency by offering to purchase $35 million in military equipment from Britain. In return the British government agreed to retain the level of the British Army of the Rhine until at least June 1967.

Close cooperation continued in other areas as well. In February 1966 an Anglo-American Radio Research project was initiated by the two Defence Departments.[69] This joint work on the important subject of long-range military communications was to be undertaken at the RAF station at Feltwell, Norfolk, and financed by the American government. A similar arrangement involving British facilities and US finance was also negotiated in secret in 1966. This agreement, which only came to light much later, involved the establishment of a refuelling and telecommunications base on Diego Garcia, one of the islands of the British Indian Ocean Territories. In order to build the base, which was considered necessary 'to meet the future defence needs of the two nations', the 1200 inhabitants of the island were resettled in Mauritius. This aspect of the agreement caused a great deal of controversy in the United States in 1975 and in the row which developed a certain amount of information about the deal between the two countries was made public.[70] In particular it was revealed that the US had funded the base by waiving the research costs charged to Britain in the Nassau Agreement for the purchase of Polaris missiles.[71]

Collaboration of the various kinds described above suggests that relations in many aspects of the defence field in the mid-1960s were perhaps rather more than just 'close'. While this was so, however, various events both of a domestic and external nature were beginning to put new and powerful strains on the relationship as a whole: strains which in a number of respects had important implications for the defence partnership.

The impact of Vietnam

The most significant of the differences to emerge in the two capitals in the middle and late 1960s centred on the American involvement in the Vietnam War. Despite the general support given to the United States by Britain during the war, important diplomatic disagreements arose from time to time, some of which involved matters of national security. Amongst the most important of these defence-related problems were issues such as: British participation in the war alongside the United States; the continuing presence of British troops east of Suez; and the implications for British and European security of American preoccupation with a conflict in the Far East.

From the first meeting between the American President and the British Prime Minister in December 1964 Lyndon Johnson repeatedly made it plain to Harold Wilson that he would welcome a British contribution to the war effort, 'even if only on a limited – even a token – basis'.[72] What mattered to the Americans was not the size of the British force but the demonstration of diplomatic support. In July 1966, as the war escalated and world opinion began to move against the American intervention, the President even suggested that 'a platoon of bagpipers'[73] would be sufficient. On each occasion that the appeal was made, however, the British leader 'courteously but firmly' declined, emphasizing Britain's past role as Co-Chairman of the Geneva Conference and her possible contribution in helping to achieve peace.[74] It is evident that despite Wilson's genuine belief in the value of his endeavours in this field President Johnson himself was irritated by the British reluctance to commit troops in Vietnam. He also had very little faith in Britain's role as a mediator. In some ways in fact he saw the two things as being interrelated. He argues in his memoirs that he had

> no doubt . . . that the British government's general approach to the war and to finding a peaceful solution would have been considerably different if a brigade of Her Majesty's forces had been stationed just south of the demilitarized zone in Vietnam.[75]

In this somewhat distrustful atmosphere disagreements arose over British peace initiatives and also over what the Americans saw as British interference. As far as the latter was concerned one incident in particular reflected the deterioration in the personal relations between the two leaders which was gradually taking place. In February 1965, when Lyndon Johnson was under pressure at home to escalate the war to counter North Vietnamese attacks, the British Prime Minister telephoned the President to urge restraint and to suggest that he might visit Washington to discuss the matter. Attlee had after all done much the same thing during the Korean War. On this occasion, however, such advice from the British, who were not prepared to involve themselves in the fighting, was ill-received in Washington. Mr Johnson apparently 'let fly in an outburst of Texan temper',[76] telling Mr Wilson: 'I won't tell you how to run Malaysia and you don't tell us how to run Vietnam. . . . If you want to help send some folks to deal with the guerrillas.[77]

Despite British military involvement in the confrontation with Indonesia the government, however, remained adamant that British troops would not be sent 'to deal with the guerrillas' in Vietnam. One of the key reasons for this cautious policy was the traditional concern in the post-war period to prevent the United States from becoming over-committed in the Far East. As with the Korean and Indo-China wars of the 1950s, the preoccupation with Asian interests threatened to deflect the US from the European theatre. It was therefore clearly in Britain's own security interests to try to make sure that this was avoided. The presence of British troops would only help to internationalize the war further and reinforce the American commitment to Vietnam. H. G. Nicholas sums up this feeling when he says:

> Britain's over-whelming concern, second only to that of not getting involved herself, was to prevent the USA from becoming bogged down in a hopeless and costly struggle that would divert her attention, her will, and her resources from her primary task, as Britain saw them, elsewhere in Europe.[78]

Britain's failure to support her ally at a difficult time, however, remained the source of considerable bitterness in Washington. Dean Rusk was apparently so annoyed that he told Louis Heren: 'All we needed was one regiment. The Black Watch would have done. But you would not, well, don't expect us to save you again. They can invade Sussex and we wouldn't do a damn thing about it.'[79] Nor were matters made any easier by the announcement in July 1967 by the British government that it was withdrawing its military forces from the east of Suez region. A combination of the end of the war in Borneo, mounting economic difficulties at home and the lure of the EEC led to a major review of Britain's foreign and defence policy in the mid-1960s and a set of decisions to concentrate politically, economically and militarily on Europe. For an American government being sucked ever deeper into the Vietnam quagmire this represented a further and even more serious demonstration of Britain's unwillingness to contribute to maintaining stability in the Far East.[80] Even if Britain was not prepared to commit forces to Vietnam, the presence of British troops in South-East Asia was something which the American government by this time welcomed.[81] In talks between Robert McNamara and Denis Healey in December 1964 the American Secretary of Defence had gone out of his way to emphasize the importance to the US of the British role east of Suez. As Healey told the Cabinet on 11 December, what the Americans wanted Britain to do 'was not to maintain huge bases but keep a foothold in Hong Kong, Malaya, the Persian Gulf, to enable us to do things for the alliance which they can't do'.[82] The Americans strongly believed, Denis Healey told his colleagues, 'that our forces are much more useful to the alliance outside Europe than in Germany'.[83]

Given this attitude in Washington, it is hardly surprising that the decision to withdraw from east of Suez, on top of the reluctance to commit troops to Vietnam, should have caused even further friction in Anglo-American relations. Richard Crossman in his memoirs describes the 'thundering telegrams of protest' which were received from President Johnson.[84] The Americans apparently lost no opportunity to express their strong disapproval. The Foreign Secretary, George Brown, for example, had a very frosty reception from the American Secretary of State, Dean Rusk, on his visit to the United States in January 1968 because of the British withdrawal. The Americans apparently expressed 'nothing but horror and consternation' and applied 'considerable pressure' for a reversal of British policy, especially as far as the Persian Gulf was concerned.[85]

Despite the irritation which British policies towards the Far East caused in Washington, by the late 1960s the Americans themselves were beginning to move along the same road. The trauma of Vietnam first led to President Johnson's announcement in March 1968 not to seek re-election and then to President Nixon's 'Guam Doctrine' in November 1969. In Britain the prospects of an American withdrawal which these events seemed to imply resulted in a mixture of relief and anxiety. Relief that the United States was now attempting to extricate itself from a debilitating war, and anxiety because of the fear that 'the great retreat' from the Asian mainland might lead to a retreat from all overseas commitments, including Europe, to a new isolation. It may be that such anxiety stemmed from an awareness that Britain had not shared the burdens in Vietnam, as she had done in Korea, and therefore she was not in a very strong position to urge the US to maintain the level of its commitments in Europe. If the reassessment of American security interests were not enough to worry British and other European leaders Senator Mansfield and his supporters in the US remained an ever present reminder that the American presence in Europe could never be taken for granted.

By the end of the decade therefore Anglo-American relations had reached a somewhat ambiguous and uncertain state. At certain levels, including many of the informal aspects of defence planning, relations remained as close as ever. At the diplomatic level also the two countries worked in close partnership during the crises caused by the Six Day War in the Middle East in July 1967 and the Soviet invasion of Czechoslovakia in August 1968.[86] Prime Minister Harold Wilson also managed to establish a rather closer relationship with President Nixon than he had achieved with President Johnson.[87] Nevertheless important divergences of interests were becoming more pronounced and the preoccupation of resolving their own national problems helped to slacken the bonds holding the two states together. As the US was beginning the slow, painful task of withdrawing 'with honour' from Vietnam, Britain was taking a second step on the equally slow, if not quite so painful path of joining the EEC.[88] As the US was looking more and more to the Soviet Union to achieve mutually satisfactory arms control arrangements,[89] Britain was looking increasingly towards the benefits of joint procurement with her European allies. For the US, relations with the Soviet Union and détente held the centre of the stage, whereas for Britain membership of the European club was becoming more of a major preoccupation.

Britain and Europe

For Britain, however, the question of whether the European, or American, circle of foreign and defence policy should be given priority remained to a large extent unresolved. The dilemma was seen particularly in the field of defence planning. The reshaping of British defence policy towards NATO and the focus on the Eurogroup[90] and joint procurement projects was balanced against the quiet but continuing spectrum of defence relations with the Americans. The uncertainty in the minds of British leaders over where the future of the nation's foreign and defence policy lay was highlighted in the discussions which took place in June 1967 between Harold Wilson and Charles de Gaulle over Britain's new application to join the EEC. At the Versailles meeting the French President once again expressed his concern about the close links between *les Anglo-Saxons* especially in the diplomatic and military fields. He accepted that British policy was in a state of transition. He told the British Prime Minister, however, that he was unsure about what this meant in terms of relations with the US. 'Was it possible for Britain at present', he asked, 'and was Britain willing – to follow any policy that was really distinct from that of the United States, whether in Asia, the Middle East or Europe? This was what France still did not know. The whole situation, however, would be very different', he concluded, 'if France were genuinely convinced that Britain really was disengaging from the US in all major matters such as *defence policy* and in areas such as Asia, the Middle East, Africa and Europe.[91]

After de Gaulle's veto of Britain's first application, the British Prime Minister remained sensitive about the 'charge' that Britain retained 'special' links with the United States, especially on security matters. Consequently, in his reply he emphasized the great changes which had taken place in British policy, especially in terms of the greater independence from the US. He pointed out that Britain was now 'less dependent on the US for military supplies' and revealed to the French President that the Cabinet had recently decided not to buy the Poseidon missile from the Americans to replace Polaris.[92] As Wilson himself puts it, 'To that extent I was presenting him not with a new Nassau in reverse. Trianon was the opposite of Rambouillet.'[93]

De Gaulle, however, remained sceptical. He welcomed the movement away from the United States (especially in certain areas of defence) and he was encouraged by the wider-ranging cooperation in the procurement of weapons systems between Britain and other European states. At the same time, however, he expressed his continuing fear that British membership of the Community would inevitably encourage a trend towards the kind of Atlanticism which he wished to avoid. He explained that 'he had always observed, in war and peace, and whether or not Britain really wanted it, that she was linked to the United States'.[94] He felt that this was probably still the case and that Britain had not fully decided where her future lay. It was perhaps this feeling, above all else, which led the French President in November 1967 to veto once again Britain's application to join the Community.

In many respects de Gaulle was right. Britain was not fully committed to Europe and especially not to the kind of Europe which the French President favoured. To the extent that the British leaders had thought about the future of the Community, they did tend to favour the kind of Atlanticism which worried the French President and which would enable Britain to achieve the benefits of European cooperation in defence as in other fields, and still retain the advantages of close ties with the United States. For the moment, however, the veto left British decision-makers in defence, as in other areas, in an atmosphere of continuing uncertainty without any clear focus upon which to plan for the future.

5 The Residual Relationship 1970–1980

The erosion of Anglo-American relations which began in the 1960s continued into the 1970s despite initial attempts by the new Conservative government in Britain to resume a 'close', or as Edward Heath called it, a 'natural' relationship, with the US.[1] As the pace of international change accelerated at the beginning of the decade, especially with the pursuit of détente, a number of the major areas of interest of the United States and Britain continued to diverge. In the early part of the decade, particularly, both countries were faced with international and domestic preoccupations which helped to distract attention from relations with each other. Apart from the task of withdrawing from Vietnam the United States became increasingly involved in the complex and delicate task of negotiating major arms control agreements with the Soviet Union[2] while at the same time pursuing a policy of rapprochement with Russia's major adversary, Communist China. At home growing economic difficulties and the trauma surrounding the Watergate scandal also absorbed the energy of policy-makers in Washington, leaving them little time to devote to European or British relations. At the same time Britain's own perennial economic problems and the determination to play a more positive role in Europe likewise contributed to a weakening of relations with the United States. The changed political and strategic circumstances meant that some of the compelling pressures for the continuation of the bilateral relationship were increasingly disappearing. Despite these changes, however, a number of important links nevertheless remained between the two countries especially in the defence field, helping to qualify the growing tendency by the United States to treat Britain as just another European state.

A return to the global alliance?

After the somewhat sour personal relations which existed at times between Harold Wilson and Lyndon Johnson in the late 1960s,[3] the new Conservative government which came to power in Britain in 1970 promised to restore the close ties with the United States.[4] For Edward Heath, the Tory leader, the need to improve the two-way communication across the Atlantic was apparently an important and immediate objective. One decision in particular taken by the new government must have been very welcome in Washington. Not only the Americans had been critical of the decision by the Labour government in 1967 to withdraw from east of Suez. The Conservative opposition criticized the government of the day for the haste involved and the instability which would be caused by such precipitate action. On resuming office the Conservatives announced that they would retain a presence in the Far East as part of a five-power defence arrangement.[5] According to the Supplementary Statement on Defence issued in October 1970, Britain would contribute land, sea and air forces to the new ANZUK arrangement.[6] The force would be small but would nevertheless represent a firm commitment 'on the ground'.

Negotiations also took place with the United States at much the same time to jointly develop further the facilities of Diego Garcia in the Indian Ocean.[7] The British Indian Ocean Territories had been made available for fifty years for the defence purposes of both countries under the 'Exchange of Notes' in 1966. By 1970 the extension of a Soviet naval presence into the Indian Ocean led to pressure from the US to establish airfield and communications facilities in the region. Following the negotiations between the two countries it was announced in December 1970 that work on an Anglo-American base would begin in March 1971 and would be financed by the US government.[8]

Britain's renewed determination 'to play her part . . . in countering threats to stability outside Europe'[9] also led to speculation that the government would reverse the decision of its predecessors to withdraw from the Persian Gulf. The Americans were known to be very concerned about the dangers of a power vacuum in the oil-rich Gulf after British forces left.[10] Thus the announcement in the 1971 Defence White Paper that 'a new round of discussions' had taken place with the Gulf rulers[11] must have led to hopes in the United States that Britain would decide to stay. Shortly afterwards, however, it was announced, no doubt to the disappointment of the US, that the protected status of the Gulf states would cease and British forces would be withdrawn by December 1971.[12] Britain's exclusive treaties were to be terminated and new treaties of friendship signed with Bahrain, Qatar, and with the United Arab Emirates which were to be formally established on 2 December 1971. The only concession Britain was prepared to make was to continue the loan of British military personnel to the local defence forces and to station a small British military force at Sharjah to give advice to those forces. It was also decided that ships of the Royal Navy and Royal Air Force aircraft would visit the Gulf regularly.

By this stage it was becoming apparent that the Conservative government's policies towards the defence of the east of Suez region were only a modification, not a reversal, of Labour's policies. For the United States it soon became clear that the hopes of Britain resuming a significant share of the world-wide responsibilities were not going to materialize.

With the return of a Labour government in March 1974, even the limited world presence maintained by the Conservatives came under attack. Faced with severe economic problems, the new government initiated what it described as 'the most extensive and thorough review of defence . . . ever undertaken by a British government in peacetime'.[13] As a result, Parliament was informed in December 1974 that defence expenditure would be reduced from 5•5 per cent to 4•5 per cent of GNP by 1984, which would involve a saving of £4700 million in projected expenditure. At the same time the policy of contracting and concentrating the defence effort on Europe begun in 1967/68 was taken a stage further. The government decided that 'it could not in future commit British maritime forces to the Mediterranean in support of NATO'[14] and it was announced that forces would be run down in Malta between 1977 and 1979 when the Military Facilities Agreement would finally expire. Further withdrawals were also to occur in the Far East. The 1975 White Paper indicated that the consultative commitment contained in the five-power defence arrangement would be maintained but that, with the exception of a small residual contribution to the integrated air defence system, Britain would withdraw the forces in Singapore and Malaysia by April 1976.[15] Force levels in Hong Kong and Cyprus were also to be reduced and the staging post on Gan as well as the naval communications station on Mauritius were to be closed.

Thus by the middle of the 1970s very little remained of the global military partnership which had begun in the Second World War and which had been revived in the post-war period. Britain had ceased to declare ground forces to the contingency plans of the South-East Asia Treaty Organization on 31 March 1969. Now, in the 1975 White Paper it was announced that British forces would no longer be designated for another of the cold war alliances, CENTO. Just as SEATO and CENTO had helped to symbolize the world-wide partnership in arms between Britain and the United States in the 1950s and early 1960s, so the withdrawal of Britain's military contribution (and the later winding up of SEATO on 1 July 1977) highlighted for many observers the erosion of the close defence relationship which had occurred by this time.

Not surprisingly perhaps, the 1974 British Defence Review and the continuation of the policy of withdrawal were badly received in Washington, just as similar policies had been in the late 1960s. The military establishment in the United States in particular was highly critical of the level of defence effort in Britain. As a result of the review and the further cuts in expenditure announced in 1975 and 1976, the Chairman of the American Joint Chiefs of Staff was moved in October 1976 to describe Britain's armed forces as 'pathetic'.[16] In a moment of perhaps calculated outspokenness, the General declared: 'They're no longer a world power, all they've got are generals, admirals and bands.'[17] Such comments not surprisingly had a chilly reception in London and led to a stir in Washington. General Brown subsequently explained that his remarks were meant more in sorrow than anything else but significantly he made little attempt to change his assessment of Britain's defence effort.[18]

European defence and the shifting relationship

Apart from the continuing erosion of the close cooperation in global defence, the 1970s also witnessed changes in attitudes on both sides of the Atlantic towards questions of European defence. For Britain the successful completion in 1972 of negotiations to join the European Economic Community resulted in an extension of the kind of Eurocentric defence policies which had increasingly emerged in the late 1960s. This involved such things as an active role by Britain in the work of the Eurogroup and its various sub-committees and also a growing commitment to greater cooperation in weapons procurement with her European allies (as the Jaguar and Tornado programmes testify). At the same time there was a parallel tendency for the United States to pay less attention to the bilateral relationship. This arose largely as a result of the Administration's wide-ranging international responsibilities and preoccupations. Of particular importance was the development of a strategic relationship with the Soviet Union which involved the Nixon, Ford and later Carter governments in a series of long and complex negotiations leadings to the SALT I Agreement in May 1972, the Vladivostok Accords in November 1974, and eventually the SALT II Agreement in June 1979.[19]

Although consultations on SALT took place between the United States and its allies, including Britain,[20] the relationship developed between the super-powers was in many respects an exclusive one. Unlike arms control negotiations of the past, Britain no longer sat 'at the top table'. For Britain, exclusion from such major negotiations not only highlighted her relative decline in power but raised the possibility of agreements which might be detrimental to her security interests. These were anxieties which were shared with other Western states and helped to strengthen the growing tendency for Britain to work more closely with her European allies. For all these states the reliability of the American guarantee had for a long time been a source of some uncertainty.[21] The tendency in the 1970s for the super-powers to negotiate on a strictly bilateral basis raised further fears in Europe that tacit understandings would be reached to fight a future war if it occurred in Europe and to preserve each other's homelands from attack. There was also some anxiety that a new SALT agreement might not only limit Soviet and American arsenals and options but also those of the allies themselves. The European states were particularly concerned that the option to develop Cruise Missiles, which held many attractions for them, might be foreclosed by such an agreement.[22] This appeared a particularly serious prospect at a time when a growing Eurostrategic imbalance was developing as a result of the Soviet deployment of the mobile SS-20 missile and the Backfire bomber. Britain thus found herself increasingly in common accord with other Eurogroup states in a collective effort to ensure that the United States did not sacrifice Europe's strategic interests in its search for accommodation with the Soviet Union.

Alongside this trend for Britain to play a greater role in European defence matters, there was also a growing preference in the United States itself to deal with Western Europe as a whole on defence issues. The shift in the Anglo-American relationship which this implied was clearly discernible in the negotiations which took place in 1974/75 to try to resolve the arguments surrounding 'the recurrent theme' of burden-sharing in NATO.

In the early 1970s American-European relations in general were strained by differences over such events as the Indo-Pakistan conflict in 1971, the Yom Kippur War in October 1973[23] and concern in Europe over the failure of the Nixon government to consult its allies, especially over the new policy towards China. Criticisms of Europe were also to be found in the United States, especially of the failure of the European allies to play their full part in their own defence. Throughout the 1960s Senators Symington and Mansfield had spearheaded a campaign to secure American troop withdrawals from Europe. Once again between 1971 and 1974 several Mansfield Amendments were introduced designed to reduce the burden on the United States of defending Western Europe. Although these moves, like those in the 1960s, failed to get majority support in the Senate, they nevertheless served notice on the Europeans that the present levels of American military support could not be taken for granted in the future.[24]

Such demands were also of concern to the United States government itself. In order partly to head off some of the more stringent pressures for US troop withdrawals, the Jackson–Nunn Amendment to the 1974 American Defence Appropriation Authorization Act required the US government 'to reduce forces in NATO Europe to the extent that their foreign exchange costs were not met by the European allies'.[25] Although the main purpose of the Amendment was recognized in Europe, not surprisingly it did little to improve relations. The somewhat mercenary overtones were widely resented by Western European governments.

During 1974, however, there was a movement away from the recriminations of the previous couple of years to a realization on both sides of the Atlantic that improvements in cooperative efforts within the alliance were necessary if the West was to match the steady buildup of Soviet military power. According to a 1973 NATO Report, duplication of armaments and research projects were costing NATO $1000 million a year compared with the kind of standardization achieved in the Warsaw Pact.[26] The former SACEUR, General Goodpaster, estimated that 30 per cent of the military efficiency of the Alliance was lost because of the lack of rationalization, standardization and interoperability.[27] In December 1974, as a result of a concerted campaign by the NATO establishment to highlight these weaknesses, the decision was made to include 'a long range defence concept' in the next NATO Ministerial Guidance for the period up to 1982. This concept, which was endorsed by the Defence Planning Committee of NATO in May 1975, was designed to set out the objectives for cooperative efforts within the framework of NATO strategy.

This campaign within NATO had its impact both in the United States and in Europe. In the United States the Callaghan Report was produced in August 1974 by the State Department which, amongst other things, proposed a transatlantic common market in defence equipment. The report suggested that this should involve a 'two-way-street' in military trade and the establishment of some form of European Defence Procurement Agency. Callaghan's initiative was followed by the Nunn Amendment to the 1975 Defence Appropriation Authorization Act. This required the American Defence Secretary to assess the economic and military costs to NATO arising out of the lack of standardization, to devise appropriate remedial measures, and to report to Congress on these measures. The importance of the Amendment derived from the fact that it forced the United States Administration to pursue more positively the goal of standardization in NATO.

The process was taken a stage further in the United States by the Culver–Nunn Amendment to the 1976 Defence Appropriation Authorization Act which highlighted various ways of overcoming the restrictive provisions of the so-called 'Buy American' Act of 1933. Under this Amendment it was henceforth to be United States policy that:

1. Equipment procured for the use of American forces in Europe should be standardized or at least interoperable with the equipment of her allies.

2. The Defence Secretary was to regard this objective 'as a sufficient condition' – for the purpose of the 'Buy-American Act' – for purchasing weapons systems overseas where necessary.

3. The Defence Secretary was required to inform Congress of any cases where it was proposed to depart from the policy of standardization or interoperability.

Despite some modification of the Amendment in the Senate, the principle of standardization and the importance of a 'two-way-street' in defence equipment with Europe was firmly recognized by the Administration and Congress in legislation passed on 1 July 1976. The legislation followed the Culver–Nunn Amendment closely and advocated that the European states themselves should work together on a united and collective basis to make a genuine 'two-way-street' possible. 'Accordingly, the Congress encourages the governments of Europe to accelerate their present efforts to achieve

European armaments collaboration among all European members of the Alliance.'[28]

At the same time that these events were occurring in the United States similar moves to achieve a greater emphasis on equipment cooperation were taking place in Europe. In June 1974, in the light of economic difficulties facing the European states (as a result of the oil embargo), the Eurogroup Ministers agreed that 'there was a need to maintain a highly developed technological, scientific and industrial base in Europe whilst also seeking to achieve the closest possible cooperation in arms production and procurement between the countries of North America and Europe'.[29] With the British Defence Secretary, Roy Mason, as Chairman of the Eurogroup in 1975, the question of a genuine 'two-way-street' and the need for some forum for greater European cooperation was pursued at various meetings both within the Eurogroup and the Defence Planning Committee. These discussions culminated with the Eurogroup proposals of November for the creation of an Independent European Programme Group (IEPG). The IEPG was to be independent of the Eurogroup and the integrated military structure of NATO and as such would enable France to become a member. But it was also designed to act within the 'spirit of the Alliance'. It was hoped that the Programme Group would help to reconcile the twin objectives of alliance standardization and the preservation of the European defence industries. The proposals were acceptable to both the United States and France and the organization was duly established at a meeting of the Eurogroup countries and France held in Rome on 2 February 1976.

The experience of the IEPG is clearly of great significance in the movement both towards increasing cooperation between the European states themselves in the procurement field and the development of a European end of the 'two-way-street'. It is also of significance, as far as the present study is concerned, in illustrating the changes which were taking place during this period in certain areas of Anglo-American defence relations. The negotiations demonstrated the growing American interest in dealing with Britain as part of a wider European grouping rather than on a purely bilateral basis. They also highlighted Britain's concern to coordinate her policies with those of her European allies and her interest in establishing a greater European identity for dealing with the United States.

Real as these trends were, however, they should not be allowed to obscure the fact that in many areas of defence, bilateralism still remained important: a residual 'special relationship' continued alongside the movement towards a wider multilateral approach. Even in the field of weapons procurement this remained the case. At the height of negotiations to establish the Independent European Programme Group, for example, in September 1975 a 'Memorandum of Understanding' (MoU) was agreed between the British and American governments relating to procurement of defence equipment. The memorandum was a follow-up to an Arrangement of May 1963 for Joint Military Development and other earlier off-set agreements between the two countries. As such the MoU was designed to achieve greater cooperation in research, development, production and procurement in areas of high technology weapons systems and other advanced items of defence equipment. The aim was also

> to make the most rational use of their respective industrial, economic and technological resources, to achieve the greatest attainable military capability at the lowest possible cost, and to achieve greater standardization and interoperability of their weapons systems.[30]

Another purpose of the agreement was to achieve 'a long term and equitable balance in reciprocal purchasing of defence equipment'.[31] Thus at a time when the final touches were being put on proposals for the IEPG to act on behalf of the European states in the attempt to develop a genuine 'two-way-street', Britain and the United States were working out their bilateral arrangements. For most of the post-war period Britain had been heavily dependent on American military equipment and in the mid-1970s she continued to buy important military items from the United States, particularly in the field of missiles, torpedoes and ECM equipment. The MOU was clearly advantageous to Britain because it created greater opportunities for the sale of British armaments in the US to redress the highly unfavourable balance which existed.

There was, however, already one important area of defence technology where Britain's expertise was such that throughout the 1970s the American government had been prepared to 'buy British': namely the VTOL Harrier Aircraft. In 1970 and 1971, in an unprecedented move, the US Marines placed orders for the Harrier.[32] This represented the first time since the First World War that the United States had bought an operational military aircraft for its own Services direct from Britain or indeed from any other country.[33] The Americans had been interested in the revolutionary Harrier project from the early days of its development. In fact it had been American aid which helped to keep the project going when the lack of resources seemed to put its future production in doubt. The lack of British government support in the early days of the project compelled the Hawker and Bristol companies to develop the VTOL P1127 as a private venture. They were able to continue with the development of the aircraft and eventually succeed in perfecting the new concept largely through the considerable financial support given by the American Mutual Development Programme Agency. The Agency apparently provided in the region of 75 per cent of the funds for the important engine development which, it is estimated, amounted to about £12½ million.

Thus through a combination of American financial help and British technical expertise, Britain was able to produce an aircraft which led the world in its concept and design. Despite continuing opposition in the

United States to buying foreign aircraft which, at times, has interrupted sales,[34] large numbers of Harriers have nevertheless been purchased by the American Marines, helping to offset some of the large costs of British purchases of American weapons systems.

Continuing nuclear cooperation

Collaboration on conventional weapons systems and arms sales were not the only, or the most vital, areas of the bilateral relationship which continued through the 1970s. Of even greater importance was the on-going nuclear partnership which included not only the exchange of information between the scientific communities but wide-ranging American support for the continuing efficacy of the British deterrent. The wider political, economic and military trends towards greater European cooperation clearly influenced the debate about the future of the British deterrent which took place periodically throughout the 1970s.[35] Nevertheless the Heath, Wilson and Callaghan governments all remained committed to the continuation of the 'special' nuclear partnership with the United States.

During the Heath government some thought was apparently given in 1972 to collaboration with the French on nuclear matters in line with the Prime Minister's ardent Europeanism.[36] The emphasis by the French government on the continuing importance of independence in the defence field, however, and France's absence from the integrated military structure of NATO, made this difficult to achieve. In evidence to the House of Commons sub-committee on Defence and External Affairs in February 1973, the Conservative Secretary of State for Defence, Lord Carrington, indicated that there were long-term possibilities of Anglo-French nuclear collaboration. He also recognized, however, that it was 'an area which bristles with political and other problems'.[37] He argued that

> The first factor is the present French Defence policy, which entirely relies on national sovereignty and is not prepared to share the decisions about defence with anybody. Therefore real collaboration is impossible.[38]

The same sub-committee which was considering the future of the British deterrent also received a memorandum from the London-based International Institute for Strategic Studies which made much the same point.[39] In line with the Defence Secretary's views, the memorandum recognized that there were technical, economic and particularly political difficulties inhibiting Anglo-French cooperation in the immediate future. These were problems, the Institute suggested, which were not susceptible to change overnight. There was 'a need for time to pass' before such difficulties might be overcome.[40]

The IISS submission also raised a number of important doubts about continuing American nuclear help for Britain in the future. In a section headed 'Fading American Cooperation' the memorandum suggested that there was considerable uncertainty

> . . . about American willingness to continue supporting Britain's nuclear deterrent, either in its present form or in terms of willingness to modernize it at a later date. This could be technical or economic, based on reluctance to support Polaris missile systems after their phasing out from the American strategic deterrent. It could also be political, derived from a combination of factors such as the development of the strategic arms limitation talks between the super-powers; friction between NATO powers which impinge on the American view of its European allies, and Britain and France in particular; attitudes in Congress where strategic nuclear policy to Britain gets caught up in largely autonomous or domestic rivalries between the legislative and executive branches or simply the continuation in the decline in the closeness of the nuclear relationship between Britain and the U.S. which has been evident in recent years.[41]

Even if the government shared these doubts there is no evidence that at this time it felt inclined to consider serious alternatives to cooperation with the United States as a consequence. Indeed there seems to have been a recognition that everything should be done to maintain the close ties. As Lord Carrington himself argued in February 1973, 'There is no doubt that we have benefited considerably from U.S. assistance with the creation of our own Polaris force, and in economic terms alone it makes sense to continue to rely on the United States whether we continue with the Polaris system in its current or in an improved form or change to another system.'[42]

After deciding to spend £40 million on improvements to the British nuclear deterrent in August 1971, Prime Minister Edward Heath raised the question of further modernizing the force on his visit to the United States in April 1973. As a result of these 'informal soundings' the Nixon government was apparently prepared to consider the question of providing Britain with further technical help. United States officials were reported as studying three possibilities.[43] These involved passing on technical information (on MRV techniques for example), or alternatively selling Britain either Poseidon or Trident. The Royal Navy, with strong backing from American naval circles, favoured Poseidon (with its MIRV capability) and urged the government to try to purchase the missile as the natural follow-on to Polaris.

British officials apparently assumed that Poseidon could be bought from the United States under the terms of the Nassau Agreement.[44] As it was, this somewhat 'questionable assumption' was never tested at the official level in Washington.[45] The Heath government decided in the end not to make a formal request for either Poseidon or Trident. Instead it was decided in April 1973 to postpone the decision on a new generation of nuclear weapons and to continue to up-date the existing system. As a result the Polaris Improvement Programme was initiated with the objective of improving the design of the British warheads and the penetration capability of the force.[46] In many respects it is significant that this relatively cheap option was made possible to a large extent by the SALT I Agreement signed by the United States and the Soviet Union in Moscow in May 1972. Under this agreement both sides agreed to limit anti-ballistic missile systems to two 'deployment areas'.[47] In so doing the agreement helped to maintain the credibility of the Polaris system and to significantly prolong the life of the British deterrent. The unrestricted deployment of ABMs by the super-powers would increasingly have raised doubts about the ability of the small British force (and other medium nuclear forces) to penetrate Soviet defences in the late 1970s and 1980s.

When the Tory government was defeated in the March 1974 election there was a widespread public feeling both in Britain and the United States that Anglo-American relations in general were in a rather poor state. Observers in Washington in particular felt that Mr Heath's advocacy of the European cause had 'allowed the rope to go slack' and 'opportunities to go unexploited'.[48] A similar view was held in NATO. The Secretary General of the Alliance, Dr Luns, complained that the Heath government had allowed the 'special relationship' to deteriorate in order to keep on good terms with Europe.[49] While there may well be some truth in these criticisms of the relationship as a whole they do not seem to reflect the state of nuclear collaboration between the two countries. In this particular field, apart from some consideration of Anglo-French cooperation, Heath and his government undoubtedly remained as determined to maintain the close habitual cooperation as any of his predecessors.[50] The United States government likewise showed no signs of wanting to break the links which it continued to regard as being valuable.

The new Labour government in 1974 inherited the Polaris improvement programme which, in many ways, represented an extension of the policy begun by the previous Labour government in the late 1960s.[51] It was announced in March 1975 that the government had no intention of moving on to a new generation of strategic nuclear weapons.[52] At the same time, however, the Wilson government remained committed to maintaining the effectiveness of the existing force. In 1974 Britain resumed nuclear testing at the American underground site at Navada and in the following four years up to November 1978 five tests occurred.[53] During this period a number of test firings of the Polaris missile also took place at the American ranges at Cape Kennedy.

The Wilson government was also concerned to extend the life of the very important bilateral nuclear exchange agreement when part of it came up for renewal.[54] In the late 1960s two amendments had been passed to the 1958 Agreement, one of which allowed the transfer of U-235 for use as submarine reactor fuel to continue until 31 December 1979[55] and the other allowed the transfer of non-nuclear parts of atomic weapons for weapons purposes to continue only until 31 December 1974.[56] In July 1974 the new government sought and achieved an agreement with the United States on a further amendment which extended the transfer of weapon parts also until 31 December 1979.[57] At the same time the Labour government, like its Conservative predecessor, showed no signs of wanting to terminate the exchange of information component of the 1958 Act which was subject to review in 1973/74.[58]

The tritium mystery

Despite the continuation by the Labour government of the close working relationship with the United States on nuclear matters, however, there was one area of cooperation which the British government itself decided to sever. This involved tritium, a radioactive isotope of hydrogen, which is important in the making of thermonuclear warheads. Britain had acquired her supplies of tritium from the United States for the past sixteen years under the terms of the 1958 nuclear exchange agreement. Then suddenly in April 1976 the government decided to stop importing the material and to produce it instead at the Chapelcross plant in Dumfries.[59] The implication was that Britain was intent on ending her dependence on the United States in this particular field and becoming self-sufficient in the manufacture of thermonuclear warheads.

The government's explanation for this move was not altogether convincing. It was announced that the decision had been made because it was 'convenient' and because it 'saved dollars'.[60] It was 'convenient' supposedly because tritium would not have to be transported from the United States to Britain (once production began at Chapelcross). This is hardly likely, however, to have been a crucial consideration. At a time when Britain was still suffering from major economic difficulties, considerations of cost, on the other hand, would clearly be of some importance. A certain amount of doubt, however, exists over whether the switch to self-sufficiency did in fact save money. In rejecting the government's explanation the former Labour Minister for Disarmament, Lord Chalfont, argued that it would in fact be enormously expensive to produce tritium in Britain;[61] possibly even more expensive than buying it from the United States. Because of the absence of any published information on the relative costs involved it is obviously difficult to come to any definite conclusions about the importance of economic considerations in the decision. There is, however, sufficient doubt to suggest that there may well have been other reasons that were just as, or even more, important than costs.

Lord Chalfont himself argued that 'A more convincing explanation is that the British government had reason to believe that the 1958 Agreement which is extendable every four years and comes up for renewal in 1978, may not in fact be renewed.'[62] Chalfont suggested that this might be the case because the Americans had decided that it was no longer in their interests to transport their nuclear secrets and materials across the Atlantic.

The weakness with this interpretation, however, is that the British decision apparently took the American government itself by surprise.[63] There had been few difficulties in extending the 1958 Act in the late 1960s and early 1970s when the various components came up for renewal or review and there is no evidence that the Americans saw any difficulties arising from further renewal at the end of the 1970s.

Another explanation put forward is that the British government recognized that substantial amounts of tritium would be needed in the 1980s to produce new nuclear weapons. It has been suggested, for example, that defence planners were concerned to provide Britain with the option of producing new (perhaps neutron) warheads for the Lance missile at a later date if the need arose.[64] Some observers have also linked the decision with preparations for a replacement to Polaris, although the government itself had said that it had no plans for a new generation of nuclear weapons.[65] None of these explanations, however, suggests why the decision was made at this particular time[66] and why the government should have wanted to end its dependency on the United States in this field.

Speculation has also centred on the question of collaboration with France in the 1980s. It is argued that self-sufficiency in the production of nuclear warheads as well as re-entry vehicles would enable Britain to work with France without the political problem caused by continuing dependence on the United States for a vital material. With her own tritium supplies Britain would be independent in the production of nuclear warheads. How significant this would be, however, is difficult to determine. Britain would still remain dependent on the United States in numerous other ways.[67] It would also presumably be very difficult for Britain to disentangle information derived from her own research efforts and that derived from the United States, which under the terms of the Nuclear Exchange Agreement cannot be passed on to a third country without American approval.[68]

The reason why the government decided to produce tritium in Britain, then, remains something of a mystery. Questions of convenience, cost, or future planning, may have played some part. All that can be said for certain is that the government decided for whatever reason to reduce its dependence on the United States in this one important area after many years of American assistance and that this took place at a time when speculation was starting to build up once again about the future of the British deterrent.[69]

Apart from the tritium decision, the Labour government quietly but effectively continued the wide-ranging nuclear cooperation with the United States right up to its defeat in the General Election in May 1979. Over the previous twenty years government officials and scientists from both countries had built up a network of close personal ties, habitual working relationships which the government clearly thought it important to continue behind the scenes regardless of the separate and diverging preoccupations of both governments in certain areas.

The continuing defence partnership

This was also true of many other areas of the defence relationship as well. Cooperation in the field of research on chemical and biological agents was one such area. Collaboration in these fields had been a little publicized but nevertheless important feature of the relationship throughout the post-war period.[70] Although some of the work had been scaled down in the 1970s and various agreements limiting stock-piling had been signed with the Soviet Union, nevertheless joint research on defensive measures against such weapons remained as vital as at any time since 1945.

The scientists of the two countries have also continued to cooperate on a wide range of weapons systems and equipment for the future. Various reports have appeared from time to time, for example, of exchanges of information which have been taking place on laser technology for defence purposes. Scientists in Britain working at the Royal Radar Establishment at Malvern have apparently been working 'for some time' in close harmony with their counterparts in the United States on charged-particle beams.[71] As a result a wide range of laser weapons and other laser devices for all three Services are being considered and, if they turn out to be practical, may well replace some of the present conventional systems towards the end of the century.

Of even greater importance has been the wide spectrum of collaboration which has continued between the intelligence agencies of both countries. Again for obvious reasons much of this work has taken place away from the public gaze. It remains, however, no less vital for that, as Professor Coral Bell has noted. 'No doubt', she suggests, 'the CIA and the Special Intelligence Service (SIS) compete in many areas . . . but it is clear from such scraps of knowledge as the outsider can gather that there is also a considerable "pooling" of information in Washington and London.'[72] It is clearly very difficult to identify the range of cooperation which does take place in this field. Some of it involves areas which, as one official put it, are 'too secret even to identify'.[73] One can assume, however, that a great deal of information relating to the security of each state and to the Western alliance as a whole is passed reasonably freely between the Intelligence communities of both countries. This no doubt includes intelligence estimates of Soviet military deployments, including information received from American satellite surveillance. With the revolution in Iran at the end of 1978 and early 1979 the US lost an important source of intelligence, which, amongst other things, would have been of great value in monitoring the domestically sensitive question of Soviet compliance with the provisions of the SALT II Agreement. It is significant that the Carter Administration went out of its way to reassure sceptics at home that other forms of surveillance still existed, including the use of 'British facilities'.[74]

It also seems a reasonable supposition that close cooperation on such things as ciphers continues between the two countries. Recent revelations about the role of 'Ultra' and 'Magic' in the Second World War has confirmed the crucial importance of this kind of work and the close ties which were built up between British and American teams.[75] Given the continuing vital nature of cryptography in peace and war it seems highly likely that both countries would have maintained and developed their joint work in this field since the war ended. Information revealed in an article in *The Times* in August 1971[76] and during an Official Secrets Act trial in Britain in September 1978[77] also seems to indicate that cooperation on military communications generally remains an important (as well as sensitive) area of the relationship.

Some of these intelligence links are centred on US military bases in Britain which since the late 1940s have contributed to the close working partnership between the armed forces of the two countries.[78] By the late 1970s there were in the region of 24,000 American airmen, sailors and soldiers based at twenty or so US military establishments in the UK. These facilities include the US nuclear submarine depot at Holy Loch and the Third Tactical Air Force bases at Bentwaters, Lakenheath and Upper Heyford which contain 40 per cent of the US air commitment to NATO. In recent years also the importance of these bases has been emphasized by the doubling of the numbers of American FIII aircraft at Lakenheath and the subsequent decision to deploy US Cruise Missiles in Britain to offset the Soviet buildup of SS-20s and Backfire bombers targeted against Western Europe.

Despite the fact that a great deal of this effort forms part of the wider NATO relationship, even within the alliance itself the central role played by Britain and the United States from 1949 onwards continues to have some relevance.[79] Apart from the exclusive nuclear partnership there are various operational planning links, such as those between CINC WESTLANT and CINC EASTLANT which are primarily the concern of the two countries. Although these tasks are undertaken on behalf of the alliance they nevertheless involve close bilateral cooperation between the respective military authorities.[80]

The close ties which derive from the presence of US bases in Britain and cooperation within the alliance framework are clearly part of a much wider relationship which continues between the defence establishments of both countries. Contacts take many different forms and include a wide range of training exercises, exchanges of officers and frequent visits by defence officials to each other's capitals; all of which help to keep both states in close touch with military developments in the other country. As far as Britain is concerned one only has to consider the size and range of activities of the British Defence Staff Washington (BDSW) to see the importance attached to these links.[81] The BDSW totals around 168 divided into:

Front-line staff
42 service officers (8 of whom have attaché status)
33 UK-based civilians
Support staff
19 servicemen
34 UK-based civilians
40 locally engaged civilians

The seventy-five 'Front-line' staff in Washington compare with seven in Bonn and ten in Paris, the capitals of Britain's two most important European allies. Apart from the Chancery in the Washington embassy who play a small role, the BDSW is responsible for most of the defence cooperation work in the United States.[82] To achieve this it is organized into nine component parts reflecting in microcosm the Ministry of Defence itself with central and single service staffs, and research and development and defence sales sections corresponding to the MOD's Procurement Executive.

The range of defence contacts which remain between the two countries was spelled out by the report of 'The Central Policy Review Staff Review of Overseas Representation' produced in March 1978. The report began by confirming that 'Although the UK's defence effort has increasingly centred on Europe it has retained a "special relationship" with the United States in defence matters which is of vital importance'.[83] It then went on to argue that Britain needed a large number of contacts throughout the United States defence establishment. According to the report:

> One way of doing this is to have liaison officers attached to particular units or establishments who do not take an active part in the work of the unit but observe and report on new ideas and equipment. There are at present 20 such officers in the United States at various staff colleges etc. Another possibility is to negotiate reciprocal arrangements so that British officers fill full-time posts in the United States and the United States officers in the U.K. (for example aircraft pilots). These are called exchange officers and the U.K. has 172 of them in the United States at present. . . . There remains a need to maintain contact with the United States defence machine in Washington and with a number of establishments throughout the country. Given the huge size of the United States

> defence programme, the complex bureaucracy in Washington and the vast number of military and civilian defence establishments spread across the United States, this task is virtually open-ended.[84]

Apart from the large resident staff in Washington, officials from the Ministry of Defence are also frequent visitors to the United States. In 1976, for example, there were as many as 2700 visits of this kind involving discussions with American officials on a wide variety of defence business.[85]

Although, therefore, the changes which have taken place in Anglo-American relations in the 1970s have had an impact on the defence field, there is nevertheless a range of military contacts between the two countries which remain close: indeed some of which retain a 'special' quality.[86] Certain areas of cooperation are so normal and habitual that they go unnoticed. Others are so important and secret that little information reaches the general public. The absence of dramatic manifestations of Anglo-American defence collaboration in the 1970s, however, should not necessarily lead to the conclusion that the partnership is withering away. After all, many of the major agreements of the 1940s, 1950s and 1960s were concluded after periods of strained relations and indeed helped to symbolize the restoration of the alliance. The fact that such symbols are no longer so necessary is in itself important.[87] The quiet working relationship which exists at the dawn of the 1980s in a wide spectrum of vitally important areas of defence is an indication of just how intimate that relationship has become.

6 A Stocktaking and Prospectus*

The picture of the Anglo-American defence relationship which emerges from the period covered by this study is far from straightforward. At a general level the defence partnership has mirrored the changing patterns and fortunes of the wider relationship between the two states. Thus when relations have been strained, part of the problem at least has often centred on differences over security issues. This was the case, as we have seen, in the immediate post-war period with the difficulties over nuclear cooperation,[1] as it was in 1956 with the Suez crisis[2] and in 1962 with the Skybolt affair.[3] Similarly, when relations in general have been harmonious this invariably has been reflected in wide-ranging cooperation in defence matters. A good illustration of this was in the late 1950s when the series of defence agreements which were negotiated[4] symbolized the restoration of the 'special relationship' after the traumatic events of 1956.

Such a generalized image, however, clearly needs to be qualified. Defence relations have taken a variety of forms and cooperation in some areas has not precluded differences in others. Thus, not surprisingly perhaps, there have been times when certain areas of military cooperation have been out of step both with the wider defence partnership and Anglo-American relations in general. This was clearly the case on a number of occasions during the Second World War. At various times between 1941 and 1945 when Britain and the United States and particularly their military establishments were working as closely in harmony as perhaps two independent states have ever done before, military and strategic differences nevertheless arose in certain areas which ran counter to the general trends of the alliance. Disagreements over strategic bombing, the second front and especially the conduct of the war against Japan, all caused varying degrees of friction despite the fundamental harmony of purpose which existed.

This also seems to have been the case after the war in the late 1940s and early 1950s in the atomic energy field. At a time when formal and informal, bilateral and multilateral military ties were being established as

*The author owes a debt to Hedley Bull for this chapter title. See H. Bull 'Arms Control: A Stocktaking and Prospectus', *Adelphi Paper,* No. 55 (London: ISS, 1969).

the Cold War gathered momentum, progress towards restoring the wartime nuclear partnership was painfully slow. Despite the 1948 *modus vivendi*, atomic energy clearly stood out against the web of inter-dependency which was being woven between the two states at this time.[5]

In the late 1940s many of the difficulties and frustrations in the atomic energy field were felt in private by British officials trying to secure the scale of cooperation which the 1948 agreement seemed to promise. The public image, however, of the close and developing partnership in various areas of defence showed few signs of the problems of nuclear collaboration which existed in private. There have been other times, however, when the reverse has occurred; when dramatic well-publicized but nevertheless temporary differences over a particular issue in the defence field which seemed to threaten the alliance have tended to obfuscate wide-ranging military cooperation which has continued almost unaffected behind the scenes. This appears to have been the case, for example, during the Skybolt affair in 1962,[6] when the cancellation of the air-launched missile which had been promised to prolong the life of Britain's V-Bomber force caused high-level friction between the two countries.[7] But the crisis and its aftermath seem to have had almost no impact on defence business being transacted in a wide variety of other areas.[8] Working and personal relationships, numerous defence contacts and information exchanges on the multiplicity of issues, unrelated to Skybolt, apparently continued in their normal largely amicable fashion between the officials of both countries.

Another caveat to the generalized image of a close correlation between the defence partnership and the wider relationship would seem to derive from the experience of the 1970s. It does seem to have been the case that as Anglo-American relations in general became gradually 'less enthusiastic',[9] so defence relations in *certain* areas also became cooler. Britain's growing interest in European weapons procurement and the US preoccupation with super-power issues as well as her propensity to deal with Western Europe as a bloc seems to confirm this. This overall impression of erosion which appears to be widely held and towards which certain events in the defence field undoubtedly contributed, does not, however, altogether correspond with what was happening in other important areas of the defence relationship, as Chapter 5 tries to show. While the public image of Anglo-American relations has been one of 'fading cooperation', the defence establishments of both countries have generally got on with the task of quietly but effectively coordinating their policies in various (often vital) areas of the defence field. To a certain extent therefore military relations in general between the two countries in recent years do seem to have stood out somewhat against the general trends of Anglo-American relations as a whole. In line with this it is probably true to say that in certain of the defence and security fields (especially atomic energy) the term 'special relationship' still seems to be applicable.[10]

The problems and benefits of the special defence relationship

The fact that Anglo-American defence relations have generally remained close for much of the period suggests that the leaders of both countries have regarded the cooperation involved as being mutually beneficial. Whether, in fact, this has been the case is, however, a matter of some dispute. Apart from the large number of supporters of the relationship there have also been a number of critics in Britain and the United States who have argued that the military partnership has been harmful to the interests of both states.

Britain and the 'special relationship'

As far as Britain is concerned criticisms of the alliance tend to centre on such things as the illusions of great-power status which have been fostered; the political opportunities which have been lost; the strategic dependence on the United States which has resulted; and the added threats to the nation's security which the alliance has brought.

It is often argued that the 'special relationship' with the United States, and especially the preferential treatment which has allowed Britain to maintain a technologically advanced nuclear deterrent, has contributed very significantly to the maintenance of the harmful illusion that Britain remained a great power. It is frequently suggested that the post-war belief in Britain that she was a major power with world-wide responsibilities at a time when the nation's economic position was rapidly declining, played an important part in the over-stretch of Britain's defence resources in the 1960s.[11] Those who hold this view point not only to the encouragement given to Britain in the nuclear field but also to the pressure from the United States on Britain to maintain her forces east of Suez to help share the burdens of global defence.[12]

The illusion of great-power status fostered by American technological, political and financial support is also often cited as having contributed to lost opportunities especially as far as Europe is concerned. Margaret Gowing has shown how the determination in Britain to re-establish nuclear cooperation with the United States in the late 1940s prevented Britain from collaborating with other European powers in this field, with all the political implications which this might have led to.[13] It has also been suggested more generally that the wide-ranging political and military ties which had been established with the United States by the early 1950s helped to reinforce Britain's determination to stay outside the European Defence Community in 1954 and the European Economic Community in 1957. Andrew Pierre is one observer of the alliance who has argued that the emphasis placed on the close defence partnership was probably 'injurious' to Britain's long-term interests 'to the extent that it encouraged

Britain to feel that she could avoid Europe'.[14] George Ball, the former US Under-Secretary of State, is another who has claimed that the Nassau Conference in particular 'encouraged Britain in the belief that she could by her own efforts – so long as she maintained a specially favoured position with the United States – play an independent great power role and thus it deflected her from coming to terms with her European destiny.[15] These arguments suggest that if Britain had not enjoyed such close links with the United States in a variety of fields, including defence, then she would have recognized the reality of her true position in the world earlier and made the adjustment to join the European Economic Community sooner than 1973.

There is clearly something in these criticisms. The wide range of material support and the preferential links with the world's most powerful military state undoubtedly helped to reinforce the belief that Britain could play a role outside Europe and delayed the process of adjustment to the realities of power. It must be said, however, that the illusion of great-power status (if illusion it was) was just as much the result of Britain's traditional role in the world and the recent experience of being one of the big three victorious powers as it was of the close association with the United States.[16] It is also perhaps worth noting that Britain's reluctance to play a part in Europe was, in part at least, due to her lack of sympathy with the views of European integration which were widely supported on the Continent and which underpinned the emerging EEC. The retention of Britain's national identity and the maintenance of close ties with the United States were seen by governments of both right and left as being of vital importance in the preservation of British interests. Such interests could not necessarily be guaranteed by the kind of European movement which was being created. Thus although the 'special relationship' may, in one sense, be regarded as a cause of Britain's lack of commitment to Europe, in another sense it can be interpreted more as a symptom of other important forces at work in British policy.

Another harmful effect of the Anglo-American defence relationship which is often cited is the loss by Britain of its strategic independence. Although Britain has remained independent in the production of certain important weapons systems nevertheless various writers have shown that in a wide area of procurement, reliance has been placed on American manufacturers. In the field of strategic delivery vehicles this has been particularly pronounced.[17]

The beginning of British strategic dependence on the United States in the post-war period, as noted earlier, dates back to 1948 when American B29s were sent to Britain at the height of the Berlin Crisis.[18] At this stage Britain had neither nuclear weapons nor an effective long-range bomber capability of her own. Under the Mutual Defence Assistance Programme, however, Britain received Super Fortresses from the US in the early 1950s which helped to fill the gap between the development of nuclear weapons and the deployment of the V-Bomber force.[19] Even at this time there were leading politicians in Britain who were concerned about the growing dependence on the United States which these events implied. Harold Wilson, writing in 1952, complained – somewhat ironically it might be thought,[20] given his later policies – that more and more American aid is being voted on conditions which involve British acceptance of American strategic decisions and control not even by Congress but by the Pentagon, H.Q. of the US Chief of Staff'.[21]

Such complaints, however, had little impact, as we have seen. Throughout the 1950s and 1960s Britain became increasingly dependent on American strategic delivery vehicles: firstly with help for Blue Streak[22] and then the agreements on the American Thor, Skybolt and finally Polaris missiles. The Nassau Agreement, in particular, led to British dependence on the United States not only for the missile itself but also a wide range of other closely related information, materials and facilities to make the nuclear deterrent as a whole effective.

The implication of US assistance in all these fields is somewhat difficult to assess. Britain's dependency is obviously more pronounced in some areas than in others.[23] There seems little doubt, however, that during the 1960s Britain 'tied herself to the American order of priorities in research, development and production and in some respects at least become partially dependent on American satellite intelligence, navigation and radio communications systems'.[24] In so doing, Andrew Pierre points out, 'she has undoubtedly lost a measure of her strategic independence'.[25]

Despite this reliance on the United States in certain fields and despite the fact that the nuclear force is assigned to NATO, in one important sense the British deterrent remains independent. Under the terms of the Nassau Agreement, as we have seen earlier, the force can be withdrawn when Britain's vital interests are at stake. There is no question that the missiles could be fired independently if ever the occasion necessitated such action. For British policy-makers throughout the 1960s and 1970s *this* has been the 'acid test' of whether the Polaris force is or is not strategically independent.[26]

Another detrimental effect of the close alliance which has often been identified is the added threat of the nuclear devastation of Britain which the link with the United States is said to have enhanced. From 1948 onwards, when the 'Airstrip One' relationship was established,[27] Britain undoubtedly became a major target for the Soviet Union in any war with the United States.[28] Apart from American strategic air bases, the vulnerable slow-reacting Thor missiles deployed in Britain in 1957 under a 'two-key system' are often cited as having particularly increased the danger to Britain. These missiles with their first-strike potential are said to have increased the possibilities of nuclear war because of the incentives they created for pre-emptive strikes against them. A great deal of concern was further expressed from 1960 onwards after it was decided to allow the

United States to set up a Polaris submarine base at Holy Loch as a sort of *quid pro quo* for the sale of Skybolt missiles to Britain. According to those who hold this view the presence of Holy Loch as well as the US bases and the close connections between the nuclear forces of both countries means that the Soviet Union has *even greater* reasons for launching missiles against Britain if war broke out, than if those ties did not exist. Robin Cook and Dan Smith for example have argued that:

> In the event of . . . a nuclear war the role of Polaris as 'an integral part of NATO's strategic nuclear force' would inevitably entrammel Britain in the exchange. Indeed mainland Britain provides a number of targets related to our strategic deterrent which no prudent Russian commander could leave out of his list of first-strike priorities – the Faslane base, the Rugby VLF Communication station, and Fylingdales early warning station. Ironically the retention of an 'independent' nuclear capability only serves to ensure that we are embroiled in *any* conflict between the Americans and the Soviet Union.[29]

It is interesting that arguments such as these were also used against the proposals of the Thatcher government in the late 1970s to set up bases for US missiles in Britain as a response to the perceived threat to Europe from the Soviet deployment of the SS20 and the Backfire bomber. Significantly on this occasion, as on previous occasions, the Soviet Union was itself at pains to point out the dangers involved in such an American presence.[30]

While accepting the close ties with the United States may have produced extra risks in one sense, there would seem nevertheless to be a strong case that *overall* Britain's security has benefited very significantly from the cooperative relationship.[31] Access to American research and development in a wide variety of weapons and equipment, as well as purchases 'off-the-shelf', has helped to cut the costs and provide Britain with technologically advanced military hardware.[32] Through this close collaboration Britain has been able to provide herself with conventional and nuclear weapons systems which almost certainly she would not have been able to afford to produce on her own. In the nuclear field for example the help provided by the 1958 Act was (and remains) of particular importance.[33] Some of the advantages of this Act to Britain were spelled out by Frederick Jandrey, the Deputy Assistant Secretary for European Affairs in July 1958 in a statement to a sub-committee of the US Joint Committee on Atomic Energy:

> The British . . . stand to gain very substantial benefits from this agreement which, in the long run, can serve only to strengthen the whole free world. In the first place, the exchange of information and certain materials which will now be possible should enable them to abandon

> the barren and costly course of continuing to develop through the advanced stages their nuclear weapons capability in the knowledge that they are in many respects merely duplicating technical progress already achieved by their major ally. The fact that we will from now on be going forward in company with them will thus have benefits of a deep psychological nature not only for the British scientists, technicians and military specialists but for the British people as a whole. In addition I believe we are in advance of the British in enough aspects of this field so that they will be able to effect substantial savings in money, trained manpower and material resources by the adoption of knowledge and techniques we have already developed.[34]

Apart from helping Britain to provide for her own security the significantly larger American nuclear deterrent force and the presence of US troops in Europe can also be regarded as being of inestimable value in providing protection and a sense of security to Britain (and to the other Western European states) throughout the post-war period. American troops in Europe in particular have also probably helped to cut the defence costs of the Western European countries, including Britain. Certainly the kind of reductions Senator Mansfield has advocated in the past would have required Britain and her allies to increase defence spending substantially if a credible defensive system was to be maintained.[35]

There have also been other economic benefits as well from cooperating with the United States, some of which have been very substantial. Apart from the vital contribution of lend-lease during the war, the special economic relationship which continued through to the late 1960s also played an important part in bolstering a declining economy.[36] There seems little doubt that Britain would have had even greater difficulties than she did in continuing to perform her numerous overseas responsibilities in the twenty years after the war if it had not been for considerable financial assistance from the American government. In some cases when the financial strain became too great, as it did in Greece and Turkey in 1947, the United States even stepped in to take over the responsibility from Britain.

An overall assessment of the defence partnership with the United States, therefore, would seem to indicate that although it may not have been unambiguously advantageous, it has nevertheless provided Britain with wide-ranging and important benefits. While this may be so it does not, of course, mean that the alliance has necessarily been useful to the United States. Andrew Pierre has argued that the 'Anglo-American relationship has been more important to Britain and for this reason, primarily, it is the British who usually undertook the burden of keeping it "special". . . . Because of the disparities in power and global responsibility, the "special relationship" as viewed from Washington, often looked less important than it appeared in London.'[37]

In general terms this would seem to be so. The alliance for example was clearly more vital to the survival of Britain in the Second World War than it was to the United States. Also since 1945 there can be little doubt that in strictly material terms Britain has received much more from cooperating with the United States on defence matters than she has given in return. Some observers point to the fact that for Britain there has only really been one 'special relationship' and that relationship has remained the corner-stone of British foreign and defence policy for much of the post-war period. Whereas for the United States there have been a number of close cooperative relationships in the defence field each of which has fitted in a different niche in the overall structure of the American global security system. It is not uncommon, it is pointed out, to hear talk of a 'special relationship' between the United States and the Canadians, Australians, Japanese, Israelis, West Germans, Saudi Arabians and, until recently at least, the Russians.[38]

While this may be so, it does not of course prove that the defence relationship with Britain has been unimportant to the United States or that the American government has regarded it in the same light as the other close relationships it has in certain areas with these other countries. The fact that the United States government has been prepared to cooperate with Britain in such a wide area of defence projects, and indeed at times to take the initiative in suggesting collaboration, hardly suggests that it regards the partnership as being unimportant. The range, exclusiveness and vital nature of some of this joint work would also suggest that overall the United States has probably seen its alliance with Britain in somewhat different terms from its other close relationships.

For some observers in the United States, however, the main criticism of the special ties with the UK is that too much emphasis has been given by their government to the relationship. There are those who argue that American governments since the war have been too influenced by the sentimental attachments and cultural links with Britain and have lost sight of the nation's true interests. George Ball, a former US Under-Secretary of State, has argued that 'the emotional baggage of the "special relationship" has got in the way of cooler American judgement'.[39] Mr Ball claims that US interests in both a strong and united Europe and the prevention of nuclear proliferation have been harmed by the over-zealous support for the partnership with Britain, especially in the defence field. The United States, he says, has frequently 'yielded to temptation either because of the subtle seductions of the "special relationship" – or for reasons of our own short term convenience (or often a confusion of the two) – to assist Britain to avoid actions, or to induce Britain to take actions that have directly conflicted with the long-range goal of a healthy Britain playing a role of leadership in Europe.'[40] Ball cites the Nassau

Conference in particular as having emphasized Britain's favoured position and in so doing helped to check the momentum towards European unity which was disadvantageous to US interests.[41]

Also, on the question of proliferation, the former Under-Secretary of State argues that the United States has made a series of mistakes in the post-war period in providing assistance for the development of the British nuclear force.[42] Without American assistance, he suggests, Britain would have been forced out of the nuclear business. He regards the 1958 Amendment of the McMahon Act in particular as being 'a major blunder in American policy',[43] because it provided encouragement to other states to follow Britain's example in the hope of getting for themselves the kind of American assistance accorded to Britain. In this sense, Mr Ball sees 'the literal phrasing of the amendment' as being 'grotesquely at variance' with America's best interest of stopping the spread of nuclear weapons.[44]

There is perhaps an element of truth in these views as far as they go. Such arguments do, however, tend to ignore the fact that although in some ways American policies were ambiguous the government had nevertheless frequently encouraged Britain to join the European Community. They also ignore the fact that the really significant American encouragement for the British deterrent did not come until Britain was well established as a nuclear power. By 1958 she had achieved on her own the capability of fabricating a variety of atomic weapons and had constructed and operated the necessary facilities such as weapons research and development laboratories; weapon manufacturing facilities; a weapons testing station; had trained the personnel to operate these facilities; and had detonated both atomic and hydrogen bombs. Indeed this was the very reason for the decision to re-open collaboration with the British. It was clear to the American government that Britain would continue with her nuclear force with or without American help. From the point of view of western security it was thought better to assist Britain in order not to duplicate and waste resources.

The evidence seems to suggest therefore that US policies are unlikely to have been decisive in Britain's attitudes either towards Europe or the decision to become a nuclear power. Even if it is conceded[45] that US help for Britain did play a part in delaying the progress towards European unity and encouraging the proliferation of nuclear weapons, it could be argued that from the American viewpoint other interests were seen as being more important (and probably *were* more important). As far as the United States was concerned, in the 1950s Britain was undoubtedly her most important ally and as such was regarded as having a significant diplomatic and military contribution to make to the Western alliance in the series of Cold War confrontations which punctuated the 1950s and 1960s. Help for the British military effort therefore probably was in US interests and the interests of the West as a whole. As one American official put it in the late 1950s:

> Our close relationship with the United Kingdom is of vital importance in today's world. Cooperation between our two countries will contribute to the growth of free world solidarity. It will also permit a strengthening of our mutual defenses coupled with a conservation of the scarce talents and resources of both countries.[46]

Some of these benefits were of a somewhat intangible nature but there were areas where cooperation provided more material advantages. The US was able to make use, for example, of various overseas British territories such as Christmas Island for high altitude hydrogen tests in the early 1960s and Diego Garcia as a naval and communications base from the mid-1960s onwards. Britain has also made important contributions over the years in conventional defence equipment and weapons. Inventions like the steam catapult, the angled-deck, improved landing aids, as well as VTOL techniques and Chobham armour, as we have seen, were all pioneered in Britain and quickly imitated in the United States.[47] Even in the nuclear field American officials have argued that Britain has had something of value to offer the United States. In justifying the 1958 Act from the American perspective Frederick Jandrey argued that

> For us, the merging of British information and know-how in a common fund with our own . . . should provide two direct benefits. Since nuclear weapons programmes have been carried out independently by each country we stand to gain from techniques developed by the British where they have solved the same problems which we faced by methods different from our own. For the same reason, where we find that British techniques developed separately are closely similar to those we have evolved, we can have added confidence in the evolution of our own program. Thus our weapons program should profit measurably through the stimulation which inevitably results from the cross-fertilization of ideas.[48]

It could also perhaps be argued that despite the generosity of the 1958 Atomic Energy Act and the subsequent Skybolt and Polaris Agreements, Britain's dependence on the US has been and remains, *in itself*, in America's interests. Because Britain relies on the United States for various vital materials and facilities the American government retains a degree of control and influence over the British deterrent and over British strategic planning. The use of this influence is likely to have been of value in gaining British support for US strategic policies in the past and could conceivably be of major importance in certain circumstances in the future where American vital interests are at stake.

There is no doubt, of course, that during the 1960s and 1970s Britain's diplomatic and military value to the United States declined, especially in terms of her contribution to the global defensive partnership. It would be wrong, however, to conclude from this that the wide-ranging residual links do not continue to serve American interests. Clearly in terms of her diplomatic support as well as her military facilities, scientific knowledge and variety of expertise Britain still has a great deal to offer the United States. The alliance remains significantly unequal but American leaders continue to recognize that in certain areas of the defence field, in particular, the close partnership with Britain remains of great importance to American security.

The future of Anglo-American defence cooperation

The fact that both states regard the defence partnership as being of mutual advantage[49] and are likely to continue to do so in the foreseeable future would seem to be borne out by significant events in the nuclear field in late 1979 and early 1980.

Towards the end of the Callaghan government and during the early months of the Conservative government which came to power in May 1979 the debate re-emerged in Britain (within fairly narrow circles) over what, if anything, should take the place of the Polaris SLBM once the system became obsolescent at the beginning of the 1990s.[50] Apart from the traditional opposition of the nuclear disarmers,[51] there were those, such as Robin Cook MP and Dan Smith, who suggested that Britain could not afford nuclear weapons as well as the projected improvements in conventional arms and that it would be better to phase out the nuclear deterrent and provide the conventional forces so badly needed by NATO.[52] There were, however, many other observers who opposed this view and argued that there *was* a strategic purpose which 'could only, or best' be served by nuclear weapons.[53]

Amongst the supporters of a continued nuclear force, there were those who favoured Anglo-French cooperation and those advocating the maintenance of the Anglo-American nuclear partnership. Although an Anglo-French strategic deterrent seems to have been a non-starter,[54] there were a number of commentators who pointed to the economic, military and particularly political advantages to be gained from looser cooperation either through some kind of commercial arrangements on the French M-4 missile or collaboration in the development of Cruise Missiles.[55] The most powerful lobby, however, during the debate came from those supporting a 'new Nassau Agreement' or at least an agreement which would be as favourable as could be achieved from the American administration.[56] Even here there were some differences between those who favoured a continuation of the existing Polaris system in new submarines and those who advocated the purchase of Poseidon, Trident or Cruise Missiles from the United States.[57]

In May 1979 before the Callaghan government could make up its mind on what form, if any, the next generation of the deterrent should take, the Labour government lost power.[58] Despite the proclaimed Europeanism of the new Prime Minister, Mrs Thatcher, the Conservative government which took its place adopted a strong Atlanticist stand from the start. Close relations with the US were seen as complementary (rather than in opposition) to Britain's role in Europe. Strong support was given to the United States in its attempt to modernize NATO's European-based missile force[59] and in the crises in Iran and Afghanistan which erupted in late 1979 and early 1980.[60] Following the Prime Minister's successful visit to Washington in December 1979 and her reaffirmation of what she called 'the extraordinary alliance'[61] the Thatcher government announced a package of diplomatic and military measures indicating a close rapport between the two governments as the climate of international relations darkened. On the military side, an announcement was made in the House of Commons in January 1980 that the Government had agreed to allow 40 launch vehicles with 160 ground-launch Cruise Missiles, owned and operated by the US, to be based in Britain.[62] At the same time the Defence Minister, Mr Francis Pym, informed the House that the hitherto secret 'Chevaline' programme, costing £1000 million and designed to improve the warhead of Britain's Polaris missiles, was near completion. The Defence Minister went out of his way to point out that although the programme had been funded and managed entirely by the United Kingdom, it had been undertaken 'with the full cooperation of the United States government'.[63]

The major question of the replacement for Polaris, however, remained (and at the time of writing continues to remain) unresolved. Strong rumours circulated in late 1979 and early 1980 that, although the Cabinet had yet to make a final decision, the purchase of the American Trident missile was the most favoured option.[64] Mr Pym's strong endorsement of the nuclear deterrent, his speculation that the new system would cost in the region of £4000 million and £5000 million, and his comment that the US would support Britain in providing a replacement, all appear to point in that direction.[65] An agreement to purchase Trident, or any other American system, if that is the decision, will clearly be of particular symbolic as well as politico-military importance.[66] The willingness of the United States to provide Britain with strategic missiles and Britain's willingness to rely on the US in this vital area of security has been, as we have seen, a continuing characteristic feature of the 'special defence relationship' from the late 1950s onwards. Thus a decision by either government not to maintain the relationship would be viewed generally, with some justification, as a further and significant manifestation of the erosion of the 'special' links between the two countries. It is true that such a decision would probably not mean in practice the end of the close partnership in defence as a whole. Cooperation between the scientists, intelligence communities, armed forces and defence departments would almost certainly continue in various ways regardless of what happens in the nuclear field. Nevertheless nuclear cooperation in the past has not only been one of the most important areas of the defence relationship but it has also played a major role in maintaining the atmosphere of trust between the two countries and, as such, has had an important impact on other areas of the defence partnership.

The purchase of Trident therefore, if it takes place, will represent an important indicator of the future prospects for defence partnership between the two countries.[67] The United States no doubt will continue to give priority to its super-power relations and to maintaining its interests in global and regional security; Britain almost certainly will continue to forge improved links in political, economic and certain military fields with her Western European neighbours; and, despite the strains caused by the crises in Iran and Afghanistan, NATO is likely to remain the most important multilateral framework for the security interests of both states. A decision in favour of an American system, however, will highlight the value which both governments continue to see in the close bilateral ties between them and indicate a common concern to maintain an intimate defence partnership in a variety of important fields in the dangerous years ahead.

Epilogue

It was announced in both London and Washington on 15 July 1980 that agreement had been reached in the form of an exchange of letters between Prime Minister Margaret Thatcher and President Carter for Britain to purchase 100 Trident missiles from the United States at a cost of just over 1000 million pounds. Britain will build the four or five new submarines and develop the re-entry vehicles for the missile herself (although a large part of the MIRV warhead and certain vital nuclear materials will also apparently be purchased from the United States).

The decision culminated a very lengthy and very sensitive set of bilateral discussions and paralleled very closely the Nassau Agreement of 1963. As in the Agreement between Prime Minister Macmillan and President Kennedy Britain will pay only 5 per cent of the research and development costs of the missile under the terms of the Trident accord. The purchase of the missile at such favourable financial terms to Britain clearly reflects the close nuclear ties which continue to exist between the two countries. At the same time it was significant that the announcement emphasized that 'close co-operation between the United States and Britain was not limited to the nuclear field'. The Trident Agreement was also reported as containing a provision that calls on Britain to man the Rapier air-defence missile system recently purchased by the United States from Britain for deployment at American bases in the United Kingdom. At the same time it was pointed out by officials in both countries that London and Washington are also cooperating in many other areas, including plans to expand the American military installations on the British-owned island of Diego-Garcia in the Indian Ocean and the deployment of US Cruise Missiles in Britain.

18 July 1980.

Appendices

Appendix 1 The Quebec Agreement, 19 August 1943

Articles of Agreement Governing Collaboration between the Authorities of the U.S.A. and the U.K. in the matter of Tube Alloys

Whereas it is vital to our common safety in the present War to bring the Tube Alloys project to fruition at the earliest moment; and whereas this may be more speedily achieved if all available British and American brains and resources are pooled; and whereas owing to war conditions it would be an improvident use of war resources to duplicate plants on a large scale on both sides of the Atlantic and therefore a far greater expense has fallen upon the United States;

It is agreed between us

First, that we will never use this agency against each other.

Secondly, that we will not use it against third parties without each other's consent.

Thirdly, that we will not either of us communicate any information about Tube Alloys to third parties except by mutual consent.

Fourthly, that in view of the heavy burden of production falling upon the United States as the result of a wise division of war effort, the British Government recognise that any post-war advantages of an industrial or commercial character shall be dealt with as between the United States and Great Britain on terms to be specified by the President of the United States to the Prime Minister of Great Britain. The Prime Minister expressly disclaims any interests in these industrial and commercial aspects beyond what may be considered by the President of the United States to be fair and just and in harmony with the economic welfare of the world.

And Fifthly, that the following arrangements shall be made to ensure full and effective collaboration between the two countries in bringing the project to fruition:

(*a*) There shall be set up in Washington a Combined Policy Committee composed of:

The Secretary of War	(United States)
Dr Vannevar Bush	(United States)
Dr James B. Conant	(United States)
Field-Marshal Sir John Dill, G.C.B., C.M.G., D.S.O.	(United Kingdom)
Colonel the Right Hon. J. J. Llewellin, C.B.E., M.C., M.P.	(United Kingdom)
The Honourable C. D. Howe	(Canada)

The functions of this Committee, subject to the control of the respective Governments, will be:

(1) To agree from time to time upon the programme of work to be carried out in the two countries.

(2) To keep all sections of the project under constant review.

(3) To allocate materials, apparatus and plant, in limited supply, in accordance with the requirements of the programme agreed by the Committee.

(4) To settle any questions which may arise on the interpretation or application of this Agreement.

(*b*) There shall be complete interchange of information and ideas on all sections of the project between members of the Policy Committee and their immediate technical advisers.

(*c*) In the field of scientific research and development there shall be full and effective interchange of information and ideas between those in the two countries engaged in the same sections of the field.

(*d*) In the field of design, construction and operation of large-scale plants, interchange of information and ideas shall be regulated by such *ad hoc* arrangements as may, in each section of the field, appear to be necessary or desirable if the project is brought to fruition at the earliest moment. Such *ad hoc* arrangements shall be subject to the approval of the Policy Committee.

Appendix 2 Declaration of Trust, 13 June 1944

THIS AGREEMENT AND DECLARATION OF TRUST is made the thirteenth day of June One thousand nine hundred and forty four by FRANKLIN DELANO ROOSEVELT on behalf of the Government of the United States of America, and by WINSTON LEONARD SPENCER CHURCHILL on behalf of the Government of the United Kingdom of Great Britain and Northern Ireland. The said Governments are hereinafter referred to as 'the Two Governments';

WHEREAS an agreement (hereinafter called the Quebec Agreement) was entered into on the Nineteenth day of August One thousand nine hundred and forty three by and between the President of the United States and the Prime Minister of the United Kingdom; and

WHEREAS it is an object vital to the common interests of those concerned in the successful prosecution of the present war to insure the acquisition at the earliest practicable moment of an adequate supply of uranium and thorium ores; and

WHEREAS it is the intention of the Two Governments to control to the fullest extent practicable the supplies of uranium and thorium ores within the boundaries of such areas as come under their respective jurisidictions; and

WHEREAS the Government of the United Kingdom of Great Britain and Northern Ireland intends to approach the Governments of the Dominions and the Governments of India and of Burma for the purpose of securing that such Governments shall bring under control deposits of the uranium and thorium ores within their respective territories; and

WHEREAS it has been decided to establish a joint organisation for the purpose of gaining control of the uranium and thorium supplies in certain areas outside the control of the Two Governments and of the Governments of the Dominions and of India and of Burma;

NOW IT IS HEREBY AGREED AND DECLARED AS FOLLOWS:

1. (1) There shall be established in the City of Washington, District of Colombia, a Trust to be known as 'The Combined Development Trust'.
   (2) The Trust shall be composed of and administered by six persons who shall be appointed, and be subject to removal, by the Combined Policy Committee established by the Quebec Agreement.
2. The Trust shall use its best endeavours to gain control of and develop the production of the uranium and thorium supplies situate in certain areas other than the areas under the jurisdiction of the Two Governments and of the Governments of the Dominions and of India and of Burma and

for that purpose shall take such steps as it may in the common interest think fit to:

a. Explore and survey sources of uranium and thorium supplies.
b. Develop the production of uranium and thorium by the acquisition of mines and ore deposits, mining concessions or otherwise.
c. Provide with equipment any mines or mining works for the production of uranium and thorium.
d. Survey and improve the methods of production of uranium and thorium.
e. Acquire and undertake the treatment and disposal of uranium and thorium and uranium and thorium materials.
f. Provide storage and other facilities.
g. Undertake any functions or operations which conduce to the effective carrying out of the purpose of the Trust in the common interest.

3. (1) The Trust shall carry out its functions under the direction and guidance of the Combined Policy Committee, and as its agent, and all uranium and thorium and all uranium and thorium ores and supplies and other property acquired by the Trust shall be held by it in trust for the Two Governments jointly, and disposed of or otherwise dealt with in accordance with the direction of the Combined Policy Committee.
(2) The Trust shall submit such reports of its activities as may be required from time to time by the Combined Policy Committee.

4. For the purpose of carrying out its functions, the Trust shall utilize whenever and wherever practicable the established agencies of any of the Two Governments, and may employ and pay such other agents and employees as it considers expedient, and may delegate to any agents or employees all or any of its functions.

5. The Trust may acquire and hold any property in the name of nominees.

6. All funds properly required by the Trust for the performance of its functions shall be provided as to one-half by the Government of the United States of America and the other half by the Government of the United Kingdom of Great Britain and Northern Ireland.

7. In the event of the Combined Policy Committee ceasing to exist, the functions of the Committee under the Trust shall be performed by such other body or person as may be designated by the President for the time being of the United States of America and the Prime Minister for the time being of the United Kingdom of Great Britain and Northern Ireland.

8. The signatories of this Agreement and Declaration of Trust will, as soon as practicable after the conclusion of hostilities, recommend to their respective Governments the extension and revision of this wartime emergency agreement to cover post war conditions and its formalization by treaty or other proper method. This Agreement and Declaration of Trust shall continue in full force and effect until such extension or revision.

(Signed) Franklin D. Roosevelt
ON BEHALF OF THE GOVERNMENT OF THE UNITED STATES OF AMERICA
(Signed) Winston S. Churchill
ON BEHALF OF THE GOVERNMENT OF THE UNITED KINGDOM OF GREAT BRITAIN AND NORTHERN IRELAND

Appendix 3 Aide-mémoire of Conversation between the President and the Prime Minister at Hyde Park, 19 September 1944

The suggestion that the world should be informed regarding tube alloys, with a view to an international agreement regarding its control and use, is not accepted. The matter should continue to be regarded as of the utmost secrecy; but when a 'bomb' is finally available, it might perhaps, after mature consideration, be used against the Japanese, who should be warned that this bombardment will be repeated until they surrender.

2. Full collaboration between the United States and the British Government in developing tube alloys for military and commercial purposes should continue after the defeat of Japan unless and until terminated by joint agreement.

3. Enquiries should be made regarding the activities of Professor Bohr and steps taken to ensure that he is responsible for no leakage of information particularly to the Russians.

Appendix 4 Washington Declaration, 15 November 1945

The President of the United States, the Prime Minister of the United Kingdom and the Prime Minister of Canada have issued the following statement:

'We recognise that the application of recent scientific discoveries to the methods and practice of war has placed at the disposal of mankind means of destruction hitherto unknown against which there can be no adequate military defence, and in the employment of which no single nation can in fact have a monopoly.

2. We desire to emphasise that the responsibility for devising means to ensure that the new discoveries shall be used for the benefit of mankind, instead of as a means of destruction, rests not on our nations alone, but upon the whole civilised world. Nevertheless, the progress that we have made in the development and use of atomic energy demands that we take the initiative in the matter, and we have accordingly met together to consider the possibility of international action:

(*a*) To prevent the use of atomic energy for destructive purposes.
(*b*) To promote the use of recent and future advances in scientific knowledge and particularly in the utilisation of atomic energy for peaceful and humanitarian ends.

3. We are aware that the only complete protection for the civilised world from the destructive use of scientific knowledge lies in the prevention of war. No system of safeguards that can be devised will of itself provide an effective guarantee against the production of atomic weapons by a nation bent on aggression, particularly since the military exploitation of atomic energy depends in large part upon the same methods and processes as would be required for industrial uses. Nor can we ignore the possibility of the development of other weapons or of new methods of warfare, which may constitute as great a threat to civilisation as the military use of atomic energy.

4. Representing, as we do, the three countries which possess the knowledge essential to the use of atomic energy, we declared at the outset our willingness, as a first contribution, to proceed with the exchange of fundamental scientific information and the interchange of scientists and scientific literature for peaceful ends with any nation that will fully reciprocate.

5. We believe that the fruits of scientific research should be made available to all nations, and that freedom of investigation and free

interchange of ideas are essential to the progress of knowledge. In pursuance of this policy, the basic scientific information essential to the development of atomic energy for peaceful purposes has already been made available to the world. It is our intention that all further information of this character that may become available from time to time shall be similarly treated. We trust that other nations will adopt the same policy, thereby creating an atmosphere of reciprocal confidence in which political agreement and co-operation will flourish.

6. We have considered the question of the disclosure of detailed information concerning the practical industrial application of atomic energy. The military exploitation of atomic energy depends, in large part, upon the same methods and processes as would be required for industrial uses. We are not convinced that the spreading of the specialised information regarding the practical application of atomic energy before it is possible to devise effective, reciprocal, and enforceable safeguards acceptable to all nations would contribute to a constructive solution of the problem of the atomic bomb. On the contrary we think it might have the opposite effect. We are, however, prepared to share, on a reciprocal basis with other of the United Nations, detailed information concerning the practical industrial application of atomic energy just as soon as effective enforceable safeguards against its use for destructive purposes can be devised.

7. In order to obtain the most effective means of entirely eliminating the use of atomic energy for destructive purposes and promoting its widest use for industrial and humanitarian purposes, we are of the opinion that at the earliest practicable date a Commission should be set up under the United Nations to prepare recommendations to the organisation. The Commission should be instructed to proceed with the utmost despatch and should be authorised to submit recommendations from time to time dealing with separate phases of its work.

In particular, the Commission should make specific proposals:

(*a*) For extending between all nations the exchange of basic scientific information for peaceful ends.
(*b*) For control of atomic energy to the extent necessary to ensure its use only for peaceful purposes.
(*c*) For the elimination from national armaments of atomic weapons and of all other major weapons adaptable to mass destruction.
(*d*) For effective safeguards by way of inspection and other means to protect complying states against the hazards of violations and evasions.

8. The work of the Commission should proceed by separate stages, the successful completion of each of which will develop the necessary confidence of the world before the next stage is undertaken. Specifically, it is considered that the Commission might well devote its attention first

to the wide exchange of scientists and scientific information, and as a second stage to the development of full knowledge concerning natural resources of raw materials.

9. Faced with the terrible realities of the application of science to destruction, every nation will realise more urgently than before the overwhelming need to maintain the rule of law among nations and to banish the scourge of war from the earth. This can only be brought about by giving wholehearted support to the United Nations Organisation, and by consolidating and extending its authority, thus creating conditions of mutual trust in which all peoples will be free to devote themselves to the arts of peace. It is our firm resolve to work without reservation to achieve these ends.'

Appendix 5 'Groves-Anderson' memorandum, 16 November 1945

(This memorandum was drawn up by Sir John Anderson and Major-General L. R. Groves during the November 1945 tripartite talks in Washington and referred to the Combined Policy Committee in December 1945)

We recommend that the following points be considered by the Combined Policy Committee in the preparation of a new document to replace the Quebec Agreement, which should be superseded *in toto*, together with all other understandings with the exception of the Combined Development Trust Agreement which should be revised in conformity with the new arrangements.

1. The three Governments, the United States, the United Kingdom, and Canada, will not use atomic weapons against other parties without prior consultation with each other;

2. The three Governments agree not to disclose any information or enter into negotiations concerning atomic energy with other governments or authorities or persons in other countries except in accordance with agreed common policy or after due prior consultation with one another;

3. The three Governments will take measures so far as practicable to secure control and possession, by purchase or otherwise, of all deposits of uranium or thorium situated in areas comprising the United States, its territories or possessions, the United Kingdom, and Canada. They will also use every endeavour with respect to the remaining territories of the British Commonwealth and other countries to acquire all available supplies of uranium and thorium. All supplies acquired under the provisions of this paragraph will be placed at the disposition of the Combined Development Trust;

4. The materials at the disposition of the Trust shall be allocated to the three Governments in such quantities as may be needed, in the common interest, for scientific research, military, and humanitarian purposes. Such supplies as are not allocated for these purposes shall be held by the Combined Development Trust and their disposal shall be determined at a later date in the light of then existing conditions and on a fair and equitable basis;

5. There shall be full and effective co-operation in the field of basic scientific research among the three countries. In the field of development, design, construction, and operation of plants such co-operation, recognised as desirable in principle, shall be regulated by such *ad hoc* arrangements as

may be approved from time to time by the Combined Policy Committee as mutually advantageous;

6. The Combined Policy Committee, already established and constituted so as to provide equal representation to the United States on the one hand and to the Governments of the United Kingdom and Canada on the other, shall carry out the policies provided for, subject to the control of their respective Governments. To this end the Committee shall:

1. Review from time to time the general programme of work being carried out in the three countries.
2. Allocate materials in accordance with the principles set forth in the fourth paragraph above.
3. Settle any questions which may arise concerning the interpretation and application of arrangements regulating co-operation between the three Governments.

The above is to be understood as being without prejudice to the consideration by the Combined Policy Committee of any matters not covered in this memorandum.

Appendix 6 The *Modus Vivendi*, January 1948

1. All agreements between the three governments or any two of them in the field of atomic energy shall be regarded as null and of no effect, with the following exceptions:

(*a*) The Patent Memorandum of 1 October 1943 as modified by subsequent agreement on 19 September 1944 and 8 March 1945.
(*b*) The Agreement and Declaration of Trust dated 13 June 1944.
(*c*) The exchange of letters between the Acting Secretary of State and the British Ambassador of 19 and 24 September 1945, concerning Brazil.
(*d*) The agreed public Declaration by the President of the United States, the Prime Minister of the United Kingdom, and the Prime Minister of Canada of 15 November 1945.

2. The Combined Policy Committee, already established, and subject to the control of the three governments, shall continue as an organ for dealing with atomic energy problems of common concern. The Committee shall consist of three representatives of the United States, two of the United Kingdom, and one of Canada, unless otherwise agreed.

3. The Committee shall *inter alia*:

(*a*) Allocate raw materials in accordance with such principles as may be determined from time to time by the Committee, taking into account all supplies available to any of the three governments.
(*b*) Consider general questions arising with respect to co-operation among the three governments.
(*c*) Supervise the operations and policies of the Combined Development Agency referred to in paragraph 4 below.

4. The Combined Development Trust, created on the thirteenth of June 1944 by the Agreement and Declaration of Trust signed by President Roosevelt and Mr Winston Churchill, shall continue in effect except that it shall henceforward be known as the Combined Development Agency. Of the six persons provided for in Clause 1(2) of the Declaration of Trust, three shall represent the United States, two the United Kingdom, and one Canada.

5. The United States, the United Kingdom and Canada will, within the limits of their respective constitutions and statutes, use every effort to acquire control of supplies of uranium and thorium situated within their respective territories. The United Kingdom will, in so far as need exists, communicate with the governments of the British Commonwealth for the

purpose of ensuring that such governments exercise control of supplies of uranium and thorium situated in their respective territories. The United Kingdom will consult with the Commonwealth Governments concerned with a view to encouraging the greatest possible production of uranium and thorium in the British Commonwealth, and with a view to ensuring that as large a quantity as possible of such supplies is made available to the United States, United Kingdom and Canada.

6. It is recognised that there are areas of information and experience in which co-operation would be mutually beneficial to the three countries. They will therefore co-operate in respect of such areas as may from time to time be agreed upon by the CPC and in so far as this is permitted by the laws of the respective countries.

7. In the interests of mutual security, classified information in the field of atomic energy will not be disclosed to other governments or authorities or persons in other countries without due prior consultation.

8. Policy with respect to international control of atomic energy remains that set forth in the Three-Nations Agreed Declaration of 15 November 1945. Whenever a plan for the international control of atomic energy with appropriate safeguards which would ensure use of atomic energy for peaceful purposes only shall be agreed upon, and shall become fully effective, the relationship of these countries in atomic energy matters will have to be reconsidered in the light thereof.

ANNEX I

Allocations

1. The agreed objective is the maintenance of the United States, United Kingdom and Canadian minimum programmes with reasonable pipeline and reserve stocks.

2. In 1948 the 1949 all supplies available from the Belgian Congo will be allocated to the United States, subject to para. 4 below.

3. In 1948 and 1949, if supplies additional to those which will flow from existing sources are required to maintain the United States minimum programme, they will be provided, subject to para. 4 below, from the unprocessed and presently unallocated supplies now in the United Kingdom, according to the following arrangements:

(*a*) The United States requirements is 2547 tons in 1948 and 2547 in 1949, including capital charge of 370 tons for one pile in each year, a pipeline stock of 2800 tons and a reserve stock of 2547 tons throughout 1948, diminishing to 2176 tons at the end of 1949.

(*b*) The United Kingdom requirement to the end of 1949 is as follows: capital charge for two piles 600 tons, pipeline stock of 770 tons, reserve stock of 660 tons.

(*c*) At the end of each quarter a balance will be struck and submitted to the CPC. If the reserve stock in the USA is below the agreed minimum, an amount equivalent to the deficit will be ear-marked from the unallocated and unprocessed stocks in the United Kingdom. At the end of the third quarter in 1948 and 1949, a review of the situation will be made by the CPC in the light of the current position and the prospective shipments in the fourth quarter of each year. In striking this balance supplies will be taken into account which are in transit from the port of shipment. Should stocks at any time before the end of the third quarter fall below seven months' supply, emergency shipments to safeguard continued operation will be made.

(*d*) According to the result of this review a shipment will be made or ear-marked supplies will be released as the case may be. A similar arrangement will apply in due course in respect of the United Kingdom programme.

(*e*) From its allocation during 1948 and 1949, the United States will furnish metal to Canada as required for the Canadian programme in amounts not to exceed the equivalent of 20 tons of U_3O_8 per year.

(*f*) It is understood that when depleted sludges are available for re-use the quantities thrown up should be taken into account.

4. An immediate review of these arrangements may be requested by any of the three governments:

(*a*) If the total unallocated supplies seem likely to be insufficient to support the agreed programme or alternatively to be materially in excess of the estimates* contained in Tab. CCC annexed to the minutes of the CPC meeting of 15 December 1947; or

(*b*) in the event of a state of emergency; or

(*c*) in the event of a change of circumstances bringing about a substantial alteration in the relationships established at this time by the CPC.

*Estimates of Uranium Ore Production 1948–52
(Dated 12 December 1947)

	1948	*1949*	*1950*	*1951*	*1952*	*Total*
Congo	2,200	1,200	1,200	1,200	1,200	7,000
United States	100	200	200	200	200	900
Canada	150	150	150	150	150	750
South Africa	–	–	125	320	825	1,270
Portugal	–	–	–	50	50	100
Total	2,450	1,550	1,675	1,920	2,425	10,020

(All in short tons U_3O_8)

ANNEX 2

Areas of Co-operation between Members of the British Commonwealth
(Approved by the Combined Policy Committee at its meeting on 7 January 1948)

Apart from the arrangements which already exist between the United Kingdom and Canada, the question has arisen of co-operation between the United Kingdom and other members of the British Commonwealth.

As a part of the combined effort during the war years, assistance to the British atomic energy project was given by scientists from New Zealand, Australia and South Africa. Some of these have worked in Canada and some in United States and from there have moved to Harwell. Several of them will shortly be returning to New Zealand and at a later stage – one year or more – there will be a similar return to Australia. It is intended to admit further scientists from these Dominions to work at Harwell.

The three CPC governments are also actively co-operating with the Dominions in the field of raw materials. South Africa in particular is likely to become an important source of raw materials and is carrying out active work on benefication of ores. In due course South African interests may be expected to extend.

With a view particularly to making secure the information held by Dominion scientists on their return to their respective countries, and of furthering full co-operation in the field of raw material investigation and supply, it is recommended that the areas of co-operation outlined below should be recognised:

(*a*) The subjects covered in Sections I and II of the proposed Declassification Guide and which are listed as 'Topics for immediate declassification'.
(*b*) *The field of health and safety,* including
  1. Experimental work from which radiation tolerances may be established.
  2. Genetics.
  3. General medical and biological studies.
  4. Instruments, laboratory design and techniques of this field.
(*c*) *Research uses of radioactive isotopes and stable isotopes, including* preparation, techniques for handling, instruments, mutual availability for research purposes.
(*d*) *Detection of a distant nuclear explosion*
  Operation of recording stations.
(*e*) Survey methods for source materials.
(*f*) Benefication of ores – co-operation with South Africa and with other Dominions of (*sic*) the work developed there.

(*g*) Extraction of low-grade ores – within the fields defined by the ores locally available.

(*h*) *Design information on research reactors*

Design information on the low-power graphite reactor build at Harwell (Gleep) to be communicated by United Kingdom to New Zealand. It is recognised that this information will be effectively available to the New Zealand Government on the return of its staff in early 1948.

(*i*) *General research experience* with the following reactors

Harwell, Gleep, to be communicated by United Kingdom to New Zealand.

Co-operation within the above classified fields will be subject to an understanding between Governments to adopt common standards in holding information secure. Transmission would also be subject to the principle of current usability.

ANNEX 3

Technical Co-operation

(Memorandum to Combined Policy Committee, approved at the meeting on 7 January 1948 as the basis of co-operation)

The sub-group has considered a wide range of subjects of common interest within the field of atomic energy and from among these has selected certain topics which were agreed upon for presentation to the Combined Policy Committee as suitable subjects in which co-operation and the exchange of information, at the present time, would be mutually advantageous.

1. Those subjects covered in Sections I and II of the 'Proposed Declassification Guide' which are listed as 'Topics for immediate declassification'.

2. *The entire field of health and safety*, including

(*a*) experimental work from which radiation tolerances may be established;

(*b*) genetics;

(*c*) general medical and biological studies; therapy of over-exposure to radiation;

(*d*) health hazards associated with reactors, such as effluent gases and their ecological effects, disposal of wastes, toxic effects of reactor materials including Be and Pu; tolerances for the various toxic substances and the various radiations;

(*e*) instruments, laboratory design and techniques of this field.

3. *Research uses of radio-isotopes and stable isotopes* including

preparation, techniques for handling instruments; mutual availability for general research purposes.

4. *Fundamental nuclear and extra-nuclear properties of all the elements* including experimental methods and instruments (e.g. particle accelerators, detection devices).

5. *Detection of a distant nuclear explosion,* including meterorological and geophysical data; instruments (e.g. seismographs, microbarographs); air sampling techniques and analysis; new methods of possible detection.

6. *Fundamental properties of reactor materials* (*i.e. solid state physics, basic metallurgy*) including moderators, fuel elements, structural materials, also liquid metal and other coolants; the reactions of materials to radiations; the preparation of moderator materials, e.g. graphite, heavy water.

7. *Extraction chemistry* including basic chemistry of processes, problems of 'scale up' of laboratory methods, techniques of remote control, concentration and storage of fission products.

8. *The design of natural uranium reactors* in which the power generated is not wasted. The economy of operation of such reactors, e.g. preferred schemes for enrichment of depleted fuel for re-use.

9. *General research experience with the following* (*low power*) *reactors*: Clinton (graphite), Argonne (graphite, heavy water), Chalk River (heavy water), Harwell (graphite).

In furthering these objectives it is considered desirable to encourage the exchange of technical experience and information in these fields. Administrative arrangements should be followed which apply the general principle that classified information shall be currently usable by the recipient.

United Kingdom:	J. D. COCKCROFT	F. N. WOODWARD
Canada:	C. J. MACKENZIE	GEORGE IGNATIEFF
United States:	V. BUSH	J. B. FISK

Appendix 7 The Burns-Templer Agreements, August 1948—January 1950

Documents Relating to the Exchange of Classified Military Information Between the United States and the United Kingdom[1]

SECRET [WASHINGTON, January 27, 1950.]

DOCUMENT A

POLICY STATEMENT REGARDING U.S.–U.K. EXCHANGE OF CLASSIFIED MILITARY INFORMATION

The U.S. and the U.K. are agreed that it is in the interests of both countries that there should be a full and frank interchange to the greatest practicable degree of all classified military information and intelligence, except in a limited number of already declared fields, it being understood that either Government may subsequently declare any newly-developed fields or projects as excepted upon due notification to the other Government.

In this connection it is agreed that the flow of information over the whole field of guided missiles shall be resumed at once.

DOCUMENT B

SECURITY AGREEMENT BETWEEN THE UNITED STATES AND THE UNITED KINGDOM CHIEFS OF STAFF

1. The United States Chiefs of Staff will make every effort to insure that the United States will maintain the military security classifications established by United Kingdom authorities with respect to military information of U.K. origin, and the military security classifications established by U.K.–U.S. agreement with respect to military information of joint U.K.–U.S. origin or development; will safeguard accordingly such military information; will not exploit such information for production for other than military purposes; and, will not disclose such military information to a third nation without U.K. consent. The British Chiefs of Staff will make every effort to insure that the United Kingdom will maintain the military security classifications established by the U.S. authorities with respect to military information of U.S. origin, and the military security classifications established by U.K.–U.S. agreement with respect to military information of joint U.K.–U.S. origin or development; will safeguard accordingly such military information; will not exploit such information

for production for other than military purposes; and will not disclose such military information to a third nation without U.S. consent. This agreement applies to military information disclosed by the United States to the United Kingdom or by the United Kingdom to the United States or exchanged between the United States and the United Kingdom on and after the date of acceptance of this agreement by the United Kingdom. The provisions contained in C.C.S. 953, 953/1, and 953/2 will apply to information disclosed by either country to the other or exchanged between the United States and the United Kingdom between 1 September 1939 and the date of acceptance of this agreement by the United Kingdom.

2. The United States Chiefs of Staff and the British Chiefs of Staff agree that, insofar as the U.S. and the U.K. are concerned, the safeguards indicated above also apply to information developed by the U.S. and U.K. jointly in collaboration with a third nation.

3. It is agreed that the provisions of C.C.S. 210/4 shall remain in full force and effect until cancelled or superseded by another agreement which shall then be controlling in this respect.

4. It is agreed in respect of classified information communicated by one country to the other, that the recipient country shall use its best endeavours within the framework of its laws and rules to prevent any loss of patent rights in the information. Specifically it is declared and agreed that:

a. Any rights of the originator to obtain patent protection in the recipient country in respect of the information communicated are not and will not be prejudiced by virtue of the introduction of the information into such country.

b. The information, so long as it remains classified, will not be used or disclosed by the recipient country in any manner likely to prejudice the rights of the originator to obtain patent protection in respect thereof, but if the recipient country desires to use or to disclose the information in any manner likely so to prejudice the rights of the originator, then the recipient country will immediately notify the country of origin of the full circumstances of such intended use or disclosure, and such use or disclosure shall not be effected until approval is given by the country of origin.

c. Each country when so requested by the other and to the extent consistent with its laws and rules will use its best endeavours.

(1) to have maintained in secrecy any patent application filed in the recipient country in respect of the information for so long as may be desired by the country of origin, and

(2) to supply reports of the manner in which the information embodied in a patent application has been used or disclosed.

5. For the purpose of this agreement the United Kingdom, the British

Dominions, and India are considered to be separate nations.

Approved August 1948.

DOCUMENT C

POLICY WITH RESPECT TO COMMONWEALTH NATIONS

1. The general principle of the security agreement will be maintained: that the Government of the United Kingdom seek the consent of the U.S. prior to the release to third nations of information of U.S. or of U.S.–U.K. origin; and that the United States Government seek the consent of the U.K. prior to the release to third nations of information of U.K. or of U.K.–U.S. origin.

2. *a*. The U.S. reserves its right to disclose information of sole U.S. origin directly to any foreign nation.

b. The U.K. reserves its right to disclose information of sole U.K. origin directly to any foreign nation.

3. However, to meet the special needs of the U.K. with respect to the other nations comprising the British Commonwealth, and to enable these nations to obtain as much information as possible in the interests of common defense, the general principle set forth in Paragraph 1 above is hereby modified in the following respects:

A. (1) The United Kingdom and Canada may exchange freely without prior United States consent classified military information of United States origin, of combined United States-Canadian origin, or of combined United States–United kingdom origin, except for information relating to Western Hemisphere defense provided that:

(*a*) Only in exceptional circumstances will the United Kingdom and Canada exchange documents originating wholly in the United States.

(2) The United States and Canada may exchange freely without prior United Kingdom consent classified military information of United Kingdom origin, of combined United Kingdom-Canadian origin, or of combined United States–United Kingdom origin provided that:

(*a*) Only in exceptional circumstances will the United States and and Canada exchange documents originating wholly in the United Kingdom.

(3) The United States and the United Kingdom may exchange freely without prior Canadian consent classified military information of Canadian origin, or combined United Kingdom-Canadian origin or of combined United States-Canadian origin except for information relating to Western Hemisphere defense provided that:

(*a*) Only in exceptional circumstances will the United States and the United Kingdom exchange documents originating wholly in Canada.[2]

B. (1) The U.K. may, at its discretion, exchange with Australia, New Zealand, South Africa, India, Pakistan, or Ceylon, without prior U.S. consent classified military information of U.S. origin or of combined U.S.–U.K. origin, provided that:

(*a*) With respect to information in the fields of strategic planning and research and development:

Such information falls within the content and scope of specific projects agreed to by the U.K. and the U.S. as being releasable projects in respects of a specified Commonwealth nation or nations.

(*b*) With respect to information in the fields of intelligence, tactical and technical doctrine and training, and materiel (military equipment which has passed the research and development stage):

Such information falls within the content and scope of specific projects agreed by the U.K. and the U.S. as being projects which the U.K. may release to any Commonwealth nation which the U.K. deems to be a suitable recipient when evaluated in accordance with the criteria set forth in Paragraph 5, below.

(*c*) When U.S. or combined U.S.–U.K. information relating to an approved project is released to a Commonwealth nation or nations, the nation or nations will be informed by the U.K. that the U.S. has agreed to the disclosure.

(*d*) The U.K. furnish to the U.S. periodic reports identifying specific documentary materials released to any of the named Commonwealth nations, when such documents are of U.S. or combined U.S.–U.K. origin.

(*e*) The U.K. and/or the other Commonwealth nation or nations concerned furnish to the U.S., when requested by the U.S., reports on the progress and results of the specific projects approved in accordance with subparagraph B(1) (*a*) and (*b*) above.

(2) While the U.S. recognizes the special relationship between the U.K. and the other Commonwealth nations and the desirability in practice for the U.K. to initiate and effect the disclosures provided for in this agreement, it is agreed as a matter of principle that the U.S. may, at its discretion, exchange with Australia, New Zealand, South Africa, India, Pakistan, or Ceylon, without prior U.K. consent classified military information of U.K. origin or of combined U.K.–U.S. origin, provided that:

(*a*) With respect to information in the fields of strategic planning and research and development:

Such information falls within the content and scope of specific projects agreed to by the U.S. and the U.K. as being releasable projects in respect of a specified Commonwealth nation or nations.

(*b*) With respect to information in the fields of intelligence, tactical and technical doctrine and training, and materiel (military equipment which has passed the research and development stage):

Such information falls within the content and scope of specific projects agreed by the U.S. and the U.K. as being projects which the U.S. may release to any Commonwealth nation which the U.S. deems to be a suitable recipient when evaluated in accordance with the criteria set forth in Paragraph 5, below.

(*c*) When U.K or combined U.K.–U.S. information relating to an approved project is released to a Commonwealth nation or nations, the nation or nations will be informed by the U.S. that the U.K. has agreed to the disclosure.

(*d*) The U.S. furnish to the U.K. periodic reports identifying specific documentary materials released to any of the named Commonwealth nations, when such documents are of U.K. or combined U.K.–U.S. origin.

(*e*) The U.S. and/or the Commonwealth nation or nations concerned furnish to the U.K., when requested by the U.K., reports on the progress and results of the specific projects approved in accordance with subparagraph B(1) (*a*) and (*b*) above.

4. At the time that a project is agreed as 'releasable' or at any time thereafter, either the U.K. or the U.S. may specify that a certain item or items within that project are not to be released to one or more of the Commonwealth nations.

5. The criteria to be taken into consideration in the establishment of 'releasable' projects under the terms of subparagraphs 3B(1) (*a*) and (*b*) and 3B(2) (*a*) and (*b*) above shall include:

A. The principle of "need to know" established for each Commonwealth nation in the light of its strategic role and of its ability or potential ability to contribute to the common defense in the fields of manpower, production, or research and development.

B. Recognition of the importance of maintaining among the Commonwealth nations the will to resist aggression and to make the maximum contribution to the common defense.

C. The principle that the U.K. should be in a position to make available to the other Commonwealth nations the most up-to-date equipment issued to the armed forces of the U.K.

D. The standard of security in the Commonwealth nation or nations concerned.

6. Agreement has been reached in respect of a specific subject as set forth in Annex 2 to Document C.

7. It is recognized that a differentiation exists between Government- and privately-owned information of U.S. or U.K. origin. Information already released by either the U.S. or the U.K. will be cleared between the two Governments on an individual item basis before release to third nations. In the future, the nation of origin will determine whether the information is privately- or Government-owned and will state whether the Commonwealth nation concerned may receive such privately-owned information.

Annex 1

Interpretation of Certain Terms Used in This Document

1. The definition of '*combined military information*' and the procedures for the resolution of differences concerning releases of combined military information to third nations are set forth in the Agreed Charter establishing the U.S.–U.K. Military Information Board.

2. *a*. '*United States Information*' does not become combined U.S.–U.K. information merely by virtue of its release by the U.S. to the U.K.

b. '*United Kingdom information*' does not become combined U.S.–U.K. information merely by virtue of its release by the U.K. to the U.S.

3. In order that the establishment of projects will not be hampered by the rigid adherence to a strictly defined term, the word '*project*' is not defined herein but shall, in general include an agreed upon area of effort, such as an undertaking to develop an item (a tank, an airplane, a weapons system, a radar system, or a principal component thereof), a tactical or doctrinal procedure, a training program, or an intelligence study.

Annex 2

Agreement has been reached in respect of the following specific subject within the framework of the above policy:

Training Publications and Instructions

United States military information, classified no higher than 'Secret', and exclusive of Intelligence and Research and Development information may, at the discretion of the U.K., be included in U.K. training publications and instructions for issue to the other Commonwealth nations. This should not be construed as implying that publications and instructions of U.S. origin of the classification of 'Secret', 'Confidential', and 'Restricted' or other information so classified, may be sent by the U.K. to the other Commonwealth nations, in their original form, without prior U.S. approval.

Document D

Charter of the U.S.–U.K. Military Information Board

It has been agreed by the appropriate United States and United Kingdom authorities to establish the U.S.–U.K. Military Information Board (MIB), hereinafter referred to as the 'Board'.

Purpose

1. The Board is established for the purpose of providing a combined body wherein proposed disclosures to third nations by either the appropriate United States or United Kingdom authorities of "combined military information", defined in (2) below, may be considered. It is intended that the Board will facilitate the implementation of the Security Agreement approved by the Combined Chiefs of Staff in August 1948, insofar as 'military information of joint [combined] U.S.–U.K. origin or development' is concerned.

Functions and Powers

2. The Board shall decide whether disclosures to third nations of combined military information proposed either by the U.S. or the U.K. shall be permitted. Combined military information is defined as follows:

(*a*) Classified military information resulting or originating from projects developed on a combined basis; or

(*b*) Other classified military information determined by the Board from time to time to be combined military information.

The criteria upon which the Board will base its determination under paragraph 2(*b*) are:

(1) The appropriate U.S.–U.K. authorities have agreed to undertake separately, different phases of a specific project; *or*

(2) The appropriate U.S.–U.K. authorities have agreed that one will assume sole project responsibility on behalf of both; *or*

(3) The appropriate U.S.–U.K. authorities have agreed at the outset of the project to adopt the best results of independent endeavours.

Membership

3. The Board shall consist of (*a*) an official of the U.S. Department of State, (*b*) an official of the British Embassy in Washington, (*c*) an officer or official from each of the U.S. military departments (Army, Navy, Air Force), (*d*) an official of the U.S. Research and Development Board, (*e*) an officer or official from each of the offices of the British Joint Services (Navy Staff, Army Staff, Air Force Staff, and Technical Services).

There may be present at meetings of the Board such U.S. or U.K. consultants or observers as desired.

Chairmanship

4. The chairmanship of the Board shall rotate monthly between the U.S. and U.K. Representatives. The U.K. shall hold the chairmanship during the first calendar month the Board meets.

Place of Meetings

5. Unless otherwise provided for, meetings of the Board shall be held in Washington.

6. A Combined Secretariat shall be established by the Board.

Decisions of the Board

7. All decisions of the Board shall be taken by unanimous agreement.

Procedures

8. (*a*) *Rules of Procedure*

Except as provided in paragraph 7, the Board shall adopt its own rules of procedure for conduct of its business, including the establishment of committees.

(*b*) *Processing of Requests*

(1) Requests normally will be processed through direct presentation to the Board by members, except that,

(2) In the processing of requests applicable to groups or combinations of nations, or states members thereof, the Board will prescribe such special procedures as it considers desirable.

Annex 1

Statement to be incorporated in first procedural paper to be prepared by the U.S.–U.K. Military Information Board.

Procedure for Processing of Requests to Disclose Combined Military Information to Member Nations of the Western Union for Western Union Purposes

1. Proposals by the United Kingdom to disclose combined military information to member nations of the Western Union for Western Union purposes shall be submitted by the United Kingdom to the United States through the U.S. delegation to the Western Union (with copy of the request forwarded by the United Kingdom to the Secretariat of the Board).

2. Proposals by the United States to disclose combined military information to member nations of the Western Union for Western Union purposes shall be submitted by the United States to the United Kingdom through the U.S. delegation to the Western Union (with copy of the request forwarded by the United States to the Secretariat of the Board).

3. Differences between the U.S. and U.K. as to a proposed disclosure under (1) or (2) above may be referred to the Board for consideration.

Annex 2

Statement to be incorporated in first procedural paper to be prepared by the U.S.–U.K. Military Information Board.

AGREED CATEGORIES OF COMBINED INFORMATION

A. Only one highly secret subject, which is already covered by special U.S.–U.K. arrangements, release of which to a third nation would be subject at the time of the request to the specific authority of the U.S. and the U.K. in each case.

B. Combined U.S.–U.K. information classified Restricted through Top Secret, the release of which to a third nation would be subject, at the time of the request, to the specific authority of both the U.S. and the U.K. in each case.

C. Combined U.S.–U.K. information relating to a specific project classified Confidential or Restricted, the release of which to a third nation may be accomplished unilaterally either by the U.K. or the U.S. subject to the following procedures:

a. At the initiation of the project or at any time thereafter the U.S. and U.K. agreed to assign this project to Category C.

b. The U.S. and U.K. mutually agree on that group of nations to which the release of the information on the particular project would be permissible.

Annex 3

The United States and British Teams agreed:

To incorporate in the first procedural paper to be prepared by the U.S.–U.K. Military Information Board a statement of understanding to the effect that the functions of the Combined Communications Board or its successor agency will be unaffected by the establishment of the U.S.–U.K. Military Information Board.

Annex 4

SUPPLEMENTARY NOTE

In the course of discussions between representatives of the United States and the United Kingdom on the subject of the exchange and/or disclosure of classified military information on January 23, 1950, the representatives of the United Kingdom requested that the following statements be placed in the record:

The representatives of the Government of the United Kingdom wish to place on record that they consider it most essential that the C.M.I.B. procedures should be expeditious in operation and should take account of factors wider than security alone. This should be made clear in the directives addressed by each Government to their representatives on the Board.

Document E

Statement Regarding Employment of Foreign Nationals

It is recognized that the employment by either the U.S. or the U.K. on work involving access to classified military information of individual nationals of third countries is a matter entirely within the discretion of the employing nation, which will be responsible for applying adequate security safeguards.

Document F

Policy Regarding the Disclosure of Certain Classified Military Information to the North Atlantic Treaty Nations

It is agreed that both the U.S. and the U.K. have the discretion to release classified U.S.–U.K. combined military information in the fields of established and published technical and tactical training and doctrine and materiel to the nations of the North Atlantic Treaty Organization to permit adequate use of equipment and materiel furnished them by either the U.S. or the U.K.

Document G

Policy Respecting the Disclosure of Guided Missiles Information to Australia

Within the framework of the 'Policy with Respect to Commonwealth Nations', the following principle has been agreed to:

The United Kingdom Government may exchange with the appropriate authorities of the Australian Government without prior U.S. consent, information of U.S. origin or of combined U.S.–U.K. origin on installation, instrumentation and operating techniques of long range proving grounds, and such classified research and development information regarding the guided missiles themselves as is necessary for the development of the general U.K.–Australian guided missiles program, subject to the conclusion of satisfactory arrangements between the U.S. and Australian Governments with respect to the safeguarding of such information. Procedures for effecting the release of such information by the U.K. authorities to the Australian authorities concerned will be reviewed in detail by the representatives of the U.K. and U.S. Governments.

NOTES

[1] The source text was attached to a memorandum by Norwood W. Watts, Secretary of the State-Defense Military Information Control Committee, which stated that the documents were for the guidance and information of the Departments of State and Defense. Document B had been approved in August 1948 and Document D, in October 1949, Documents A, C, E, F, and G were approved by the representatives of the United States and United Kingdom at meetings in Washington between January 20 and January 27, 1950. No United States record of these meetings has been found in the Department of State files, but a British record of the meeting on January 20 is in file 611.41/1–2050. The seven documents were circulated within the Departments of State and Defense as MIC 206/70 and became known as the Burns–Templer Agreements, named after the heads of the respective delegations, Maj. Gen. James H. Burns, Assistant to the Secretary of Defense and Lt. Gen. Sir Gerald Templer, Vice Chief of the Imperial General Staff.
Source: *Foreign Relations of the United States, (FRUS)*, Western Europe, 1950, Vol. III (Department of State Publication).

[2] In the source text the pages for paragraph 3A bear the typewritten notation '(Revised October 9, 1951).' Another copy of MIC 206/70 provides the following text for paragraph 3A, presumably as written at the time of approval by the representatives of the United States and United Kingdom:

'3. However, to meet the special needs of the U.K. with respect to the other nations comprising the British Commonwealth, and to enable these nations to obtain as much information as possible in the interests of common defense, the general principle set forth in Paragraph 1 above is hereby modified in the following respects:

'*A*. (1) The U.K. may exchange freely with Canada without prior U.S. consent classified military information of U.S. origin, of combined U.S.-Canadian origin, or of combined U.S.–U.K. origin, except for information relating to Western Hemisphere defense, and provided that:

'(*a*) The Canadian Government concurs in this position.

'(*b*) The U.K. and/or Canada furnish to the U.S. periodic reports identifying the specific documentary materials released by the one to the other, when such documents are of U.S., combined U.S.–U.K., or combined U.S.-Canadian origin,

'(2) The U.S. may exchange freely with Canada without prior U.K. consent classified military information of U.K. origin, of combined U.K.-Canadian origin, or of combined U.K.–U.S. origin, provided:

'(*a*) The Canadian Government concurs in this position.

'(*b*) The U.S. and/or Canada furnish to the U.K. periodic reports identifying the specific documentary materials released by the one to the other, when such documents are of U.K.-Canadian origin.'

Appendix 8 Agreement[1] between the Government of the United Kingdom of Great Britain and Northern Ireland and the Government of the United States of America for co-operation regarding atomic information for mutual defence purposes. Signed at Washington on 15 June 1955

The Government of the United Kingdom of Great Britain and Northern Ireland and the Government of the United States of America,

Recognising that their mutual security and defence requires that they be prepared to meet the contingencies of atomic warfare,

Recognising that their common interests will be advanced by the exchange of information pertinent thereto,

Believing that the exchange of such information can be undertaken without threat to the security of either country, and

Taking into consideration the United States Atomic Energy Act of 1954, which was prepared with these purposes in mind.

Agree as follows:–

Article I

1. While the United Kingdom and the United States are participating in international arrangements for their mutual defence and security and making substantial and material contribution thereto, each Government will from time to time make available to the other Government atomic information which the Government making such information available deems necessary to–

(*a*) the development of defence plans;
(*b*) the training of personnel in the employment of and defence against atomic weapons; and
(*c*) the evaluation of the capabilities of potential enemies in the employment of atomic weapons.

2. Atomic information which is transferred by either Government pursuant to this agreement shall be used by the other Government exclusively for the preparation and implementation of defence plans in the mutual interests of the two countries.

Article II

1. All transfers of atomic information to the United Kingdom by the

United States pursuant to this agreement will be made in compliance with the provisions of the United States Atomic Energy Act of 1954 and any subsequent applicable United States legislation. All transfers of atomic information to the United States by the United Kingdom pursuant to this agreement will be made in compliance with the United Kingdom Official Secrets Acts, 1911–1939, and the United Kingdom Atomic Energy Act of 1946.

2. Under this Agreement there will be no transfers by the United Kingdom or the United States of atomic weapons or special nuclear material, as these terms are defined in Section 11 d. and Section 11 t. of the United States Atomic Energy Act of 1954.

Article III

1. Atomic information made available pursuant to this Agreement shall be accorded full security protection under applicable security arrangements between the United Kingdom and the United States and applicable national legislation and regulations of the two countries. In no case shall either Government maintain security standards for safeguarding atomic information made available pursuant to this Agreement lower than those set forth in the applicable security arrangements in effect on the date this Agreement comes into force.

2. Atomic information which is exchanged pursuant to this Agreement will be made available through channels existing or hereafter agreed for the exchange of classified defence information between the two Governments.

3. Atomic information received pursuant to this Agreement shall not be transferred by the recipient Government to any unauthorised person or, except as provided in Article V of this Agreement, beyond the jurisdiction of that Government. Each Government may stipulate the degree to which any of the categories of information made available to the other Government pursuant to this Agreement may be disseminated, may specify the categories of persons who may have access to such information, and may impose such other restrictions on the dissemination of such information as it deems necessary.

Article IV

As used in this Agreement, 'atomic information' means:

(*a*) so far as concerns the information provided by the United States, Restricted Data, as defined in Section II r. of the United States Atomic Energy Act of 1954, which is permitted to be communicated pursuant to the provisions of Section 144 b. of that Act, and information relating primarily to the military utilisation of atomic weapons which has been removed from the Restricted Data category in accordance with the provisions of Section 142 d. of the United States Energy Act of 1954;

(*b*) so far as concerns the information provided by the United Kingdom, information exchanged under this Agreement which is either classified atomic energy information or other United Kingdom defence information which it is decided to transfer to the United States in pursuance of Article I of this Agreement.

Article V

Nothing herein shall be interpreted or operate as a bar or restriction to consultation and co-operation by the United Kingdom or the United States with other nations or regional organisations in any fields of defence. Neither Government, however, shall communicate atomic information made available by the other Government pursuant to this Agreement to any nation or regional organisation unless the same information has been made available to that nation or regional organisation by the other Government in accordance with its own legislative requirements and except to the extent that such communication is expressly authorised by such other Government.

Article VI

This Agreement shall enter into force on the date on which each Government shall receive from the other Government written notification that it has complied with all statutory and constitutional requirements for the entry into force of such an agreement, and shall remain in effect until terminated by mutual agreement of both Governments.

DONE at Washington this fifteenth day of June, 1955, in two original texts.

For the United Kingdom of Great Britain and Northern Ireland:
R. H. SCOTT

For the United States of America:
C. Burke ELBRICK

NOTES

[1] Came into force on 21 July 1955, in accordance with the provisions of article VI.
Source: *United Nations Treaty Series,* 1955, Vol. 214, No. 2905, pp 302, 304.

Appendix 9 Exchange of notes constituting an agreement[1] between the United States of America and the United Kingdom of Great Britain and Northern Ireland relating to intermediate range ballistic missiles. Signed at Washington, 22 February 1958

I

The Secretary of State to the British Ambassador

DEPARTMENT OF STATE

WASHINGTON

Feb. 22, 1958

Excellency:

I have the honor to refer to discussions which have taken place between representatives of the Government of the United Kingdom of Great Britain and Northern Ireland and of the Government of the United States of America on the subject of the supply by the United States Government to the United Kingdom Government of intermediate range ballistic missiles.

I also have the honor to record that, pursuant to the agreement in principle reached between the Prime Minister of the United Kingdom and the President of the United States at Bermuda on March 22, 1957, and in support of the purposes of the North Atlantic Treaty and of the obligations of the parties thereto, the representatives of the two Governments have agreed to the terms set out in the memorandum annexed hereto regarding the proposed supply of intermediate range ballistic missiles.

Accordingly, I have the honor to propose that this Note and Your Excellency's reply to that effect shall be regarded as constituting an Agreement between the two Governments in the terms set out in the annexed memorandum and that such Agreement shall have effect from the date of Your Excellency's reply.

Accept, Excellency, the renewed assurances of my highest consideration.

For the Secretary of State:
Christian A. HERTER

Enclosure:
Memorandum

His Excellency Sir Harold Caccia, K.C.M.G., K.C.V.O.
British Ambassador

MEMORANDUM

1. The Government of the United States shall supply to the Government of the United Kingdom an agreed number of intermediate range ballistic missiles and their related specialized equipment and make available training assistance in order to facilitate the deployment by the Government of the United Kingdom of the said missiles. The missiles shall be located only in the United Kingdom at such sites and under such conditions as may be agreed upon between the two Governments.

2. The United Kingdom Government shall provide the sites and supporting facilities required for the deployment of the missiles.

3. Ownership of the missiles and related equipment shall pass to the United Kingdom Government under established United States Mutual Assistance Program procedures as soon as the United Kingdom Government is in a position to man and operate the missiles.

4. The missiles will be manned and operated by United Kingdom personnel, who will be trained by the United States Government for the purposes of this project at the earliest feasible date.

5. For the purposes of this Agreement, training and test-firing of missiles will normally take place on United States instrumented ranges but by agreement with the United States Government the United Kingdom Government may arrange with the Government of the Commonwealth of Australia for missiles to be test-fired on the Woomera Range in Australia.

6. Material, equipment, and training provided by the United States Government to the United Kingdom Government pursuant to the arrangements recorded herein will be furnished pursuant to the United States Mutual Security Act of 1954, as amended, acts amendatory or supplementary thereto, appropriations acts thereunder or any other applicable United States legislative provisions.

7. The decision to launch these missiles will be a matter for joint decision by the two Governments. Any such joint decision will be made in the light of the circumstances at the time and having regard to the undertaking the two Governments have assumed in Article 5 of the North Atlantic Treaty.

8. References to intermediate range ballistic missiles in this Agreement do not include the nuclear warheads for such missiles. The United States Government shall provide nuclear warheads for the missiles transferred to the United Kingdom Government pursuant to this Agreement. All nuclear warheads so provided shall remain in full United States ownership, custody and control in accordance with United States law.

9. The arrangements recorded herein are made in consonance with the North Atlantic Treaty and in pursuance of the Mutual Defense Assistance Agreement between the United Kingdom Government and the United States Government, signed January 27, 1950, as supplemented, and related agreements, and are subject to the applicable provisions thereof.

10. This Agreement shall be subject to revision by agreement between the two Governments and shall remain in force for not less than five years from the date of the Agreement but may thereafter be terminated by either Government upon six months' notice.

Washington, February 22, 1958

II

The British Ambassador to the Under Secretary of State

BRITISH EMBASSY

WASHINGTON, D. C.

February 22, 1958

Sir,

I have the honour to acknowledge receipt of your Note of today's date with reference to discussions which have taken place between representatives of the Government of the United States of America and of the Government of the United Kingdom of Great Britain and Northern Ireland on the subject of the supply to the United Kingdom of intermediate range ballistic missiles . . .

I have the honour to inform you that the proposal made in your Note is acceptable to the Government of the United Kingdom and to confirm that your Note, together with this reply, shall constitute an Agreement between the two Governments in the terms set out in the memorandum annexed to your Note, a copy of which memorandum is enclosed, such Agreement to have effect from the date of this Note.

I avail myself of this opportunity to renew to you the assurance of my highest consideration.

Harold CACCIA

The Honourable Christian A. Herter
Under Secretary of State

NOTES

[1] Came into force on 22 February 1958 by the exchange of the said notes.
Source: *United Nations, Treaty Series,* 1958, Vol. 307, No. 4451, pp. 208–214.

Appendix 10 Agreement[1] between the Government of the United Kingdom of Great Britain and Northern Ireland and the Government of the United States of America for co-operation on the uses of atomic energy for mutual defense purposes. Signed at Washington, on 3 July 1958 (1958 atomic energy agreement)

The Government of the United Kingdom of Great Britain and Northern Ireland on its own behalf and on behalf of the United Kingdom Atomic Energy Authority and the Government of the United States of America,

Considering that their mutual security and defense require that they be prepared to meet the contingencies of atomic warfare;

Considering that both countries have made substantial progress in the development of atomic weapons;

Considering that they are participating together in international arrangements pursuant to which they are making substantial and material contributions to their mutual defense and security;

Recognizing that their common defense and security will be advanced by the exchange of information concerning atomic energy and by the transfer of equipment and materials for use therein;

Believing that such exchange and transfer can be undertaken without risk to the defense and security of either country; and

Taking into consideration the United States Atomic Energy Act of 1954, as amended, which was enacted with these purposes in mind,

Have agreed as follows:

Article I

General Provision

While the United States and the United Kingdom are participating in an international arrangement for their mutual defense and security and making substantial and material contributions thereto, each Party will communicate to and exchange with the other Party information, and transfer materials and equipment to the other Party, in accordance with the provisions of this Agreement provided that the communicating or transferring Party determines that such cooperation will promote and will not constitute an unreasonable risk to its defense and security.

Article II

Exchange of Information

A. Each Party will communicate to or exchange with the other Party such classified information as is jointly determined to be necessary to:

1. the development of defense plans;
2. the training of personnel in the employment of and defense against atomic weapons and other military applications of atomic energy;
3. the evaluation of the capabilities of potential enemies in the employment of atomic weapons and other military applications of atomic energy;
4. the development of delivery systems compatible with the atomic weapons which they carry; and
5. research, development and design of military reactors to the extent and by such means as may be agreed.

B. In addition to the cooperation provided for in paragraph A of this Article each Party will exchange with the other Party other classified information concerning atomic weapons when, after consultation with the other Party, the communicating Party determines that the communication of such information is necessary to improve the recipient's atomic weapon design, development and fabrication capability.

Article III

Transfer of Submarine Nuclear Propulsion Plant and Materials

A. The government of the United States will authorize, subject to terms and conditions acceptable to the Government of the United States, a person to transfer by sale to the Government of the United Kingdom or its agent one complete submarine nuclear propulsion plant with such space parts therefore as may be agreed by the Parties and to communicate to the Government of the United Kingdom or its agent (or to both) such classified information as relates to safety features and such classified information as is necessary for the design, manufacture and operation of such propulsion plant. A person or persons will also be authorized, for a period of ten years following the date of entry into force of this Agreement and subject to terms and conditions acceptable to the Government of the United States, to transfer replacement cores or fuel elements for such plant.

B. The Government of the United States will transfer by sale agreed amounts of U-235 contained in uranium enriched in the isotope U-235 as needed for use in the submarine nuclear propulsion plant transferred pursuant to paragraph A of this Article, during the ten years following the date of entry into force of this Agreement on such terms and conditions as may be agreed. If the Government of the United Kingdom so requests, the Government of the United States will during such period reprocess any material sold under the present paragraph in facilities of the Government of the United States, on terms and conditions to be agreed, or authorize such reprocessing in private facilities in the United States. Enriched uranium recovered in reprocessing such materials by either Party may be purchased by the Government of the United States under terms and conditions to be agreed. Special nuclear material recovered in reprocessing such materials and not purchased by the Government of the United States may be returned to or retained by the Government of the United Kingdom and any U-235 not purchased by the Government of the United States will be credited to the amounts of U-235 to be transferred by the Government of the United States under this Agreement.

C. The Government of the United States shall be compensated for enriched uranium sold by it pursuant to this Article at the United States Atomic Energy Commission's published charges applicable to the domestic distribution of such material in effect at the time of the sale. Any purchase of enriched uranium by the Government of the United States pursuant to this Article shall be at the applicable price of the United States Atomic Energy Commission for the purchase of enriched uranium in effect at the time of purchase of such enriched uranium.

D. The Parties will exchange classified information on methods of reprocessing fuel elements of the type utilized in the propulsion plant to be transferred under this Article, including classified information on the design, construction and operation of facilities for the reprocessing of such fuel elements.

E. The Government of the United Kingdom shall indemnify and hold harmless the Government of the United States against any and all liabilities whatsoever (including third-party liability) for any damage or injury occurring after the propulsion plant or parts thereof, including spare parts, replacement cores or fuel elements are taken outside the United States, for any cause arising out of or connected with the design, manufacture, assembly, transfer or utilization of the propulsion plant, spare parts, replacement cores or fuel elements transferred pursuant to paragraph A of this Article.

Article IV

Responsibility for use of Information, Material, Equipment and Devices

The application or use of any information (including design drawings and specifications), material or equipment communicated, exchanged or transferred under this Agreement shall be the responsibility of the Party receiving it, and the other Party does not provide any indemnity, and does not warrant the accuracy or completeness of such information and does not warrant the suitability or completeness of such information, material or equipment for any particular use or application.

Article V

Conditions

A. Cooperation under this Agreement will be carried out by each of the Parties in accordance with its applicable laws.

B. Under this Agreement there will be no transfer by either Party of atomic weapons.

C. Except as may be otherwise agreed for civil uses, the information communicated or exchanged, or the materials or equipment transferred, by either Party pursuant to this Agreement shall be used by the recipient Party exclusively for the preparation or implementation of defense plans in the mutual interests of the two countries.

D. Nothing in this Agreement shall preclude the communication or exchange of classified information which is transmissible under other arrangements between the Parties.

Article VI

Guaranties

A. Classified information, materials and equipment communicated or transferred pursuant to this Agreement shall be accorded full security protection under applicable security arrangements between the Parties and applicable national legislation and regulations of the Parties. In no case shall either Party maintain security standards for safeguarding classified information, materials or equipment made available pursuant to this Agreement less restrictive than those set forth in the applicable security arrangements in effect on the date this Agreement comes into force.

B. Classified information, communicated or exchanged pursuant to this Agreement will be made available through channels existing or hereafter agreed for the communication or exchange of such information between the Parties.

C. Classified information, communicated or exchanged, and any materials or equipment transferred, pursuant to this Agreement shall not be communicated, exchanged or transferred by the recipient Party or persons under its jurisdiction to any unauthorized persons, or, except as provided in Article VII of this Agreement, beyond the jurisdiction of that Party. Each Party may stipulate the degree to which any of the information, materials or equipment communicated, exchanged or transferred by it or persons under its jurisdiction pursuant to this Agreement may be disseminated or distributed; may specify the categories of persons who may have access to such information, materials or equipment; and may impose such other restrictions on the dissemination or distribution of such information, materials or equipment as it deems necessary.

Article VII

Dissemination

Nothing in this Agreement shall be interpreted or operate as a bar or restriction to consultation or cooperation in any field of defense by either Party with other nations or international organizations. Neither Party, however, shall communicate classified information or transfer or permit access to or use of materials, or equipment, made available by the other Party pursuant to this Agreement to any nation or international organization unless authorized to do so by such other Party, or unless such other Party has informed the recipient Party that the same information has been made available to that nation or international organization.

Article VIII

Classification Policies

Agreed classification policies shall be maintained with respect to all classified information, materials or equipment communicated, exchanged or transferred under this Agreement. The Parties intend to continue the present practice of consultation with each other on the classification of these matters.

Article IX

Patents

A. With respect to any invention or discovery employing classified information which has been communicated or exchanged pursuant to Article II or derived from the submarine propulsion plant, material or equipment transferred pursuant to Article III, and made or conceived by the recipient Party, or any agency or corporation owned or controlled thereby, or any of their agents or contractors, or any employee of any of the foregoing, after the date of such communication, exchange or transfer but during the period of this Agreement:

1. in the case of any such invention or discovery in which rights are owned by the recipient Party, or any agency or corporation owned or controlled thereby, and not included in subparagraph 2 of this paragraph, the recipient Party shall, to the extent owned by any of them:

(*a*) transfer and assign to the other Party all right, title and interest in and to the invention or discovery, or patent application or patent thereon, in the country of that other Party, subject to the retention of a royalty-free, non-exclusive, irrevocable license for the governmental purposes of the recipient Party and for the purposes of mutual defense; and

(*b*) grant to the other Party a royalty-free, non-exclusive, irrevocable license for the governmental purposes of that other Party and for purposes of mutual defense in the country of the recipient Party and third countries, including use in the production of material in such countries for sale to the recipient Party by a contractor of that other Party;

2. in the case of any such invention or discovery which is primarily useful in the production or utilization of special nuclear material or atomic energy and made or conceived prior to the time that the information it employs is made available for civil uses, the recipient Party shall:

(*a*) obtain, by appropriate means, sufficient right, title and interest in and to the invention or discovery, or patent application or patent thereon, as may be necessary to fulfill its obligations under the following two subparagraphs;

(*b*) transfer and assign to the other Party all right, title and interest in and to the invention or discovery, or patent application or patent thereon, in the country of that other Party, subject to the retention of a royalty-free, non-exclusive, irrevocable license, with the right to grant sublicenses, for all purposes; and

(*c*) grant to the other Party a royalty-free, non-exclusive, irrevocable license, with the right to grant sublicenses, for all purposes in the country of the recipient Party and in third countries.

B. 1. Each Party shall, to the extent owned by it, or any agency or corporation owned or controlled thereby, grant to the other Party a royalty-free, non-exclusive, irrevocable license to manufacture and use the subject matter covered by any patent and incorporated in the submarine propulsion plant and spare parts transferred pursuant to paragraph A of Article III for use by the licensed Party for the purposes set forth in paragraph C of Article V.

2. The transferring Party neither warrants nor represents that the submarine propulsion plant or any material or equipment transferred under Article III does not infringe any patent owned or controlled by other persons and assumes no liability or obligation with respect thereto, and the recipient Party agrees to indemnify and hold harmless the transferring Party from any and all liability arising out of any infringement of any such patent.

C. With respect to any invention or discovery, or patent application or patent thereon, or license or sublicense therein, covered by paragraph A of this Article, each Party:

1. may, to the extent of its right, title and interest therein, deal with the same in its own and third countries as it may desire, but shall in no event discriminate against citizens of the other Party in respect of granting any license or sublicense under the patents owned by it in its own or any other country;

2. hereby waives any and all claims against the other Party for compensation, royalty or award, and hereby releases the other Party with respect to any and all such claims.

D. 1. No patent application with respect to any classified invention or discovery employing classified information which has been communicated or exchanged pursuant to Article II, or derived from the submarine propulsion plant, material or equipment transferred pursuant to Article III, may be filed:

(*a*) by either Party or any person in the country of the other Party except in accordance with agreed conditions and procedures; or

(*b*) in any country not a party to this Agreement except as may be agreed and subject to Articles VI and VII.

2. Appropriate secrecy or prohibition orders shall be issued for the purpose of giving effect to this paragraph.

Article X

PREVIOUS AGREEMENTS FOR COOPERATION

Effective from the date on which the present Agreement enters into force, the cooperation between the Parties being carried out under or envisaged by the Agreement for Cooperation Regarding Atomic Information for Mutual Defense Purposes, which was signed at Washington on June 15, 1955, and by paragraph B of Article I *bis* of the Agreement for Cooperation on Civil Uses of Atomic Energy, which was signed at Washington on June 15, 1955, as amended by the Amendment signed at Washington on June 13, 1956, shall be carried out in accordance with the provisions of the present Agreement.

Article XI

DEFINITIONS

For the purposes of this Agreement:

A. 'Atomic weapon' means any device utilizing atomic energy, exclusive of the means for transporting or propelling the device (where such means is a separable and divisible part of the device), the principal purpose of which is for use as, or for development of, a weapon, a weapon prototype, or a weapon test device.

B. 'Classified information' means information, data, materials, services or any other matter with the security designation of 'Confidential' or higher applied under the legislation or regulations of either the United Kingdom or the United States, including that designated by the Government of the United States as 'Restricted Data' or 'Formerly Restricted Data' and that designated by the Government of the United Kingdom as 'ATOMIC.'

C. 'Equipment' means any instrument, apparatus or facility and includes any facility, except an atomic weapon, capable of making use of or producing special nuclear material, and component parts thereof, and includes submarine nuclear propulsion plant, reactor and military reactor.

D. 'Military reactor' means a reactor for the propulsion of naval vessels, aircraft or land vehicles and military package power reactors.

E. 'Person' means:

1. any individual, corporation, partnership, firm, association, trust, estate, public or private institution, group, government agency or government corporation other than the United Kingdom Atomic Energy Authority and the United States Atomic Energy Commission; and
2. Any legal successor, representative, agent or agency of the foregoing.

F. 'Reactor' means an apparatus, other than an atomic weapon, in which a self-supporting fission chain reaction is maintained and controlled by utilizing uranium, plutonium or thorium, or any combination of uranium, plutonium or thorium.

G. 'Submarine nuclear propulsion plant' means a propulsion plant and includes the reactor, and such control, primary, auxiliary, steam and electric systems as may be necessary for propulsion of submarines.

H. References in this Agreement to the Government of the United Kingdom include the United Kingdom Atomic Energy Authority.

Article XII

DURATION

This Agreement shall enter into force on the date on which each Government shall have received from the other Government written notification that it has complied with all statutory and constitutional requirements for the entry into force of this Agreement, and shall remain in force until terminated by agreement of both Parties, except that, if not so terminated, Article II may be terminated by agreement of both Parties, or by either Party on one year's notice to the other to take effect at the end of a term of ten years, or thereafter on one year's notice to take effect at the end of any succeeding term of five years.

IN WITNESS WHEREOF, the undersigned, duly authorized, have signed this Agreement.

DONE at Washington, this third day of July, 1958, in two original texts.

For the Government of the United Kingdom of Great Britain and Northern Ireland:
HOOD

For the Government of the United States of America:
John Foster DULLES

NOTES

[1] Came into force on 4 August 1958, the date on which each Government received from the other Government written notification that it had complied with all statutory and constitutional requirements for the entry into force of the Agreement, in accordance with article XII.

Source: *United Nations Treaty Series,* 1959, Vol. 326, No. 4707, pp. 4-20.

Appendix II Amendment to 1958 Atomic Energy Agreement. Signed at Washington on May 1959

Official text: English.

Registered by the United Kingdom of Great Britain and Northern Ireland on 4 March 1960.

The Government of the United Kingdom of Great Britain and Northern Ireland, on its own behalf and on behalf of the United Kingdom Atomic Energy Authority, and the Government of the United States of America;

Desiring to amend in certain respects the Agreement for Cooperation on the Uses of Atomic Energy for Mutual Defense Purposes (hereinafter referred to as the Agreement for Cooperation) signed at Washington on the third day of July, 1958;

Have agreed as follows:

Article I

The following new Article shall be inserted after Article III of the Agreement for Cooperation:

'Article III *bis*

'TRANSFER OF MATERIALS AND EQUIPMENT

'A.—The Government of the United States shall transfer to the Government of the United Kingdom the following in such quantities, at such times prior to December 31, 1969, and on such terms and conditions as may be agreed:

'1. non-nuclear parts of atomic weapons which parts are for the purpose of improving the United Kingdom's state of training and operational readiness;

'2. other non-nuclear parts of atomic weapons systems involving Restricted Data which parts are for the purpose of improving the United Kingdom's state of training and operational readiness when in accordance with appropriate requirements of applicable laws;
'3. special nuclear material for research on, development of, production of, or use in utilization facilities for military applications; and
'4. source, by-product and special nuclear material, and other material, for research on, development of, or use in atomic weapons when, after consultation with the Government of the United Kingdom, the Government of the United States determines that the transfer of such material is necessary to improve the United Kingdom's atomic weapon design, development or fabrication capability.

'B.—The Government of the United Kingdom shall transfer to the Government of the United States for military purposes such source, by-product and special nuclear material, and equipment of such types, in such quantities, at such times prior to December 31, 1969, and on such terms and conditions as may be agreed.

'C.—1. With respect to by-product material, special nuclear material and other material transferred from one Party to the other under this Article, the recipient Party agrees not to use any such material for purposes other than those for which it was received, provided that material which has lost its identity as a result of commingling with other material of the recipient Party may be put to other uses if the recipient Party retains an equivalent amount of its own material for the purpose for which the other Party's material was received.

'2. For material or equipment transferred from one Party to the other Party, the recipient Party shall pay or reimburse, as may be agreed, all packaging, transportation and related costs. Packaging, shipping containers and methods of shipment shall be as may be agreed.

'3. Should either Party desire to acquire materials or components for use in the manufacture or in preparation for manufacture of atomic weapons from any source within the jurisdiction of the other Party, the procuring Party shall inform the other Party of the proposed procurement in order that such other Party may determine whether the proposed procurement involves classified information and if so whether the proposed procurement is in compliance with its applicable laws and regulations.'

Article 2

Article VII of the Agreement for Cooperation shall be amended to read as follows:

'Article VII

'DISSEMINATION

'Nothing in this Agreement shall be interpreted or shall operate as a bar or restriction to consultation or cooperation in any field of defense by either Party with other nations or international organizations. Neither Party, however, shall communicate classified information or transfer or permit access to or use of materials, or equipment, made available by the other Party pursuant to this Agreement to any nation or international organization unless:

'A.—it is notified by the other Party that all appropriate provisions and requirements of such other Party's applicable laws, including authorization by competent bodies of such other Party, have been complied with as necessary to authorize such other Party directly so to communicate to, transfer to or permit access to or use by such other nation or international organization; and further that such other Party authorizes the recipient Party so to communicate to, transfer to or permit access to or use by such other nation or international organization; or

'B.—in the case of communication of classified information and access to materials or equipment, such other Party has informed the recipient Party that such other Party has so communicated such classified information to, or permitted access to such materials or equipment by, such other nation or international organization; or

'C.—in the case of material which has lost its identity as a result of commingling with other material of the recipient Party, the recipient Party retains an amount under its jurisdiction equivalent to that made available to it by the other Party under this Agreement.'

Article 3

Article IX of the Agreement for Cooperation shall be amended as follows:

(1) The words 'Article III' shall be deleted from paragraph A, subparagraph 2 of paragraph B, and subparagraph 1 of paragraph D, and the words 'Articles III or III *bis*' shall be substituted therefor.
(2) The words 'submarine propulsion plant and spare parts transferred pursuant to paragraph A of Article III' shall be deleted from subparagraph 1 of paragraph B, and the words "submarine propulsion plant, spare parts or equipment transferred pursuant to paragraph A of Article III or paragraph A or paragraph B of Article III *bis*" shall be substituted therefor.

Article 4

Article XI of the Agreement for Cooperation shall be amended as follows:

(1) Paragraph C shall be amended by adding at the end thereof the following:

'"Equipment" also includes non-nuclear parts of atomic weapons and other non-nuclear parts of atomic weapons systems involving Restricted Data.'

(2) After paragraph H add the following:

'I. "Non-nuclear parts of atomic weapons" means parts of atomic weapons which are specially designed for them and are not in general use in other end products and which are not made, in whole or in part, of special nuclear material; and "other non-nuclear parts of atomic weapons systems involving Restricted Data" means parts of atomic weapons systems, other than non-nuclear parts of atomic weapons, which contain or reveal atomic information and which are not made, in whole or in part, of special nuclear material.

'J. "Atomic information" means information designated "Restricted Data" or "Formerly Restricted Data" by the Government of the United States and information designated "ATOMIC" by the Government of the United Kingdom.'

Article 5

Article XII of the Agreement for Cooperation shall be amended as follows:

The words 'to take effect at the end of a term of ten years,' shall be deleted and the words 'to take effect on December 31, 1969,' shall be substituted therefor.

Article 6

This Amendment which shall be regarded as an integral part of the Agreement for Cooperation, shall enter into force on the date on which each Government shall have received from the other Government written notification that it has complied with all statutory and constitutional requirements for the entry into force of this Amendment.

IN WITNESS WHEREOF, the undersigned, duly authorized, have signed this Amendment.

DONE at Washington this seventh day of May, 1959, in two original texts.

For the Government of the United Kingdom of Great Britain and Northern Ireland:
Harold CACCIA

For the Government of the United States of America:
Christian A. HERTER

NOTES

Source: *United Nations Treaty Series,* 1960, Vol. 351, No. 4707, pp. 458–464.

Appendix 12 Polaris sales agreement[1] between the Government of the United States of America and the Government of the United Kingdom of Great Britain and Northern Ireland. Signed at Washington, on 6 April 1963

The Government of the United States of America and the Government of the United Kingdom of Great Britain and Northern Ireland, recalling and affirming the 'Statement on Nuclear Defense Systems' included in the joint communiqué issued on December 21, 1962[2] by the President of the United States of America and the Prime Minister of Her Majesty's Government in the United Kingdom of Great Britain and Northern Ireland;

Have agreed as follows:

Article I

1. The Government of the United States shall provide and the Government of the United Kingdom shall purchase from the Government of the United States Polaris missiles (less warheads), equipment, and supporting services in accordance with the terms and conditions of this Agreement.

2. This Agreement shall be subject to the understandings concerning British submarines equipped with Polaris missiles (referred to in paragraphs 8 and 9 of the Nassau 'Statement on Nuclear Defense Systems') agreed by the President of the United States and the Prime Minister of the United Kingdom at their meeting held in the Bahamas between December 18 and December 21, 1962.

Article II

1. In recognition of the complexity of the effort provided for in this Agreement and the need for close coordination between the contracting Governments in giving effect to its terms, the two Governments shall promptly establish the organizational machinery provided for in the following paragraphs of this Article.

2. The Department of Defense, acting through the Department of the Navy, and the Admiralty, or such other agency as the Government of the United Kingdom shall designate, will be the Executive Agencies of their respective Governments in carrying out the terms of this Agreement. Appropriate representatives of the Executive Agencies are authorized to enter into such technical arrangements, consistent with this Agreement, as may be necessary.

3. A Project Officer will be designated by each Government's Executive Agency with direct responsibility and authority for the management of the activities of that Government under this Agreement. Each Project Officer will designate liaison representatives, in such numbers as may be agreed, who will be authorized to act on his behalf in capacities specified in technical arrangements and who will be attached to the Office of the other Project Officer.

4. A Joint Steering Task Group will be established by the Project Officers to advice them, *inter alia*, concerning the development of new or modified equipment to meet specific requirements of the Government of the United Kingdom, and concerning interfaces between the equipment provided by the two Governments respectively. The Joint Steering Task Group will comprise the Project Officers (or their representatives), and principal liaison representatives, and may include selected leaders from among the scientists, industrialists and government executives of the United States and of the United Kingdom. The Joint Steering Task Group will meet approximately every three months alternately in the United Kingdom and in the United States under the chairmanship of the resident Project Officer.

Article III

1. The Government of the United States (acting through its Executive Agency) shall provide, pursuant to Article I of this Agreement, Polaris missiles (less warheads), equipment, and supporting services of such types and marks and in such quantities as the Government of the United Kingdom may from time to time require, and in configurations and in accordance with delivery programs or time tables to be agreed between the Project Officers. In the first instance the missiles, equipment, and supporting services provided by the Government of the United States shall be sufficient to meet the requirements of a program drawn up by the Government of the United Kingdom and communicated to the Government of the United States prior to the entry into force of this Agreement.

2. The missiles, equipment, and supporting services referred to in paragraph 1 of this article are the following:

a. Polaris missiles (less warheads but including guidance capsules);
b. missile launching and handling systems;
c. missile fire control systems;
d. ships navigation systems;
e. additional associated, support, test, and training equipment and services including, but not limited to:
  (i) test and check-out equipment, specialized power supplies, power distribution systems and support equipment associated with the items enumerated in subparagraphs *a, b, c,* and *d* of this paragraph and adequate in type and quantity to meet the requirements of installations both aboard ship and ashore;

(ii) specialized equipment including the types specified in subparagraphs *a, b, c, d,* and *e* (i) of this paragraph for use in such support and training facilities as may be provided by the Government of the United Kingdom;

(iii) construction spares and spare parts adequate in scope and quantity to ensure the continued maintenance of the equipment specified in subparagraphs *a, b, c, d,* (i), and *e* (ii) of this paragraph;

(iv) (*a*) latest available United States technical documentation including specification, blueprints, and manuals covering the missiles and equipment listed in subparagraphs *a, b, c, d, e* (i), *e* (ii) and *e* (iii) of this paragraph in sufficient scope and quantity to cover safety requirements and permit successful transport, installation, operation, and maintenance by the Government of the United Kingdom of all equipment purchased under the terms of this Agreement;

(*b*) latest available United States technical documentation, as may be necessary from time to time in individual cases, to permit manufacture by the Government of the United Kingdom to the extent necessary for the maintenance, repair, and modification of the items listed in subparagraphs *a, b, c, d, e* (i), *e* (ii) and *e* (iii) of this paragraph;

(v) services, including:

(*a*) use, as appropriate, of existing support and missile range facilities in the United States;

(*b*) assistance in program management techniques and, in addition, those engineering and lead shipyard services required to ensure proper system integration, installation, and check-out in the United Kingdom; to the extent required and available, appropriate modification, maintenance, and overhaul of the equipment listed in subparagraphs *a, b, c, d, e* (i), *e* (ii), and *e* (iii) of this paragraph;

(*c*) research, design, development, production, test, or other engineering services as may be required to meet specific United Kingdom requirements;

(*d*) training of naval and civil personnel in the service of the Government of the United Kingdom and United Kingdom contractors to the extent to which they are involved in the inspection, installation, operation, maintenance, repair, and modification of the equipment listed in sub-paragraphs *a, b, c, d, e* (i), *e* (ii), and *e* (iii) of this paragraph.

Article IV

Future developments relating to the Polaris Weapon System, including all modifications made thereto, by the Government of the United States or the Government of the United Kingdom shall, in the areas enumerated in Article III, be made reciprocally available through their Executive Agencies in accordance with the terms of this Agreement, reciprocally applied.

Article V

The Government of the United Kingdom will provide the submarines in which will be installed the missiles and equipment to be provided under this Agreement, and will provide the warheads for these missiles. Close coordination between the Executive Agencies of the contracting Governments will be maintained in order to assure compatibility of equipment. Information concerning the hull, auxiliary machinery, and equipment of United States submarines transmitted under the authority of this Agreement will be such as is necessary to obtain a satisfactory interface between the equipment provided by the two Governments respectively. This Agreement does not, however, authorize the sale of, or transmittal of information concerning, the nuclear propulsion plants of United States submarines.

Article VI

1. In carrying out this Agreement, the Government of the United States will use, to the extent practicable, established Department of Defense contracting procedures and existing Polaris contracts. In any event contracts for production or work for the Government of the United Kingdom will be incorporated in or placed on the same terms as those for the Government of the United States. When appropriate the United States Project Officer will direct that amendments he sought to existing contracts and that terms be incorporated in new contracts to safeguard any special requirements of the Government of the United Kingdom in the contract subject matter which may arise in connection with this Agreement, for example, to provide for any alterations or any reduction of quantities which may be necessary.

2. The missiles and equipment provided by the Government of the United States under this Agreement shall be fabricated to the same documentation and quality standards as are the counterparts for the United States Polaris Program.

3. The missiles and equipment provided by the Government of the United States under this Agreement will be integrated with the scheduled United States Polaris Program and will be fabricated on a schedule which will make the most efficient and economical use of existing United States production lines. Deliveries will be made upon a schedule to be defined by the Government of the United Kingdom, but which is consonant with the above fabrication schedule.

Article VII

1. The Government of the United States shall ensure that all supplies (which term throughout this Article includes, but without limitation, raw materials, components, intermediate assemblies and end items) which it will provide under this Agreement are inspected to the same extent and in the same manner (including the granting of waivers and deviations) as are the counterparts for the United States Polaris Program. The United Kingdom Project Officer or his designated representative may observe the inspection process and offer his advice to the United States Government Inspector regarding the inspection, without delay to, or impairment of the finality of, the inspection by the Government of the United States.

2. The United States Project Officer through appropriate procedures will notify the United Kingdom Project Officer when final inspection of each end item will take place, and will furnish a certificate or certificates upon completion of each such inspection stating that this inspection has been made and that such end item has been accepted as having met all requirements of the relevant acceptance documentation (subject to any appropriate waivers and deviations). Copies of acceptance documentation and quality standards, together with reports required thereby, will be furnished to the United Kingdom Project Officer or his designated representative.

3. The Government of the United Kingdom will take delivery of the supplies as agreed pursuant to Article X following inspection, acceptance and certification by the Government of the United States. Delivery to the Government of the United Kingdom shall not relieve the Government of the United States from continuing responsibility for using its best endeavours thereafter to secure the correction or replacement of any items found not to have been manufactured in strict accordance with the documentation and quality standards referred to in Article VI or to be otherwise defective. Such corrections or replacements will be at the expense of the Government of the United Kingdom to the extent they are not covered by warranty or guaranty or otherwise recoverable by the Government of the United States.

4. The Government of the United States will use its best endeavors to obtain for or extend to the Government of the United Kingdom the benefit of any guarantees or warranties negotiated with United States contractors or subcontractors.

Article VIII

The Government of the United Kingdom shall indemnify and hold harmless the Government of the United States against any liability or loss resulting from unusually hazardous risks attributable to Polaris missiles or equipment identifiable, respectively, as missiles or equipment supplied or to be supplied to the Government of the United Kingdom under this Agreement. Unusually hazardous risks, for the purposes of this Agreement, are those defined by applicable statutes of the United States, or by any appropriate administrative act under the authority of such statutes, or held to exist by a court of competent jurisdiction. The Government of the United States shall give the Government of the United Kingdom immediate notice of any suit or action filed or of any claim made to which the provisions of this Article may be relevant. Representatives of the United Kingdom may be associated with the defense, before a court of competent jurisdiction, of any claim which may be borne in whole or in part by the Government of the United Kingdom. In procurement contracts for supplies and services made pursuant to this Agreement the Government of the United States is authorized to include unusually hazardous risk indemnification provisions substantially similar to those included in its own corresponding contracts.

Article IX

1. The Government of the United States will follow its normal procurement practices in securing all rights it considers to be essential to enable it to provide the missiles and equipment to be supplied to the Government of the United Kingdom under this Agreement. In addition, the Government of the United States shall notify the Government of the United Kingdom of any claim asserted hereafter for compensation for unlicensed use of patent rights alleged to be involved in the supply of such missiles and equipment to the Government of the United Kingdom, and the two Governments will consult as to the appropriate disposition of such claim.

2. The Government of the United Kingdom shall reimburse the Government of the United States for any payments made by the Government of the United States in settlement of liability, including cost and expenses, for unlicensed use of any patent rights in the manufacture or sale of the missiles and equipment supplied or to be supplied to the Government of the United Kingdom under this Agreement.

Article X

1. Delivery of equipment other than missiles to be provided under this Agreement for installation in submarines or supporting facilities to be provided by the Government of the United Kingdom shall be the responsibility of the Government of the United States and shall be made to those locations within the United Kingdom where the equipment is required. In addition to delivery of such equipment, the Government of the United States shall, subject to reimbursement for costs incurred, be responsible for providing such technical installation and testing services as are required

by the Government of the United Kingdom for the satisfactory installation, check-out and testing of that equipment in submarines and supporting facilities of the United Kingdom.

2. Delivery of all missiles shall be made to appropriate carriers of the United Kingdom or, if it is agreed, of the United States, at such United States supply points as are agreed by the Executive Agencies of both Governments. The Government of the United States shall be responsible for the initial check-out of all missiles provided under this Agreement.

Article XI

1. The charges to the Government of the United Kingdom for missiles, equipment, and services provided by the Government of the United States will be:

a. The normal cost of missiles and equipment provided under the joint United States-United Kingdom production program integrated in accordance with Article VI. This will be based on common contract prices together with charges for work done in United States Government establishments and appropriate allowance for use of capital facilities and for overhead costs.
b. An addition of 5% to the common contract prices under subparagraph 1 *a* of this Article for missiles and equipment provided to the United Kingdom, as a participation in the expenditures incurred by the Government of the United States after January 1, 1963, for research and development.
c. Replacement cost of items provided from United States Government stock or, with respect to items not currently being procured, the most recent procurement cost.
d. The actual cost of any research, design, development, production, test or other engineering effort, or other services required in the execution of this Agreement to meet specific United Kingdom requirements.
e. The cost of packing, crating, handling and transportation.
f. The actual costs of any other services, not specified above, which the Project Officers agree are properly attributable to this Agreement.

2. Payments by the Government of the United Kingdom in accordance with paragraph 1 of this Article shall be made in United States dollars. Payments to United States agencies and contractors shall be made, as they become due, from a trust fund which will be administered by the United States Project Officer. All payments out of the Trust Fund shall be certified to be in accordance with the terms of the Agreement. The Trust Fund will consist initially of a sum to be paid as soon as possible after entry into force of this agreement and to be equivalent to the payments estimated to fall due during the first calendar quarter of program operations. Before the end of that quarter and of each succeeding quarter

deposits shall be made by the Government of the United Kingdom with the object of having sufficient money in the Fund to meet all the calls which will be made upon it in the succeeding three months.

3. If at any time the unexpended balance in the Trust Fund established pursuant to paragraph 2 of this Article falls short of the sums that will be needed in a particular quarter by the Government of the United States to cover:

a. payment for the value of items to be furnished from the stocks of, or services to be rendered by, the Government of the United States;

b. payment by the Government of the United States to its suppliers for items and services to be procured for the Government of the United Kingdom; and

c. estimated liability or costs that may fall to be met by the Government of the United States as a result of termination of such procurement contracts at the behest of the Government of the United Kingdom;

the Government of the United Kingdom will pay at such time to the Goverment of the United States such additional sums as will be due. Should the total payments received from the Government of the United Kingdom prove to be in excess of the final total costs to the Government of the United States, appropriate refund will be made to the Government of the United Kingdom at the earliest opportunity with final adjustment being made within thirty days after determination of said final costs.

4. The United States Project Officer will maintain a record of expenditures under this Agreement in accordance with established Navy Special Projects Office accounting procedures which record will be available for audit annually by representatives of the Government of the United Kingdom.

Article XII

1. The provisions of this Article concerning proprietary rights shall apply to the work referred to in subparagraph 1 *d* of Article XI of this Agreement (hereinafter called in this Article 'the work').

2. The Government of the United States shall ensure that the Government of the United Kingdom will receive a royalty-free, non-exclusive, irrevocable license for its governmental purposes:

a. to practice or cause to be practiced throughout the world all inventions conceived or first actually reduced to practice in the performance of the word; and

b. to use or cause to be used throughout the world all technical information first produced in the performance of the work.

3. In addition, the Government of the United States shall take the following steps to ensure the right of the Government of the United

Kingdom to reproduce, by manufacturers of its own choice, items developed in the performance of the work. In respect of those elements of this right not included in subparagraphs 2 *a* and 2 *b* of this Article, the Government of the United States shall:

a. to the extent that it owns or controls such elements, accord free user rights to the Government of the United Kingdom;

b. obtain the agreement of contractors and subcontractors performing the work to make available to the Government of the United Kingdom, on fair and reasonable terms and conditions, those elements which the contractor or subcontractor owns or controls at the commencement of the work or acquires during the performance of the work;

c. use its best endeavors to obtain for the Government of the United Kingdom or to assist the Government of the United Kingdom to obtain directly or through its own manufacturers, on fair and reasonable terms and conditions, elements of this right not covered by subparagraphs 2 *a* and 2 *b* of this Article.

4. The Government of the United States shall also ensure that the Government of the United Kingdom will receive the same rights as those referred to in paragraphs 2 and 3 of this Article in respect of any material now or hereafter covered by copyright produced or delivered in the performance of the work.

5. The Government of the United States shall furnish to the Government of the United Kingdom, in such quantities as may be agreed:

a. all documentation obtained by the Government of the United States under contracts placed for the performance of the work;

b. all documentation, owned or controlled by the Government of the United States, necessary for reproduction, by or on behalf of the Government of the United Kingdom, of items developed during the performance of the work.

6. It is understood that the Government of the United States will obtain for itself such of the rights referred to in subparagraphs 2 *a*, 2 *b*, and 3 of this Article as it may require for its governmental purposes.

7. The term 'owned or controlled' as used in this Article means the right to grant a license without incurring liability to any private owner of a proprietary or other legal interest.

8. The Government of the United States will use its best endeavors to ensure that there will be made available by United States manufacturers to the Government of the United Kingdom, on fair and reasonable terms and conditions, such technical assistance–for example, loan of engineers, or training–as the Government of the United Kingdom desires in order to permit the production by manufacturers of its own choice of the items developed in the performance of the work.

9. The Government of the United States will insert suitable provisions in all prime contracts for the work to ensure the availability to the Government of the United Kingdom of the rights set forth in this Article, including a requirement that similar provisions be placed in subcontracts.

Article XIII

1. The Government of the United States, to the extent that it can do so without incurring liability to any private owner of a proprietary or other legal interest, shall grant to the Government of the United Kingdom: (i) the right to reproduce and use, royalty-free, the technical documentation referred to in subparagraph 2 *e* (iv) of Article III for the purposes stated in that subparagraph; and (ii) a non-exclusive, royalty-free license to practice or cause to be practiced any invention for these purposes.

2. In respect of any part of the technical documentation referred to in paragraph 1 of this Article which the Government of the United States cannot furnish to the Government of the United Kingdom without incurring a liability to a private owner of a proprietary or other legal interest, the Government of the United States will use its best endeavors to assist the Government of the United Kingdom in securing for the Government of the United Kingdom on fair and reasonable terms and conditions the right to use such documentation for the purposes stated in subparagraph 2 *e* (iv) of Article III.

Article XIV

1. The Government of the United Kingdom shall not, without the prior express consent of the Government of the United States, transfer, or permit access to, or use of, the missiles, equipment, services, or documents or information relating thereto which are provided by the Government of the United States under this Agreement, except to a United Kingdom officer, employee, national or firm engaged in the implementation of this Agreement.

2. The Government of the United Kingdom shall undertake such security measures as are necessary to afford classified articles, services, documents or information substantially the same degree of protection afforded by the Government of the United States in order to prevent unauthorized disclosure or compromise.

Article XV

Annually, on or before the first of July, the Project Officers will prepare a formal joint report to the contracting Governments of action taken and progress made under this Agreement and a forecast of schedules and costs for completion. In addition, other more frequent joint reports will be submitted, as agreed upon by the Project Officers, to the heads of the Executive Agencies.

Article XVI

This Agreement shall enter into force on the date of signature.

IN WITNESS WHEREOF the undersigned, being duly authorized thereto by their respective Governments, have signed this Agreement.

DONE in duplicate at Washington this sixth day of April, 1963.

For the Government of the United States of America:
Dean RUSK

For the Government of the United Kingdom of Great Britain and Northern Ireland:
David ORMSBY-GORE

NOTES

[1] Came into force on 6 April 1963, upon signature, in accordance with article XVI.

[2] United States of America: *Department of State Bulletin,* 14 January 1963.

Source: *United Nations Treaty Series,* 1963, Vol. 474, No. 6871, pp. 50–68.

Appendix 13 Amendment to 1958 Atomic Energy Agreement. Signed at Washington on 27 September 1968

Authentic text: English.

Registered by the United Kingdom of Great Britain and Northern Ireland on 24 November 1969.

The Government of the United Kingdom of Great Britain and Northern Ireland on its own behalf and on behalf of the United Kingdom Atomic Energy Authority and the Government of the United States of America;

Desiring to amend in certain respects the Agreement for Cooperation on the Uses of Atomic Energy for Mutual Defense Purposes signed at Washington on the third day of July, 1958, as amended

Have agreed as follows:

Article 1

Subparagraph A. 3 of Article III *bis* of the Agreement for Cooperation shall be deleted and subparagraph A. 4 of Article III *bis* shall be renumbered as subparagraph A. 3 thereof.

Article 2

Paragraphs B and C of Article III *bis* of the Agreement for Cooperation shall be renumbered as paragraphs C and D thereof, respectively, and a new paragraph B shall be inserted to read as follows:

> 'B. The Government of the United States shall transfer to the Government of the United Kingdom special nuclear material, and authorize the transfer of other material, for research, on development of, production of, or use in utilization facilities for military applications, in such quantities, at such times prior to December 31, 1979, and on such terms and conditions as may be agreed.'

Article 3

Article IX of the Agreement for Cooperation shall be amended as follows: The words 'paragraph A or paragraph B of Article III *bis*' shall be deleted from subparagraph 1 of paragraph B and the words 'paragraph A, paragraph B, or paragraph C of Article III *bis*' shall be substituted therefor.

Article 4

This Amendment, which shall be regarded as an integral part of the Agreement for Cooperation, shall enter into force on the date on which each Government shall have received from the other Government written notification that it has complied with all statutory and constitutional requirements for the entry into force of this Amendment.

IN WITNESS WHEREOF, the undersigned, duly authorized, have signed this Amendment.

DONE at Washington, in duplicate, this twenty-seventh day of September, 1968.

For the Government of the United Kingdom of Great Britain and Northern Ireland:
Patrick DEAN

For the Government of the United States of America:
John M. LEDDY
Gerald F. TAPE

NOTES

Source: *United Nations Treaty Series,* 1969, Vol. 700, No. 4707, pp 344–346.

Appendix 14 United States/United Kingdom Collaboration

Memorandum by Ministry of Defence 1968/69

The United States and the United Kingdom collaborate in defence research and development both through common membership of certain multilateral organisations and bilaterally through formal machinery and informal contacts.

The Technical Co-operation Programme (TTCP)

2. Following a Declaration of Common Purpose by the President of the United States and the Prime Minister of the United Kingdom in 1957, to which Canada also immediately subscribed, a Tripartite Technical Co-operation Programme was established. Its name was changed to The Technical Co-operation Programme with the admission of Australia in 1965. The programme is directed by a high-level Committee which meets about once a year. A permanent group of deputies in Washington supervises the day-to-day work of the numerous sub-groups, with specialist panels where appropriate, through which information is regularly exchanged.

Other multilateral collaboration

3. Collaboration is also conducted multilaterally on a single service basis. There is a Basic Standardisation Agreement among the Armies of the United States, United Kingdom, Canada and Australia (known for short as ABCA). This Agreement aims to achieve interoperability between the Armies through material and non-material standardisation; and to obtain the greatest possible economy through combining resources and effort. It seeks to keep each Army fully informed of the others' research and development programmes and to guide these along lines compatible with the requirements of all four Armies. Consultations within ABCA were the origin of the agreement by the four countries to develop collaboratively the Mallard tactical trunk communications system.

4. The Air Standardisation Co-ordination Committee and The Naval Tripartite Standardisation Programme (U.S., U.K. and Canada only) perform similar functions in their respective fields.

5. The U.S. and the U.K. also take part in multilateral collaboration through the machinery established in N.A.T.O. for this purpose.

Bilateral arrangements

6. Following an agreement between Mr. Thorneycroft and Mr. McNamara in 1963, the purpose of which was to promote complementary R and D effort in the two countries, an Anglo/U.S. Steering Committee was set up to supervise purely bilateral collaboration. Agreement has been reached on a number of U.S./U.K. collaborative research projects, including work on an advanced lift engine, automatic astro-navigation, beryllium, lasers and fuel cells.

7. There are also bilateral agreements covering the exchange of information. The U.S.N. and R.N. operate Information Exchange Projects under which information, in both general and specific areas, is exchanged direct according to recognised administrative procedures. Mintech also operate technical information exchange agreements with the U.S.A. The information obtained is exploited in this country to the maximum extent possible consistent with military and commercial security.

Informal and ad hoc collaboration

8. In addition to the work carried on within the formal machinery described above, a great deal of activity takes place in the way of informal information exchanges, laboratory and industrial visits and attendance at symposia. In all this, representatives of the U.K. Research and Development Establishments play their full part. A note on the relationship between DOAE and U.S. Operational Analysis Institutions is attached at Annex.

General

9. There are thus, a variety of ways in which the U.S. and U.K. collaborate in defence research and development. The choice in each case depends on the scope and opportunity for collaboration. The existence of more than one channel provides flexibility without leading to duplication.

10. Some limitations are imposed by U.S. security requirements and there are for financial reasons restrictions on the numbers of visits to the U.S. by U.K. officials. Nevertheless the exchange of information and the collaboration on research projects described above are a valuable aid to the U.K.'s own R and D effort. The sharing of scientific information through for example the TTCP helps to ensure that our long-term equipment programmes have as sound a technical basis as possible.

11. The search for collaborative development projects is more difficult. There are differences in operational requirements and in the timing of defence procurement plans which are not easy to overcome. There are commercial interests in both countries which have to be reconciled. With the disparity between the production requirements of the two countries it is not easy to devise a development programme which can be allocated broadly in proportion to those requirements, yet give the U.K. an adequate share of development work. These difficulties, however, are not necessarily insuperable, as the Mallard project demonstrates. There are in

addition restraints on both sides on the exploitation of information for other than military purposes.

12. In sum, a great deal of collaboration takes place between the two countries and both the machinery and the goodwill are there to ensure that this continues.

ANNEX

The Relationship between DOAE and U.S. Operational Analysis Institutions

Although representatives from DOAE take part in the formal arrangements for co-operation (e.g. TTCP), there is no formal machinery for collaboration between the Establishment as such and institutions in the United States such as the RAND Corporation. Liaison has been maintained informally, both by participation in various conferences and by visits to government and "semi-official" agencies in the U.S. engaged or on operational analysis.

2. The main purpose of liaison visits is to maintain the cross fertilisation of ideas and to ensure that developments in operational analysis techniques and methodologies are proceeding in parallel. A team from DOAE recently returned from discussions at RAND and elsewhere which had been concerned with methods of wargaming and cost modelling. There is considerable enthusiasm for co-operation of this kind, and there is no doubt that the exchanges of ideas in these "state of the art" discussions provide valuable assistance to the work undertaken at DOAE and in the U.S.

3. The possibility of more specific co-operation, e.g. exchanging data and results in studies of mutual interest has proved more difficult. The work of many of the U.S. studies operational analysis institutions has no helpful parallel with the central policy studies carried out at DOAE, nor does it offer any useful basis for discussion. Moreover, much of the work is undertaken under contract for single service departments and this limits the extent to which the work can be discussed.

4. It has, therefore, been concluded that DOAE would, initially at least, gain most benefit from liaison with that part of the U.S. Defense Department engaged on operational analysis. A valuable though informal relationship has been built up, resulting in visits by both Ministry of Defence and U.S. teams for discussions of central Defence problems of common interest, and the exchange of information.

14th February, 1969.

NOTES

Taken from the *Second Report from the Select Committee on Science and Technology: Defence Research, Session 1968–69,* No 213, Appendix 56, pp 553–4 (London: HMSO, 1969).

Appendix 15 UK Dependence on the United States[1]

The degree of British dependence on the US in the nuclear field varies in different fields.

Missiles

Britain apparently has 102 Polaris A3 missiles which were bought 'off-the-shelf' from the United States under the Sales Agreement. Dependence in this field is virtually complete because Britain has no ability at present to produce these missiles for herself or the major components such as the rocket motors and solid propellants. Although Britain has undoubtedly learned a lot about the Polaris missile, unlike France she has effectively opted out of this important field of military technology and in so doing has become dependent on continuing American support. Having been out of this field of research and development for so long any decision in the future to produce an indigenous missile system would involve a major technical and economic effort on Britain's part.

Submarines, Re-entry Vehicles and Warheads

Although the four British nuclear submarines, the re-entry systems and nuclear warheads for the missiles, were all designed and built in Britain, even in these fields considerable American assistance has been received and continues. Apart from the important help, for example, on nuclear propulsion reactors provided under the 1955 and 1958 Agreements, Britain also apparently requires certain specialized materials from the United States. These include zirconium (used in the cladding of the reactor fuel elements); hafnium (for neutron absorption in the submarine reactors); and from 1962 on highly enriched uranium (for use in submarine reactor fields). It has also been reported that even the high-stress steel for the submarine hulls has to be purchased from the United States. Apart from these important materials the submarines themselves continue to depend on the use of American trial facilities at Cape Canaveral (previously Cape Kennedy) and the US Eastern Test Range.

The British-produced re-entry vehicles and nuclear warheads are also to a certain extent reliant on American help. As far as the re-entry vehicles are concerned it is widely assumed that use is made of American flight test facilities. Similarly, because of Britain's lack of suitable nuclear testing areas, the United States underground test site in Nevada has been used on numerous occasions for testing British nuclear warheads. Britain has also received certain vital materials such as highly enriched uranium, polonium and, in the past, tritium, for use in warhead production.

Intelligence

Apart from British reliance on the United States for these important components for the nuclear deterrent, there also seem to be other areas in which Britain is not perhaps dependent, but where US assistance is nevertheless of great value. Because Britain, for example, does not have an ability of her own to collect intelligence by the use of satellites, it seems likely, given the apparent range of intelligence cooperation, that any assistance needed in this field is provided by the American authorities. According to Ian Smart, as far as information 'on Soviet targets and Soviet strategic defences (including ABM and air defences) is derived from satellite surveillance, it must be assumed that Britain is dependent for such intelligence on the United States'. Whether such intelligence is vital or whether Britain could provide adequate information for her needs from her own intelligence resources is difficult to gauge. Nevertheless US assistance in this field no doubt remains of value.

Navigation and Communications

Much the same seems to be true in the fields of submarine navigation and communications. Britain has bought SINS navigation equipment from the US and some reports suggest that the submarines also make use of American navigation satellites and US submarine beacons for checking the submarine's position which is provided by the SINS system. Whether Britain can produce (or has produced) similar equipment herself and is able to confirm the positions of the submarines from other sources without American help has, however, not been revealed. On the question of communications between the command authorities on shore and the submarine at sea, Britain has her own VLF radio facilities (at Rugby). There has been some speculation, however, that contingency arrangements may well exist for communication through American VLF (or ELF) stations if an emergency should make that necessary.

NOTES

[1] See Ian Smart, *The Future of the British Nuclear Deterrent: Technical Economic and Strategic Issues* (The Royal Institute of International

Affairs 1977), Appendix 3; and J. Simpson, 'The Anglo-American nuclear relationship and its implications for the choice of a possible successor to the current Polaris force', Appendix 6, *Sixth Report from the Expenditure Committee: The Future of the United Kingdom's Nuclear Weapons Policy*, 348, (HMSO, 1979).

Appendix 16 US Military Installations in the UK[1]

THIRD AIR FORCE BASES AND UNITS

A. MAIN OPERATING BASES

RAF ALCONBURY, Nr Huntingdon, Cambridgeshire
10th Tactical Reconnaissance Wing (one squadron of RF-4C Phantoms and one 'Aggressor' squadron of F-5E Tiger IIs)

RAF BENTWATERS/RAF WOODBRIDGE, Woodbrige, Suffolk
81st Tactical Fighter Wing (three squadrons of A-10 Thunderbolt IIs, to be increased to six squadrons)
67th Aerospace Rescue and Recovery Squadron (HC-130 Hercules and HH-53 Super Jolly Green Giant rescue helicopters) (a Military Airlift Command unit)

RAF CHICKSANDS, Nr Shefford, Bedfordshire
7274th Air Base Group
6950th Electronic Security Group (an Electronic Security Command unit)

RAF FAIRFORD, Fairford, Gloucestershire
7020th Air Base Group
11th Strategic Group (a Strategic Air Command Unit controlling KC-135 Stratotankers)

RAF LAKENHEATH, Nr Brandon, Suffolk
48th Tactical Fighter Wing (four squadrons of F-111F all-weather strike aircraft)

RAF MILDENHALL, Nr Mildenhall, Suffolk
Headquarters, Third Air Force
513th Tactical Airlift Wing (EC-135 airborne command and control aircraft)
306th Strategic Wing (a Strategic Air Command unit controlling KC-135 Stratotankers)
313th Tactical Airlift Group (a military Airlift Command unit controlling C-130 Hercules aircraft)
627th Military Airlift Support Squadron (a military Airlift Command unit providing support for transiting C-141 Starlifters and C-5 Galaxies)

RAF UPPER HEYFORD, Upper Heyford, Oxfordshire
20th Tactical Fighter Wing (three squadrons of F-111E all-weather strike aircraft)

B. STANDBY DEPLOYMENT BASES

RAF GREENHAM COMMON, Newbury, Berkshire
 7273rd Air Base Group
RAF SCULTHORPE, Nr Fakenham, Norfolk
 Detachment 1, 48th Tactical Fighter Wing
RAF WETHERSFIELD, Nr Braintree, Essex
 Detachment 1, 10th Tactical Reconnaissance Wing
 819th Civil Engineering Squadron (Red Horse)

C. US AIR FORCE COMMUNICATIONS FACILITIES

1 RAF Barford St John
2 RAF Barkway
3 Botley Hill Radio Relay
4 Bovington Radio Relay
5 RAF Chicksands
6 RAF Christmas Common Radio Relay
7 Cold Blow Radio Relay
8 RAF Croughton
9 Daventry Radio Relay
10 RAF Dunkirk Communications Station
11 Great Bromley Radio Relay
12 High Wycombe Air Station
13 Hillington
14 RAF Martlesham Heath Radio Relay
15 Mormond Hill Communications Station (Scotland)
16 RAF St Mawgan Communications Station
17 RAF Swingate Communications Station
18 RAF Wethersfield
19 Flyingdales Moor (one of the three radars in the BMEWS network)

D. OTHER USAF INSTALLATIONS

RAF FELTWELL, Feltwell, Norfolk
 A support installation of RAF Lakenheath
HIGH WYCOMBE AIR STATION, High Wycombe, Buckinghamshire
 Detachment 1, 20th Tactical Fighter Wing
RAF MOLESWORTH, Nr Kimbolton, Cambridgeshire
 Defense Property Disposal Office, UK (Air Force Logistics Command unit)
RAF WELFORD, Nr Newbury, Berkshire
 7551st Ammunition Supply Squadron

E. US NAVY

1. Holy Loch, Squadron 14 (10 SSBNs services by one submarine tender, the USS *Holland*)
2. Edzell (Scotland) – Naval Security Group facility
3. Thurso (Scotland) – Naval Radio Station
4. Brawdy (Wales) – Oceanographic observation facility
5. 7 North Audley Street, London – HQ US Navy Europe

F. US ARMY

1. Burtonwood	Depot: Army Material Command
2. Felixstowe	US Army Terminal

US Military Personnel in the UK

Air Force	19,617
Navy	2,133
Marine Corps	310
Army	141
	22,201

NOTE

[1] The author is grateful to Mr Peter R. Sommer, Political-Military Attaché at the US Embassy in Britain for some of the information contained in this list. Other information has been derived from a paper by the Congressional Research Service on 'US Foreign Policy Objectives and Overseas Military Bases'.

Notes on Sources

To write a book about Anglo-American defence relations which covers the period from the Second World War to the present day raises at least two major difficulties. The first stems from the differences in the sources available for the wartime and post-war periods. For the period from 1939 to 1945 most of the official documents are available to researchers in both Britain and the United States. With the exception of the first three or four years after the war, however, most of the documents covering post-war British defence policy remain closed and writers on the period have to make do with published government reports, White Papers, secondary sources and interviews with contemporary officials or observers. Because this book deals mainly with the period since 1945 it was felt that the use of detailed official sources for the introductory chapter followed by the use of largely secondary sources for the rest of the book would lead to a somewhat unbalanced treatment of the subject. Consequently the decision was taken not to make detailed reference to the wartime records but instead to rely on the official histories and the relevant secondary literature. In so doing it was hoped to provide a more uniform and general coverage of the period which would fit in with the rest of the study.

The secondary literature on the post-war period tends to concentrate either on the defence policies of the two states (such as R. Rosecrance's *Defense of the Realm*, C. J. Bartlett's *The Long Retreat*, P. Darby's *British Defence Policy East of Suez 1947–1968*, S. Huntington, *The Common Defense* and M. E. Smith and C. J. Johns ed., *American Defense Policy*), or on Anglo-American relations more generally (such as H. G. Nicholas, *The United States and Britain*, H. C. Allen's *Great Britain and the United States* or C. Bell's *The Debatable Alliance*). There are, however, two main sources which are invaluable for the student of Anglo-American defence relations. One is Professor Margaret Gowing's *Independence and Deterrence*, Volumes I and II, and the other is Andrew Pierre's *Nuclear Politics*. Margaret Gowing's study is the first official history for the peacetime period to be produced. The two volumes cover the history of the British atomic energy programme from 1945 to 1952 and Professor Gowing was given free access to the British official documents on the subject, including those relating to Anglo-American relations. Andrew Pierre's book covers a much wider period of the post-war nuclear partnership but he did not have the benefit of access to either the American or British records. He was, however, a State Department official for a number of years and was on the staff of the US embassy in Britain during an important period of Anglo-American relations. As such, through his own personal experience, range of contacts, and detailed research he was able to produce an authoritative and widely respected book on an important area of the defence partnership. Both these sources have been widely used by this author.

Apart from the problems raised by the thirty-year rule in Britain,the absence of published official documents and the limited nature of the secondary literature on Anglo-American defence relations, there is another and related difficulty which arises from the sensitivity (sometimes understandable, sometimes less so) which exists in public circles over research into questions of national security. It is significant, for example, that although many of the British documents for the years 1946–9 have recently been opened, many of those relating to defence matters remain unavailable to the researcher. In the United States, where there is a somewhat more liberal attitude to these matters, the Freedom of Information Act provides researchers with access to government documents. Even here, however, it is the author's experience that documents relating to security and especially defence relations with foreign states are often difficult or impossible to see – even those covering the ten years after the war.*

One way of partially overcoming this problem is through correspondence and interviews with retired and serving officials (both military and civilian) who directly participated in the events covered by the research. The present author has undertaken a wide range of correspondence and conducted a large number of interviews with British and American officials in order to supplement the secondary sources used. One of the problems associated with this technique is that some officials, particularly those still serving, were only prepared to talk off-the-record and on no account were willing to be identified or quoted. Where this has happened the author has tried to use published references to support the point made. On occasions, however, this has not been possible. In these cases the fact that the information derived from an interview is recorded. This is not an altogether satisfactory arrangement but in most instances the information relates to interpretations of already known events rather than new or original information. In these circumstances the author felt justified in adopting this approach.

* The publication of the *Foreign Relations of the United States* (FRUS) series, up to 1951 at the time of writing, has to a certain extent helped to overcome this.

Notes

PREFACE

1. John Mander, *Great Britain or Little England?* (London: Penguin, 1963), p.21. He sees the 'special relationship' as ending on Tuesday, 23 October 1962. See p.75.
2. Lord Chalfont and Louis Heren have put forward this view.
3. *The Concise Oxford Dictionary* (Oxford: Oxford University Press, 1964).
4. A.C. Turner, *The Unique Partnership: Britain and the United States* (New York: Pegasus, 1971), p.5.
5. *Ibid., loc.cit.*
6. *Ibid., loc.cit.*
7. *Ibid., loc.cit.*
8. *Ibid.*, p.4.
9. H.C.Allen, *Great Britain and the United States: A History of Anglo-American Relations (1783–1952)* (London: Odhams Press, 1954), p.27.
10. H.G.Nicholas, *The United States and Britain* (Chicago: University of Chicago Press, 1975).
11. *Ibid.*, p.67.
12. C.Bell, *The Debatable Alliance* (London: Oxford University Press, 1964) and 'The special relationship' in M.Leifer (ed.), *Constraints and Adjustments in British Foreign Policy* (London: Allen & Unwin, 1972).
13. *Britain and the United States* (Council on Foreign Relations, New York and the Royal Institute of International Affairs, London, 1953), pp.vii and 7.
14. *Ibid.*
15. R.R.James, *Winston Churchill: His Complete Speeches, 1897–1963*, Vol. VII (London: Chelsea House Publishers, 1974), p.7289.
16. *Ibid., loc.cit.*
17. Turner, *op.cit.*, pp.1-2.
18. B.Brogan, *American Aspects* (New York: Harper & Row, 1964), p.71.
19. Turner, *op.cit.*, p.24.
20. G.Ball, *The Discipline of Power* (London: Bodley Head, 1968), p.91.
21. It is, of course, debatable whether this is true today although it is argued here that in the defence field at least a 'residual special relationship' does still exist.
22. Bell, 'The special relationship', *op.cit.*, p.119.
23. General Marshall's *Biennial Report*, 'The winning of the war in Europe

and the Pacific', (Biennial Report of the Chief of Staff of the US Army, 1 July 1943 to 30 June 1945, to Secretary of War).
24. C.Thorne, *Allies of a Kind: The United States, Britain and the War against Japan* (London: Hamish Hamilton, 1979), p.701.

INTRODUCTION: The Wartime Relationship

1. Thorne, *op.cit.*, p.699, Quoting from Nicholas, *op.cit.*, p.101.
2. See pp.21–2.
3. F.H.Hinsley with E.E.Thomas, C.F.G.Ransom and R.C.Knight, *British Intelligence in the Second World War*, Vol.I (London: HMSO, 1979) p.311. See also M.Matloff and E.Snell, *Strategic Planning for Coalition Warfare 1941–1942* (Washington: Office of the Chief of Military History, Dept. of the Army, 1953). Roosevelt also made his famous proposal for a conference to arrest the slide into war but it was turned down by the British Prime Minister, Neville Chamberlain.
4. See J.P.Lash, *Roosevelt and Churchill, 1939–1941: The Partnership that Saved the West* (New York: W.W.Norton & Company, 1976), p.63. See also K.J.Hagan (ed.), *In Peace and War: Interpretations of American Naval History 1775–1978* (London: Greenwood Press, 1978), p.239. I wish to express my thanks to my colleague Dr Ritchie Ovendale for information about the Ingersoll Mission and the Hampton visit.
5. T.B.Kittredge, *United States–British Naval Cooperation, 1940–45*, ms. study on microfilm at the New York Public Library, pp.37-58. An Air Mission was also sent to the United States in the spring of 1938. See H.D.Hall. *North American Supply* (London: HMSO, 1955), p.105.
6. Lash, *op.cit.*, p.64.
7. Nicholas, *op.cit.*, p.90.
8. The argument about President Roosevelt's 'indecision' is not one which is shared by all authors. See, for example, Lash, *op.cit.*, p.10.
9. Hall, *op.cit.*, pp.44-5.
10. *Ibid.*, p.44.
11. Quoted in *Ibid.*, p.45.
12. *Ibid.*, p.44.
13. J.R.M.Butler, *Grand Strategy*, Vol. II (London: HMSO, 1957), p.417.
14. Hall, *op.cit.*, pp.72-5.
15. *Ibid.*, pp.131-5.
16. Butler, *op.cit.*, p.240. This didn't necessarily mean that US interests were viewed in Washington, as they tended to be viewed by Churchill, as being one and the same. See Thorne, *op.cit.*, p.78.
17. Butler, *op.cit.*, p.239.
18. Hall, *op.cit.*, p.136.
19. Butler, *op.cit.*, pp.44-5.
20. *Ibid.*, p.245.
21. *Ibid., loc.cit.*

22. *Ibid., loc.cit.*
23. Hall, *op.cit.*, p.140.
24. W.S.Churchill, *Their Finest Hour* (London: Cassell, 1949), p.409.
25. *Ibid.* Churchill went on to say: 'I could not stop it if I wished: no one can stop it. Like the Mississippi it just keeps rolling along.'
26. Hall, *op.cit.*, p.140.
27. *Ibid.*, pp.156-7, 170-1 and 193.
28. Butler, *op.cit.*, p.341.
29. Hall, *op.cit.*, p.191.
30. Butler, *op.cit.*, p.423.
31. *Ibid.* See also Nicholas, *op.cit.*, p.96. Despite the importance of these talks in the development of a closer partnership between the two countries there apparently 'existed a wariness on the American side concerning what was thought to be an inbred British skill at manouvering and self-seeking'. Thus, for example, presidentially-approved instructions to the American representatives at the 1941 Washington Staff talks stated: 'It is believed we cannot afford, nor do we need, to entrust our national future to British direction . . . it is to be expected that the proposals of the British representatives will have been drawn up with chief regard for the British Commonwealth. Never absent from British minds are their post-war interests, commercial or military. We should likewise safeguard our own eventual interests.' See K.R.Greenfield, *Command Decisions* (Washington: Department of the Army, 1960) p.32.
32. H.D.Hall and C.C.Wrigley, *Studies of Overseas Supply* (London: HMSO, 1956), pp.360-1.
33. M.Gowing, *Britain and Atomic Energy 1939–45*, (London: Macmillan, 1964), p.64.
34. Hall and Wrigley, *op.cit.*, p.375. See also W.Stevenson, *A Man Called Intrepid: The Secret War 1939–45*, (London: Macmillan, 1976), p.174.
35. Hall, *op.cit.*, p.299.
36. Hinsley, *et al, op.cit.*, pp.311-14.
37. See p.1
38. A number of books have recently been written about William Stephenson. These include H.Hyde, *The Quiet Canadian* (London: Hamish Hamilton, 1962) and William Stevenson, *op.cit.* It is difficult from the material made available so far to discover what is fact or fiction in these accounts. There is enough evidence available, however, to suggest that they should be treated with some circumspection. See F.H.Hinsley, *op.cit.*, pp.487-95, and D.Hunt, 'Looking-glass war' in *The Times Literary Supplement*, 28 May 1976.
39. Hinsley, *op.cit.*, p.312.
40. *Ibid.*
41. *Ibid.*
42. *Ibid.* p.313. Trust between the two countries in the intelligence field was not, however, complete in the pre-Pearl Harbour period. Britain apparently broke at least one of the codes used by the State Department itself. Churchill wrote to Roosevelt on 25 February

1942 saying that 'some time ago . . . our experts claimed to have discovered and constructed some tables used by your Diplomatic Corps. From the moment when we became allies [i.e., presumably, December 1941] I gave instructions that this work should cease. However, the danger of our enemies having achieved a measure of success cannot, I am advised, be dismissed.' WSC to FDR, 25 Feb. 1942, Roosevelt Papers, MR box 7A. Quoted in Thorne, *op.cit.*, p.112. Speculation in brackets added by Thorne.

43. Intelligence components of the British Army and Naval Delegations to the Joint Staff Mission were formed in April 1941. The Air Ministry, however, didn't set up a special intelligence section in Washington until after the American entry into the war. *Ibid.*, pp.313-14.
44. *Ibid.*, p.313.
45. *Ibid.*, p.314.
46. Hall, *op.cit.*, p.209.
47. Allen, *op.cit.*, pp.812-13. See also Nicholas, *op.cit.*, p.95 and Lash *op.cit.*, p.263.
48. Allen, *op.cit.*, p.810 and Nicholas, *op.cit.*, p.96.
49. Hall, *op.cit.*, p.255.
50. Nicholas, *op.cit.*, p.96.
51. I.S.MacDonald, *Anglo-American Relations since the Second World War* (London: David & Charles, 1974), pp.18-19.
52. R.E.Sherwood, *Roosevelt and Hopkins* (New York: Harper & Brothers, 1948), pp.270-1. Robert Sherwood identifies nine developments in the 'common-law alliance' which had occurred by the spring of 1941.
53. *Ibid.*, p.374.
54. R.E.Sherwood, *The White House Papers of H.L.Hopkins*, Vol.I (London: Eyre & Spottiswoode, 1948), p.384.
55. The point here is not that the United States had made the most of the period from the outbreak of war to Pearl Harbour to prepare for war, but that, given the prevailing attitude in Congress to stay out of the war, the US were perhaps better prepared than might have been expected.
56. J.M.A.Gwyer, *Grand Strategy*, Vol.III, Part I (London: HMSO, 1964), p.349.
57. J.Ehrman, *Grand Strategy*, Vol.V (London: HMSO, 1956), p.19.
58. Gwyer, *op.cit.*, p.383.
59. Hall, *op.cit.*, p.403.
60. The Plan involved a pooling of production. See Gwyer, *op.cit.*, p.396.
61. *Ibid.*, p.399. For the limitations of the Combined Boards see Hall, *op.cit.*, p.378 and J.R.M.Butler and J.M.A.Gwyer, *Grand Strategy*, Vol.III, Part 2 (London: HMSO, 1964), pp.545 and 558-9.
62. Hall and Wrigley, *op.cit.*, p.233.
63. Hall, *op.cit.*, p.60.
64. Quoted in Hall, *op.cit.*, p.352. Hall suggests that 'nowhere else was there this personal intimacy, this deep mutual trust and confidence,

this degree of sharing secrets, this daily routine of working together in collaboration'. *Ibid.*, pp.348-9.

65. H.L.Stimson and M.Bundy, *On Active Service in Peace and War* (New York: Harper & Brothers, 1948), pp.413-14.
66. *Ibid.*
67. Hall and Wrigley, *op.cit.*, p.211.
68. P.Gore-Booth, *With Great Truth and Respect* (London: Constable, 1974), p.121.
69. Thorne, *op.cit.*, p.725.
70. Butler and Gwyer, *op.cit.*, pp.630-4.
71. See M. Howard, *Grand Strategy*, Vol.IV (London: HMSO, 1972), p.xv.
72. *Ibid., loc.cit.*
73. Butler and Gwyer, *op.cit.*, p.563.
74. K.Sainsbury, 'Second front in 1942: Anglo-American differences over strategy', *British Journal of International Studies (BJIS)*, Vol.4, No.1, April 1978, p.55.
75. *Ibid., loc.cit.*
76. Thorne, *op.cit.*, p.136.
77. See Howard, *op.cit.*, pp. XV-XXV.
78. Allen, *op.cit.*, pp.846-7.
79. J.Ehrman, *Grand Strategy* Vol.VI (London: HMSO, 1956), p.89. According to Robert Sherwood, however, 'One can read the official minutes without suspecting that a single harsh word had been exchanged'. R.Sherwood, *The White House Papers of Harry L. Hopkins, op.cit.*, p.848.
80. See Howard, *op.cit.*, pp.25-6 and the various volumes of S.W.Roskill, *The War at Sea* (London: HMSO, 1954-61) and C.Webster and A.N.Frankland, *The Strategic Air Offensive against Germany 1939–45* (London: HMSO, 1961).
81. Ehrman, *op.cit.*, Vol.V, pp.284-5.
82. There were, of course, also differences between the two countries over Japan before September 1939 and between the outbreak of war and Pearl Harbour. See Thorne, *op.cit.*, Part 1 and R.Callahan, *The Worst Disaster: The Fall of Singapore* (London: Associated University Presses, 1977).
83. This was due largely to the rapid pace of the Japanese advances.
84. Ismay to Auckinleck, 8 Dec. 1944, *Ismay Papers*, IV/Con/1/1H. Quoted in Thorne, *op.cit.*, p.719.
85. See R.Callahan, *Burma 1942–45* (London: Davis-Poynter, 1978).
86. R.E.Sherwood, *The White House Papers of Harry L.Hopkins, op.cit.*, p.776.
87. Thorne, *op.cit.*, pp.409-10.
88. *Ibid.*
89. Davies to Hopkins, 16 Jan. 1944, Roosevelt Papers, M.R.box 10. Quoted in Thorne, *loc.cit.*
90. Ehrman, *op.cit.*, Vol.V, p.490.
91. There were also differences over the attitudes to China; the future of

Hong Kong; the British fleet in the Pacific; and the French in Indochina.

92. Thorne, *op.cit.*, p.725.
93. *Ibid.*
94. *Ibid.*
95. *Ibid.*
96. *Ibid.*
97. See below p. 5. See also Gowing, *op.cit.*, p. 64.
98. *Ibid.*, pp.45-89.
99. *Ibid.*, p.80.
100. The Maud Report had a decisive influence on Dr Bush and Dr Conant in the United States. Professor Gowing regards this as being more important in its impact on US policy than the report of Professors Pegram and Urey. *Ibid.*, p.121.
101. *Ibid.*, p.123.
102. *Ibid.*, p.125. Much of the collaboration which subsequently took place occurred between Britain, the United States *and* Canada. Consideration here, however, is only given to Anglo-American cooperation.
103. *Ibid.*, p.97.
104. *Ibid., loc.cit.*
105. *Ibid.*, p.123. Discussions took place between Mr Hovde, the US scientific liaison officer in London and Sir John Anderson at the end of November 1941. In these discussions Sir John Anderson told Mr Hovde (somewhat ironically in the light of the subsequent case of Dr Fuchs) that, although the British government wanted to collaborate with the United States, they were concerned about the leakage of information to the enemy.
106. *Ibid.*, p.122.
107. The British scientists felt that they were still ahead on the theoretical work but they discovered that American scientists were moving ahead of them on all the processes of producing fissile material. *Ibid.*, pp.128-31.
108. W.Churchill, *The Second World War*, Vol.IV, *The Hinge of Fate* (London: Cassell, 1951), pp.374-81.
109. The decision by Bush and Conant to go slow on collaboration with Britain was supported by the President and Mr Stimson, the Secretary of War.
110. Gowing, *ibid.*, pp.155-60.
111. Churchill received promises of a resumption of information exchange at both conferences but nothing came from the American assurances.
112. The Americans refused to accept Mr Akers as the British technical adviser to the Combined Policy Committee set up by the Quebec Agreement because of his industrial connections with ICI.
113. An agreement was drafted by Churchill and Anderson to give the Americans assurances about Britain's commercial disinterestedness which was later to constitute the first four articles of the Quebec Agreement.

114. Gowing, *op.cit.*, p.169.
115. See Appendix 1.
116. Article 4.
117. Article 5(b).
118. Article 5(c). This stemmed largely from pressure from the US military to restrict the range of information exchange and reflected the view expressed in the Conant memorandum. See below p.17.
119. Gowing, *op.cit.*, p.234.
120. *Ibid., loc.cit.*
121. *Ibid.*, p.287.
122. See Appendix 3.
123. Article 2 (author's emphasis).
124. Apart from Roosevelt and Churchill, the only other people to know about the President's post-war intentions were Dr Bush and Lord Cherwell. None of the atomic energy people in Washington from Mr Stimson, the Secretary of War down, was to know of the Agreement until April 1945 (when they had to ask the British government to supply them with a copy).
125. Dr Bush apparently 'said nothing' when Roosevelt talked to him and Lord Cherwell about post-war cooperation. Gowing, *op.cit.*, p.341.
126. The first atomic bomb test in New Mexico took place on 16 July.
127. These include Hinsley *et al, op.cit.*, Hyde, *op.cit.*, F.W.Winterbotham *The Ultra Secret* (London: Weidenfeld & Nicolson, 1974), D.Khan, *The Codebreakers* (London: Weidenfeld & Nicolson, 1974), R.Lewin, *Ultra goes to War: The Secret Story* (London: Hutchinson, 1978).
128. Stevenson, *op.cit.*, p.16.
129. Hinsley *et al., op.cit.*, p.491.
130. See p.6.
131. W.Stevenson has suggested that Intrepid (William Stephenson) acted as a go-between for Churchill and Roosevelt from 1940 and passed on occasional carefully selected items of ULTRA intelligence. There is, as yet, however, no firm documentary evidence to suggest that Roosevelt was informed about ULTRA itself, although intelligence (from that source) may have been passed on.
132. R.Lewin, *Ultra goes to War: The Secret Story* (London: Hutchinson, 1978), pp.238-9. At the time of writing F.Hinsley's second volume of *British Intelligence in the Second World War* has not been published. Considerably more information about intelligence cooperation between the two countries will no doubt be contained in this and the third volume when they appear.
133. *Ibid.*, p.245.
134. *Ibid.*, p.239.
135. See *Ibid.*, pp.240-2. The close relationship between SIS and the Office of Strategic Services (OSS) set up by Colonel Donovan in July 1941 apparently led to friction with the FBI under J.Edgar Hoover. He resented the emergence of a rival intelligence agency like the OSS. The friction between BSC and the FBI is dealt with by Kim Philby in his book *My Silent War* (London: MacGibbon & Kee, 1968). Philby himself, however, is also reported as having sabotaged

the close links between the intelligence agencies. See W.Stevenson, *op.cit.*, pp.419, 432.

136. According to Sir William Stephenson, 'Battles were won because we had advance knowledge of enemy plans, could influence those plans, and could anticipate enemy actions by methods heretofore concealed'. Stevenson, *op.cit.*, p.16.
137. Lewin, *op.cit.*, p.262.
138. W.Churchill, *The Grand Alliance* (London: Cassell, 1950), pp.608-9.
139. *General Marshall's Biennial Report, op.cit.*
140. Ehrman, Vol.VI, *op.cit.*, p.350.
141. Hall, *op.cit.*, p.304.
142. Nicholas, *op.cit.*, p.98.

CHAPTER 1: DISCORD AND COLLABORATION 1945–49

1. See below p.2. Churchill had dreams during the war of some form of Anglo-American 'reunification', perhaps by means of a common citizenship. There are those who argue, of course, that the Prime Minister had a somewhat idealistic view of the relationship. See Thorne, *op.cit.*, pp.277-8.
2. Nicholas, *op.cit.*, p.94.
3. M. Gowing, *Independence and Deterrence: Britain and Atomic Energy, 1945–52*, Vol.I (London: Macmillan, 1974), p.94. This chapter owes a great debt to this particular source.
4. *Ibid., op.cit.* The British raised the possibility of the continuation, on a regular basis, of the Combined Chiefs of Staff machinery after the war ended. Little, however, came of this initiative. The Americans 'returned only unofficial benevolent replies'. See Ehrman, Vol.6, *op.cit.*, p.347.
5. Gowing, *Britain and Atomic Energy*, pp.241-3.
6. See Appendix 3. Roger Makins (now Lord Sherfield) has said that 'on strict interpretation', the Quebec and Hyde Park Agreements were 'valid for the war period only, and they therefore provided a rather weak basis for the claim that collaboration and exchange of information should continue in time of peace'. See Rt.Hon.Lord Sherfield, 'Britain's nuclear story, 1945–52: Politics and technology', *Round Table*, April 1975, No.258, p.194. David Carlton has suggested that this throws 'a great deal of doubt on . . . Professor Gowing's judgements' about the Agreements. See D.Charlton, 'Great Britain and nuclear weapons: the academic inquest', *British Journal of International Studies,* Vol.2, No.2, July 1976. The present author, however, would tend to agree with Elizabeth Young's view that 'A look at the agreements shows that Lord Sherfield's 1975 statement throws doubt on the quality of his own recollection rather than on Mrs Gowing's judgement'. See the *British Journal of International Studies*, Vol.3. No.1, April 1977, p.119.
7. For a discussion of the passage of the McMahon Act see Gowing, *Independence and Deterrence*, pp.104-12. (Further references to M.Gowing in this chapter refer to this study.)

8. See below p.19.
9. Early in September 1945 Truman himself agreed that 'we must take Russia into our confidence'. Less than a month later, however, he suggested that he might share scientific knowledge but not engineering secrets with the Soviet Union. See R.G.Hewlett and O.Anderson, *The History of USAEC: The New World* Vol.I, (Pennsylvania: Pennsylvania U.P., 1962), pp.419, 455-9.
10. James Byrnes, the US Secretary of State, in particular opposed sharing secrets with the Soviet Union.
11. Ernest Bevin for a time believed that 'we should take the risk of giving information to the Russians' as did the British Ambassador in Moscow, Sir Archibald Clark-Kerr. Further problems with Russia, however, led Bevin to adopt a 'tougher line'. The COS advised that failure to achieve international control would mean that Britain would require a deterrent 'of our own' to safeguard national security. See Gowing, *op.cit.*, pp.67-72.
12. Gouzenko was a cipher clerk in the office of the Soviet Military Attache in Ottawa. He defected on 6 September 1945, revealing an extensive Russian spy network in Canada.
13. See Gowing, *op.cit.*, pp.82-4. See Appendix 4. Although this study focuses on Anglo-American relations it is the case that in the nuclear field especially many of the early agreements included Canada.
14. *Ibid.*, p.75.
15. *Ibid.*, p.76.
16. *Ibid., loc.cit.*
17. The 'Groves–Anderson' memorandum of 16 November 1945. *Ibid.*, pp.85-6. See Appendix 5.
18. In a meeting of the Combined Policy Committee (CPC) in April 1946 Byrnes told the British Ambassador that he had not seen either the November 1945 Washington Agreement or the 'Groves–Anderson' memorandum before that meeting. In fact Byrnes had been chairman of the CPC meeting in December 1945 at which both documents were discussed. Dr Bush also told Chadwick at this time that he believed in full collaboration with Britain and yet there is evidence that he was in fact opposed to close cooperation with Britain because he believed it would impede international control. See Hewlett and Anderson, *op.cit.*, pp.459, 469. See also Gowing *op.cit.*, p.100.
19. *Ibid.*, p.101. Truman's reply seemed like a 'solicitor's letter' to the Canadians. The British Ambassador, Lord Halifax, advised the government 'that the President is not very well informed on the whole matter and that his telegrams on the subject were probably drafted for him by others'. *Ibid.*, p.109.
20. F.Williams, *A Prime Minister Remembers* (London: Heineman, 1961), p.117. See Note 6, p.211.
21. 'His Majesty's Government do not accept the view . . . that we have ceased to be a Great Power. . . .' Hansard's Parliamentary Debates, Fifth series, House of Commons, Vol.437, col.1965 (16 May 1947) (hereafter H.C.Deb).

22. Gowing, *op.cit.*, pp.179-85.
23. Williams, *op.cit.*, pp.118-19.
24. See below pp.72–4.
25. Gowing, *op.cit.*, p.115.
26. See Sir Leonard Owen, 'Nuclear Engineering in the United Kingdom: The First Ten Years', *Journal of the British Nuclear Energy Society*, January 1963.
27. Gowing, *op.cit.*, p.114.
28. See Chapter 3.
29. Gowing, *op.cit.*, p.94.
30. *Ibid., loc.cit.*
31. See Appendix 2.
32. Lord Sherfield, *op.cit.*, p.194.
33. *Ibid.*, pp.194-5.
34. *Ibid., loc.cit.*
35. See R.R.James (ed.), *Winston S. Churchill: His Complete Speeches, 1897–1963* Vol. VII, *op.cit.*, pp.7285–93.
36. *Ibid., loc.cit.* See also Turner, *op.cit.*, pp.1-3.
37. See Gowing, *op.cit.*, p.94.
38. W.Millis (ed.), *The Forrestal Diaries* (London: Cassell, 1952), p.185-185-6.
39. Field-Marshal Montgomery, *The Memoirs of Field-Marshal the Viscount Montgomery of Alamein, K.G.* (London: Collins, 1958), p.437.
40. *Ibid.*, p.440. (This is not to say that British politicians were not considering the possibility of a Soviet threat. See War Cabinet Minutes of 3 April 1945, WM(45) 39th. Conclusions, Minute I, Confidential Annex, *CAB 65/52.*)
41. *Ibid.*, p.441.
42. *Ibid.*, p.442.
43. *Ibid.*, p.441.
44. *Ibid.*, p.442.
45. *Ibid., loc.cit.*
46. *Ibid., loc.cit.*
47. *Ibid.*, pp.442-3.
48. *Ibid.*, p.450.
49. See C.J.Bartlett, *The Long Retreat: A Short History of British Defence Policy, 1945–70* (London: Macmillan, 1972), p.47.
50. Gowing, *op.cit.*, p.258.
51. *Ibid.*, p.413.
52. 'Notes of the month', *The World Today*, Vol.16, No.8, August 1960, p.319.
53. *Ibid., loc.cit.*
54. Gowing, *op.cit.*, p.117.
55. *Ibid., loc.cit.*
56. This was also a feature of many of the other exclusive agreements and arrangements which were to follow.
57. Gowing, *op.cit.*, p.94.
58. R.N.Rosecrance, *Defense of the Realm: British Strategy in the*

Nuclear Epoch (London: Columbia University Press, 1968), p.50.
59. See Field-Marshal Montgomery, *op.cit.*, p.442.
60. In some respects a new 'Common-law' alliance was being established. It was not until December 1947 that 'Britain began to think of a military alliance, and even then US policy-makers held back'. Rosecrance, *op.cit.*, p.50.
61. *Ibid.*, pp. 50-1.
62. *Foreign Relations of the United States* (*FRUS*), 1947, Vol.5, Department of State Publication (DOS), 8592, p.485.
63. Gowing, *op.cit.*, p.91.
64. *ibid.*, 242. Bevin first raised the subject with Marshall after the London Foreign Ministers Conference in December, 1947.
65. Millis (ed.), *op.cit.*, p.392. For an analysis of British wartime planning on a European Security Group see T.A. Imobighe, *War-time Influences affecting Britain's Attitude to a post-war Continental Commitment* Ph.D. Thesis, University of Wales, October 1975).
66. Millis, *op.cit.*, p.400.
67. G.Williams and B.Reed, *Denis Healey and the Policies of Power* (London: Sidgwick & Jackson, 1971), p.71.
68. Rosecrance, *op.cit.*, p.76.
69. Millis, *op.cit.*, p.448.
70. See P.Williams, 'The United States and Western Europe: A conditional commitment', *Interstate*, Vol.3, No.2, 1978, pp.16-20.
71. Millis, *op.cit.*
72. *Ibid., loc.cit.*
73. Gowing, *op.cit.*, p.242.
74. See *The World Today, op.cit.*, The initial decision was taken on 28 June 1948.
75. *Ibid.*, pp.319-20.
76. Millis, *op.cit.*, p.430.
77. See Gowing, *op.cit.*, p.310 fn.
78. *The World Today, op.cit.*, p.320.
79. Gowing, *op.cit.*, p.312.
80. *Ibid., loc.cit.*
81. *The World Today, op.cit.*, pp.322-3.
82. *Ibid., loc.cit.* The 'Attlee-Churchill Understandings' were reiterated as an arrangement with the Eisenhower administration after discussions between Eden and Dulles in Washington in March 1953.
83. Gowing, *op.cit.*, p.242.
84. *Ibid.*, p.243.
85. A.Pierre, *Nuclear Politics: The British Experience with an Independent Strategic Force, 1939–1970* (London: Oxford University Press, 1972), p.129. This study has provided the author with a major source on Anglo-American nuclear relations.
86. Gowing, *op.cit.*, p.243.
87. R.G.Hewlett and F.Duncan, *The History of USAEC: Atomic Shield*, Vol.II, *1947–52* (Pennsylvania, Pennsylvania State University Press, 1969), p.279 and *passim* (author's emphasis).

88. This was a general declaration of intent designed to establish a working relationship between the two countries (and Canada).
89. Lord Sherfield described this as 'a Roland for an Oliver'. He argues that 'Clause 2 was intolerable to the Americans, Clause 4 was intolerable to the British. . . . They were well out of the way.' Lord Sherfield takes issue with Professor Gowing's criticism of the decision to drop Clause 2. He describes it as 'unrealistic and unenforceable'. He also sees abrogation of Clause 4 as being very important from the British point of view. See 'Britain's Nuclear Story', *op.cit.*, p.195. In a letter to the author (8 September 1978) Professor Gowing has rejected this interpretation. She points out that Britain had begun its industrial project in 1946 and 'so Sherfield's point that Clause 4 abrogation was essential to the British carries no weight'. 'It is noteworthy', she says, 'that the Groves–Anderson memorandum of November 1945 in recommending the terms of a new Agreement replaced Clause 2 of Quebec but not Clause 4'.
90. This view is attributed to Lord Sherfield by Professor Gowing, *op. cit.*, p.252.
91. A report produced by Zinn and Weil in mid-1948 after a visit to Britain emphasized that the British were concentrating on plutonium production and the military applications of nuclear energy. This apparently shook 'everyone in the USAEC' and 'caused a terrific sensation in the Joint Congressional Committee'. *Ibid.*, pp.255, 258.
92. Professor Gowing suggests that 'the egg of the *modus vivendi* was addled' but like the curate's egg it was 'good in parts'. She concludes, however, that 'it is doubtful whether the good parts were ever worth what had been given up for them'. *Ibid.*, p.264.
93. *Ibid.*, p.253.
94. *Ibid.*, p.254.
95. Lord Sherfield, *op.cit.*, p.195.
96. *Ibid., loc.cit.*
97. *Ibid.*, pp. 275, 282-8. See also *The Journals of David E. Lilienthal, Vol.II: The Atomic Energy Years, 1945–1950* (London: Harper & Row, 1964), p.548.
98. Gowing, *op.cit.*, p.278.
99. More specifically the British proposals involved: providing the US with the raw materials for an expanded programme; full technical cooperation; the US to supply Britain with U-235 in exchange for plutonium (but Britain would retain freedom to build a high-separation plant if US supplies were not forthcoming); the US to fabricate most of the cores and initiators for British bombs (but Britain would retain freedom to build prototype plants); Britain would not object to the storage of the larger part of nuclear components of weapons in Canada; Britain would drop her third pile but keep the low-separation plant; there would be common test grounds. *Ibid.*, p.293.
100. The British Chiefs of Staff wanted definite assurances from the US about the creation of a stockpile of about twenty atomic bombs in the UK. Dawson and Rosecrance see this decision as an 'extra-

ordinary act of self-abnegation'. They suggest that this indicates that traditional affinities rather than calculations of national interest are at the heart of the alliance. See R.Dawson and R.Rosecrance, 'Theory and reality in the Anglo-American Alliance', *World Politics*, Vol.19, 1966–7. For a critique of this view see J.Baylis, 'The Anglo-American relationship in defence', in *British Defence Policy in a Changing World* (London: Croom Helm, 1977), p.73.

101. The Americans were urging a merged weapons project involving an 'integrated effort of raw materials, brains and plants'. They were not happy about a stockpile of bombs in Britain or a binding agreement. Gowing, *op.cit.*, p.298.
102. *Ibid., loc.cit.*

CHAPTER 2: COLLABORATION AND DISCORD 1950–56

1. *FRUS*, 1950 Western Europe, Vol.3. 'Documents Relating to the Exchange of Classified Military Information Between the United States and the United Kingdom', Secret, 611.41/1-1750, pp.1617-27. The seven documents were circulated within the Departments of State and Defence as MIC 206/70. Maj. Gen. James H.Burns was Assistant to the Secretary of Defence and Lt.Gen. Sir Gerald Templer was Vice Chief of the Imperial General Staff. See Appendix 7.
2. Document A, 'Policy Statement regarding US–UK Exchange of Classified Military Information', *ibid.*, p.1617.
3. Gowing, *op.cit.*, p.242.
4. See p.125.
5. See p.95.
6. The British were apparently given to expect £500 million over a three-year period, but no formal pledge was received from the US. See Rosecrance, *op.cit.*, p.139.
7. *Ibid.*, p.140.
8. R.Rose, *The Relation of Socialist Principles to British Labour Foreign Policy, 1945–51* (unpublished D.Phil. thesis, Oxford 1959), pp.333-4.
9. *Observer*, 27 August 1950.
10. Rosecrance, *op.cit.*, p.141. Rose also argued that 'one factor behind the rearmament programme was the attempt to show the United States that Britain was making great sacrifices for defence, and thus ensure American assistance in the defence of Europe'.
11. *FRUS*, 1950, Vol.3, Western Europe, Conference Files: Lot 59 D95: CF49, 'Final Communiqué Agreed to by President Truman and Prime Minister Attlee', Secret, DOS, Washington, 8 December 1950, pp.1783-7.
12. R.B.Manderson-Jones, *The Special Relationship: Anglo-American Relations and Western European Union 1947–56* (London: Weidenfeld & Nicolson, 1972), p.75.
13. *Congressional Record, Appendix*, 81st Congress, 1st Session, p.A5690 (7 September 1949).
14. *FRUS*, 1950, Vol.3, Western Europe, *op.cit.*, pp.1706-87. At a

meeting between Truman and Attlee in December 1950 arrangements were made to establish closer informal contact between US and UK military authorities. It was proposed that there should be regular weekly meetings and special *ad hoc* meetings at times of emergency between representatives of the British Chiefs of Staff in Washington and the American Chiefs of Staff. See *Ibid.*, 'US and UK Liaison Arrangements', p.1782-3.

15. *Washington Post*, 22 July 1949.
16. *Congressional Record, op.cit.* In the words of Hubert Humphrey: 'Make no mistake about it. Britain is our one and only powerful ally. An insolvent and impoverished Britain will be a liability. A solvent, productive Britain can act as our outer fortress.'
17. T. Geiger and H. van B. Cleveland, *Making Western Europe Defensible.* Quoted in Bartlett, *op.cit.*, p.269, fn.27.
18. 486 H.C. Deb., 19 April 1951, Col.2007.
19. For a discussion of Anglo-American differences over the Korean War and especially the friction over China see B. Porter, *Britain and the Rise of Communist China* (London: Oxford University Press, 1967) and R. Boardman, *Britain and the People's Republic of China 1959–74* (London: Macmillan, 1976).
20. See Manderson-Jones, *op.cit.*, p.113. Both Dulles and Eisenhower emphasized at this time that the 'special relationship was over'. Eisenhower made a conscious effort 'to treat Britain more or less as just another ally'.
21. See *The Memoirs of Sir Anthony Eden: Full Circle* (London: Cassell, 1960), pp.96-9.
22. H. Macmillan, *Tides of Fortune, 1945–55* (London: Macmillan, 1969), p.499.
23. Eden, *op.cit.*, pp.34-6.
24. *Ibid.*, pp.32-4.
25. *Ibid.*, p.47.
26. *Ibid.*, p.55.
27. *Ibid.*, p.57.
28. *Ibid.*, pp.57-8.
29. *Ibid., loc.cit.*
30. Nicholas, *op.cit.*, p.152.
31. Restraints were also placed upon West German development of nuclear weapons.
32. Eden, *op.cit.*, p.166.
33. Gowing, *op.cit.*, p.304.
34. *Ibid.*, p.307.
35. *Ibid., loc.cit.*
36. *Ibid.*, p.308.
37. *Ibid.*, p.315.
38. *Ibid.*, p.316.
39. *Ibid.*, pp.413-4. Churchill, however, did not succeed in improving all aspects of the defence relationship. See pp.45 and 52.
40. *Ibid.*, p.414.
41. Rosecrance, *op.cit.*, p.159.

42. Gowing, *op.cit.*, pp.440-3.
43. *Ibid.*, p.441.
44. *Ibid., loc.cit.*
45. Rosecrance, *op.cit.*, p.169.
46. See S.M.R.Robinson, *The Global Strategy Paper: The Context and Significance of the Chiefs of Staff Paper, 1952, in British Defence Policy* (unpublished M.Sc. (Econ) Dissertation, University of Wales, Aberystwyth 1973).
47. Gowing, *op.cit.*, p.407.
48. *Ibid.*, pp.407, 410-11.
49. *Ibid.*, p.411.
50. 505 H.C.Deb. Col.1270-1 (23 October 1952). Chapman Pincher has argued that a group called *The Nomination Committee*, consisting of British and American Scientists, was in fact set up in 1953 to exchange intelligence about Russia's atomic activities. See *Inside Story: A Documentary of the Pursuit of Power* (London: Book Club Associates, 1978), pp.148-9. It is difficult to establish how accurate this claim is.
51. Pierre, *op.cit.*, p.137.
52. *Ibid., loc.cit.*
53. *Public Law* 703, 83rd Congress, 2nd Session.
54. *Agreement for Co-operation on the Peaceful Uses of Atomic Energy*, Cmd.9560 and the *Agreement for Co-operation Regarding Atomic Information for Mutual Defence Purposes*, Treaty Series, No.2905, Cmd.9555. See Appendix 8 for the latter.
55. R. Rosecrance argues that negotiations began in 1955 on 'what has been one of the most fruitful but least talked about areas of Anglo-American nuclear co-operation', that of plutonium-uranium 235 exchange. This in fact does not seem to have been achieved until 1959, see p.60; see also Rosecrance *op.cit.*, p.217.
56. Pierre, *op.cit.*, p.139.
57. *Ibid., loc.cit.*
58. This in some ways foreshadowed a later agreement in May 1959 which led to the *sale* of a marine nuclear propulsion plant for the first British nuclear submarine, *Dreadnought*. See the *Amendment to the Agreement between the Government of Great Britain and Northern Ireland and the Government of the United States of America for co-operation on the Uses of Atomic Energy for Mutual Defence Purposes* of 3 July 1958. Cmnd. 859. UN Treaty Series 4707, See Appendix 11. Polaris missiles could theoretically be fired from surface ships (see later MLF proposals, p.77). They were, however, designed mainly for use from submarines.
59. Both Eisenhower and Dulles were critical of the British emphasis on a continuing 'special relationship' with the US at this time. See *The Times*, 26 January 1980, and 28 January 1980.
60. Nicholas, *op.cit.*, p.153.
61. See for example S.Lloyd, *Suez 1956: A Personal Account* (London: Jonathan Cape, 1978); H.Thomas, *The Suez Affair* (London: Weidenfeld & Nicolson, 1966); K.Love, *Suez, the Twice-Fought War* (London:

Longmans, 1970); C.Pineau, *1956 Suez* (Paris: R.Lamont, 1976); M.Dayan, *Diary of the Sinai Campaign* (London: Weidenfeld & Nicolson, 1966) and *Story of My Life* (London: Weidenfeld & Nicolson, 1976); A.J.Barker, *Suez: The Seven Days War* (London: Faber & Faber, 1967).

62. Dawson and Rosecrance, *op.cit.*, p.40. There is also evidence, however, of a certain support for British actions amongst the US military. See R.Fullick and G.Powell, *Suez: The Double War* (London: Hamish Hamilton, 1979), p.36.
63. As H.G.Nicholas has said: '. . . as far as Anglo-American relations are concerned, the basic trouble was that in connection with the complex of issues which Suez represented there was no mutuality of interests between Britain and America.' *Op.cit.*, p.155.

CHAPTER 3: THE PREFERENTIAL RELATIONSHIP 1957–1962

1. See Dawson and Rosecrance, *op.cit.*, pp.41, 48-9.
2. H.Macmillan, *Riding the Storm* (London: Macmillan, 1971), p.176.
3. I am grateful to the owners of the Churchill copyright for permission to reproduce this letter.
4. Macmillan, *Riding the Storm, loc.cit.*
5. *Ibid.*, p.245.
6. *Ibid.*, p.260. See the 'Exchange of notes (with enclosed memorandum) constituting an agreement relating to intermediate range ballistic missiles', Washington, 22 February 1958, *United Nations Treaty Series*, 1958. No.4451. Appendix 9.
7. D.D.Eisenhower, *Waging Peace* (New York: Doubleday, 1965), p.124.
8. *The Times*, 26 October 1957.
9. Macmillan, *Riding the Storm*, p.322.
10. *Ibid.*, p.316.
11. *Ibid.*, p.324.
12. *Ibid.*, pp.756-9 (author's emphasis).
13. See Appendix 10, *Treaty Series* 4707.
14. Senate Report 1634, House Report 1859, 85 Congress, 2 sess., p.12. See also R.E.Osgood, *NATO: The Entangling Alliance* (London: University of Chicago Press, 1962), p.403.
15. The Act was amended in 1959, 1968, 1969 and 1974. See Appendices 10, 11 and 13. See pp.109-110. The 1958 Act was divided into three main aspects. The first aspect was a general one 'allowing communication of information and transfer of equipment and materials'. The second component extended the scope of the information exchanges authorized by the 1955 military agreement to include 'the development of delivery systems compatible with the atomic weapons which they carry' and research development, and design of military reactors. It also allowed 'the exchange of classified information on atomic weapons if this would improve the recipients' atomic weapon design, development and fabrication capability'. The third aspect provided for

the transfer to the UK by the US of a submarine nuclear propulsion reactor and limited quantities of U-235 to fuel it. See 'The Anglo-American Nuclear Relationship and its implications for the choice of a possible successor to the current Polaris force', Memorandum by Dr John Simpson to the Defence and External Affairs Sub-Committee, February 1979. *Sixth Report from the Expenditure Committee: The Future of the United Kingdom's Nuclear Weapons Programme*, session 1978-79, No.348, p.226 (hereafter *Sixth Report*).

16. See Appendix 11. The amendment to the 1958 Act (Cmnd.859) was signed on 7 May 1959 and came into force on 20 July 1959. A new article was included on the 'Transfer of Materials and Equipment'. The author is grateful for information about this amendment received from Sylvia Penney of the United Kingdom Atomic Energy Authority, in a letter of 28 August 1979.
17. Pierre, *op.cit.*, pp.164-5.
18. Dawson and Rosecrance see this as perhaps the major influence; *op. cit.*, p.49-50. Eisenhower and Macmillan had known each other since they worked together on the Anglo-American landings in North Africa in November 1942 and this was clearly an important factor in their close relationship. Interview with Harold Macmillan 28 August 1979.
19. Pierre, *op.cit.*, p.143. See also Macmillan, *op.cit.*, p.329.
20. 600 H.C.Deb. Col.1325 (26 February 1959).
21. See below p.27.
22. Pierre, *op.cit.*, p.144 (author's emphasis). Eisenhower told his officials not 'to be too lawyer-like. A great alliance requires, above all, faith and trust on both sides.' Eisenhower, *op.cit.*, p.219.
23. Andrew Pierre argues that relations between the two air forces were 'excellent and far more intimate than they were between the other respective services of the two countries'. *Op.cit.*, pp.148-51.
24. Quoted in 600 H.C.Deb. Col.1419 (24 February 1959).
25. Letter to the author from Air Vice-Marshal S.W.B. Menaul, CB, CBE, DFC, AFC, 2 April 1976. Clearly this relationship continued after 1968 as well. See also Pierre, *op.cit.*, p.174.
26. See L.W.Martin, 'The market for strategic ideas in Britain: The "Sandys era" *American Political Science Review*, Vol.56, March 1962.
27. J.C.Garnett, 'British Strategic Thought', in J.Baylis (ed.), *British Defence Policy in a Changing World* (London: Croom Helm, 1977), pp.162-4.
28. See A.J.R.Groom, *British Thinking about Nuclear Weapons* (London: Frances Pinter, 1974).
29. See R.Ovendale, 'The English-Speaking Alliance: the Anglo-American Special Relationship', *Interstate*, No.2, 1975-6. p.22.
30. Nicholas, *op.cit.*, p.157. See also Macmillan, *Riding the Storm*, pp.213-14, 217, 237-8.
31. Quoted in D.Maclean, *British Foreign Policy since Suez* (London: Hodder & Stoughton, 1970), p.66.
32. Quoted in Macmillan, *Riding the Storm*, p.534.
33. *Ibid.*, p.474.

34. *Ibid., loc.cit.*
35. *Ibid.*, p.475.
36. *Ibid.*, p.494.
37. H.Macmillan, *Pointing the Way, 1959–61* (London: Macmillan, 1972), p.237.
38. *Ibid.*, p.238.
39. *Ibid., loc.cit.* See also *The World Today, op.cit.*
40. In 1960-1 there was also Anglo-American cooperation on two new early warning systems, BMEWS and MIDAS. The BMEWS system involved the establishment of a large radar station at Fylingdales in Yorkshire which would give the US fifteen minutes' warning of a missile attack and Britain four minutes' warning.
41. Pierre, *op.cit.*, p.198. The 'pioneering' work was in underground 'hardening'. Blue Streak was cancelled after £65 million had been spent and the estimated cost had risen to £600 million.
42. It was later used for space research as Britain's contribution to the European Launcher Development Organization. See 'The end of Blue Streak', *The Times*, 14 April 1960 and 'What for?' *Observer*, 1 May 1960.
43. Macmillan, *Pointing the Way*, p.252.
44. And as yet no real nuclear submarine capability.
45. Macmillan, *Pointing the Way*, p.253.
46. *Ibid.*, p.252 (author's emphasis). This was confirmed by Harold Macmillan in an interview on 28 August 1979. It is perhaps significant that in October 1958 a British staff officer was added to the Naval Staff delegation in Washington to liaise with the Special Projects Office. Then in 1960-61 a team of senior technical personnel went to the US – to familiarize themselves with the plans and philosophy of the US Polaris programme (led by Mr Palmer).
47. *Ibid.*, p.254. The Holy Loch agreement was in line with earlier agreements allowing the forward deployment of the US deterrent forces.
48. *Ibid.*, p.255.
49. Quoted in D.Nunnerley, *President Kennedy and Britain* (London: Bodley Head, 1972), p.129.
50. *Ibid.*, p.130.
51. Pierre, *op.cit.*, p.228.
52. Nunnerley, *op.cit.*, p.133.
53. *Ibid.*, p.137.
54. T.C.Sorensen, *Kennedy* (New York: Harper & Row, 1965), pp.564–5. pp.564-5.
55. Nunnerley, *op.cit.*, p.135.
56. Michael Howard wrote at the time: 'Whitehall has been inexcusably naive if it really expected the United States to develop at vast expense a weapon they no longer need, so that we could pursue a policy of which they disapprove; loyalty to allies has its limits.' *The Sunday Times*, 23 December 1962.
57. Nunnerley, *op.cit.*, p.135.
58. H.Brandon, 'Skybolt: The full inside story of how a missile nearly split the West', *The Sunday Times*, 8 December 1963.

59. Letter to the *Daily Telegraph*. Reprinted in *Survival*, Vol.V, No.3, March–April 1963, p.51.
60. Nunnerley, *op.cit*., p.148.
61. Quoted in *ibid., loc.cit.*
62. Pierre, *op.cit*., pp.208-9. See also *The Times*, 19, 20, 23 June 1962 and *Observer*, 17, 24 June 1962.
63. Nunnerley, *op.cit*., p.146. Arthur Schlesinger describes the meeting as 'a Pinero drama of misunderstanding'. *A Thousand Days* (London: Deutsch, 1965), pp.285-6.
64. Pierre, *op.cit*., p.230.
65. Brandon, *The Sunday Times, op.cit.*
66. Nunnerley, *op.cit*., p.147.
67. He also said that Britain's attempt 'to play a separate power role . . . based on a "special relationship" . . . is about played out.' See *ibid*., p.1.
68. Pierre, *op.cit*., p.225.
69. *Ibid., loc.cit.*
70. Nunnerley, *op.cit*., pp.127-8.
71. *Ibid*., p.149.
72. H.Macmillan, *At the End of the Day* (London: Macmillan, 1973), p.357.
73. *Ibid*., p.358.
74. *Ibid*., p.360.
75. *Ibid. loc.cit.*
76. Nunnerley, *op.cit*., p.158.
77. *Ibid., loc.cit.*
78. *Ibid*., p.160.
79. Quoted in *ibid., loc.cit.*
80. See Joint Communiqué issued on 21 December 1962. See also Appendix 12.
81. Pierre, *op.cit*., p.237.
82. Macmillan, *At the End of the Day*, p.360.
83. *Ibid*., p.363.
84. *Ibid., loc.cit.*
85. *Ibid., loc.cit.*
86. Pierre, *op.cit*., p.242. The final agreement had been largely the work of the Zuckerman–Begg Mission to Washington in early 1963 and the negotiations conducted by J.M.Mackay.
87. Mander, *op.cit*., p.21.
88. See Nunnerley, *op.cit*., p.76 and R.Crossman in the *Guardian*, 26 October 1962.
89. Macmillan, *At the End of the Day*, p.219.
90. A.Howard, 'Caution in Westminster', *New Statesman*, 26 October 1962.
91. Macmillan, *At the End of the Day*, p.220. Mr Macmillan reinforced this point in an interview with the author on 28 August 1979.
92. *Ibid*., p.182.
93. *Ibid*., p.220.

CHAPTER 4: THE 'CLOSE RELATIONSHIP' 1963–1969

1. See pp.73–4.
2. See G.W.Ball, *The Discipline of Power* (London: Bodley Head, 1968) and Pierre, *op.cit.*, p.235.
3. Pierre, *op.cit.*, p.251.
4. Ball, *op.cit.*, pp.102-8.
5. Pierre, *op.cit.*, pp.250-1.
6. *Ibid., loc.cit.*
7. H.Wilson, *The Labour Government 1964-70* (London: Penguin, 1974), p.70.
8. Schlesinger, *op.cit.*, p.875.
9. Pierre, *op.cit.*, p.251.
10. *Ibid.*, p.246.
11. *Ibid.*, p.247. See also *Guardian*, 28 September 1963 and *Observer*, 15 September 1963.
12. *Ibid.*, p.248. See also *The Times*, 26 June and 3 July 1964.
13. *Ibid.*, p.249.
14. *Ibid., loc.cit.*
15. 484 H.C.Deb. Col.49 (12 November 1963).
16. 670 H.C.Deb. Col.962 (30 January 1963).
17. *Ibid., loc.cit.*
18. Pierre, *op.cit.*, p.256.
19. See A.Jones, 'Does nuclear independence make sense?' *Observer*, 26 May 1963 and P.Worsthorne, 'Trust America more', *Sunday Telegraph*, 6 January 1963. See also A.Jones in 690 H.C.Deb. Col.484-93 (26 February 1964).
20. See P.G.Walker, 'The Labour Party's Defence and Foreign Policy', *Foreign Affairs*, Vol.XLII, No.3, April 1964 and Pierre, *op.cit.*, pp.262-4.
21. Pierre, *ibid.*, p.271.
22. Walker, *op.cit.*
23. *Ibid., loc.cit.* (author's emphasis).
24. 684 H.C.Deb. Col.498 (15 November 1963).
25. *Ibid., loc.cit.*
26. See Pierre, *op.cit.*, pp.268–9.
27. Pierre, *ibid.*, p.269.
28. Walker, *op.cit.*
29. 690 H.C.Deb. Col.480-1 (26 February 1964).
30. 687 H.C.Deb. Col.443-4 (16 January 1964).
31. P.Johnson, 'Will Wilson keep the Bomb', *New Statesman*, 13 December 1963.
32. N.Beloff, 'Labour unlikely to scrap bomb', *Observer*, 17 November 1963.
33. 'Paradox of Defence Policy', Election Paper No.3, *The Times*, 13 April 1964.
34. 'Britain's Bomb', 12 September 1964.
35. *The Times* (leader article), 7 October 1964.
36. Wilson, *op.cit.*, p.73.

37. A.Buchan, 'The Multilateral Force: An historical perspective', p.10. Quoted in Pierre, *op.cit.*, p.251.
38. *Ibid., loc.cit.*
39. Wilson, *op.cit.*, p.75.
40. Professor Neustadt published the essence of his report in a book entitled *Alliance Politics* (New York: Columbia University Press, 1970).
41. Neustadt had argued in his report to the President that there was a need to avoid situations where 'differences of interest are compounded by each side's misreading of the pressures and procedures on the other side'.
42. Wilson, *op.cit.*, p.76.
43. 704 H.C.Deb. Col.432-7 (16 December 1964).
44. *Ibid., loc.cit.*
45. See *Financial Times*, 30 October 1964.
46. As Andrew Pierre says, this was not a very convincing argument. There was little stopping the government from re-negotiating the contract if it had been determined to do so. *Op.cit.* p.285.
47. 704 H.C.Deb. Col.694 (17 December 1964).
48. *Ibid., loc.cit.*
49. *Ibid., loc.cit.*
50. Wilson, *op.cit.*, p.81.
51. Pierre, *op.cit.*, p.280.
52. See Wilson, *op.cit.*, p.69.
53. *Ibid.*, p.82.
54. See Pierre, *op.cit.*, p.279.
55. Wilson, *op.cit.*, p.85.
56. *Ibid.*, p.86.
57. *Ibid., loc.cit.*
58. *Ibid.*, pp.85-6.
59. *Ibid.*, p.87.
60. 729 H.C.Deb. Col.276-7 (24 May 1966).
61. Wilson, *op.cit.*, p.80.
62. For a discussion of Wilson's personal commitment to very close relations with the US see R.Crossman, *The Diaries of a Cabinet Minister*, Vol.II, (London: Hamish Hamilton and Jonathan Cape, 1976), pp.181-3.
63. Pierre, *op.cit.*, p.293. See Appendix 15.
64. *Ibid., loc.cit.* The Sales Agreement (and its confidential annex) led to the exchange of liaison offices in London and Washington; US specialist advisers in Barrow, Birkenhead and Faslane; the setting up of a Joint Steering Task Group to discuss financial and technical collaboration; direct teleprinter links; British participation in the US teletype communications system (AUTODIN); and the training of British personnel at POMFLANT (the naval weapons annex at Charleston, S. Carolina).
65. Wilson, *op.cit.*, p.113.
66. R.S.Crossman, *Diaries of a Cabinet Minister*, Vol.I, (London: Hamish Hamilton and Jonathan Cape, 1975), p.94.

67. *Ibid., loc.cit.*
68. Cmnd. 2853, *Report of the Committee of Inquiry into the Aircraft Industry*. See Wilson, *op.cit.*, p.248.
69. See *The Times*, 18 February 1966.
70. See *Guardian*, 11 December 1975 and *New York Times* 17 October 1975.
71. *Ibid.*
72. Wilson, *op.cit.*, p.79.
73. *Ibid.*, p.341.
74. *Ibid., loc.cit.*
75. L.B.Johnson, *The Vantage Point 1963–69* (London: Weidenfeld & Nicolson, 1971), p.255. The different interpretations of Wilson's peace initiatives are brought out in the discussions of the 'Palm-Tree Meetings'. See Johnson, p.254 and Wilson, pp.442-9.
76. Wilson, *op.cit.*, p.116. See also L.Heren, *No Hail, No Farewell* (London: Harper & Row, 1970).
77. *Ibid., loc.cit.*
78. H.G.Nicholas, *op.cit.*, p.167.
79. Quoted in L.Heren, *op.cit.*, p.231. Louis Heren does, however, suggest this outburst may have been the result of a little too much to drink!
80. The presence of British troops east of Suez at least represented a commitment by another Western state to the security of the region. Their withdrawal was therefore of great symbolic importance. Some writers see the British decision to withdraw as marking the real end of the 'special relationship'. Lord Chalfont argued at the time that the relationship ceased to be 'special' when Britain devalued the pound and withdrew from east of Suez because these acts ended the world-wide alliance to keep the peace and significantly reduced Britain's value to the US. Much the same point has been made by Heren, *op.cit.*, p.184.
81. Traditional American criticisms of British imperialism had for some time been replaced by an awareness of the value of the British presence east of Suez in the global struggle against communism.
82. Crossman, *op.cit.*, Vol.I, p.95.
83. *Ibid., loc.cit.*
84. *Ibid.*, pp.679-80.
85. Crossman, *op.cit.*, Vol.II, p.646.
86. See Wilson, *op.cit.*, p.509.
87. See, for example, Henry Kissinger's account of the relationship between Wilson and Nixon in *The White House Years* (London: Weidenfeld and Nicolson, 1979) pp.89-96. For a discussion of Kissinger's and Nixon's continuing acceptance of the term 'special relationship' see pages 90-1, *ibid.*
88. H.Wilson, *op.cit.*, pp.495-501.
89. Negotiations on a Strategic Arms Limitation Treaty began between the United States and the Soviet Union in November 1969.
90. The Eurogroup was established in 1970 largely as a result of initiatives by Denis Healey in the late 1960s.
91. Wilson, *op.cit.*, p.523.

92. *Ibid.*, p.522.
93. *Ibid., loc.cit.*
94. *Ibid.*, p.525.

CHAPTER 5: THE RESIDUAL RELATIONSHIP 1970–1980

1. See *Daily Telegraph*, 19 December 1970 and 21 December 1970.
2. The SALT I Agreement was signed in May 1972 and was followed by the Vladivostok Accords of November 1974. After a protracted period of negotiations the SALT II Agreement was finally signed in June 1979.
3. See Heren, *op.cit.*, pp.127, 157, 183. Harold Wilson plays down the difficulties in his relations with Lyndon Johnson in his memoirs arguing that contrary to the public view of friction many of his visits to the US were highly successful. The degree of tension has perhaps been exaggerated but there can be no doubt that relations were at times sorely strained. See the *Guardian*, 5 August 1970.
4. Mr Heath's visit to the United States in December 1970 was designed partly at least to achieve this objective.
5. See *Statement on the Defence Estimates* 1971 and 1972, Cmnd. 4592 and Cmnd. 4891.
6. *Supplementary Statement on Defence*, Cmnd. 4521.
7. *Guardian*, 16 November 1970 and *The Times*, 16 November 1970.
8. *The Times*, 17 November 1970.
9. Cmnd. 4592.
10. This point was made to Mr Heath during his visit to Washington in December 1970.
11. Cmnd. 4592.
12. Cmnd. 4891.
13. See Cmnd. 5976.
14. *Ibid.*
15. *Ibid.*
16. *The Times*, 19 October 1976.
17. *Ibid.*
18. *Ibid.*
19. At the time of writing the SALT II Agreement has yet to be ratified by the US Senate.
20. Because of her nuclear expertise Britain may have been consulted rather more than some of the other allies – the fact remains, however, that Britain was not a party to these negotiations.
21. See 'Seven lean years', *The Economist*, 30 December 1978. See also the 'Memorandum submitted by Mr Geoffrey Pattie M.P., to the Defence and External Affairs Sub-Committee of the Expenditure Committee', *Sixth Report, op.cit.*, pp.128-32.
22. Cruise Missiles were very much in 'fashion' in the middle 1970s. Towards the end of the decade, however, expert opinion became very much more critical of them. See 'Memorandum by Admiral of the Fleet Sir Peter Hill-Norton, GCB', *Ibid.*, pp.204-10. SALT II did place

certain restrictions on Cruise Missiles. Article 4 (para.14) of the Treaty limited the deployment of Air-launched Cruise Missiles (ALCM) with a range in excess of 600 kilometers: 'Each party undertakes not to deploy at any one time heavy bombers equipped for Cruise Missiles capable of a range in excess of 600 kilometers, a number of such Cruise Missiles which exceeds the product of 28 and the number of such bombers'. Article II of the protocol also banned the deployment of land-based and sea-based Cruise Missiles with ranges over 600 kilometers.

23. See *Guardian*, 26 October 1973 and *The Times*, 1 November 1973.
24. See Williams, 'The U.S. and Western Europe: A conditional commitment', *op.cit.*
25. See D.C.R. Heyhoe, 'The Alliance and Europe: Part VI, The European Programme Group', *Adelphi Paper*, No.129 (London: the International Institute for Strategic Studies, 1977), p.2.
26. *Guardian*, 27 April 1973.
27. Quoted in Heyhoe, *op.cit.*, p.4. See also *Guardian*, 14 November 1974 and *Financial Times*, 19 November 1974.
28. Quoted in Heyhoe, *op.cit.*, p.5.
29. Quoted in *ibid.*, p.6.
30. *Memorandum of Understanding between the Government of the United States and the Government of the United Kingdom of Great Britain and Northern Ireland Relating to the Principles Governing Cooperation in R. & D., Production, and Procurement of Defence Equipment*, 24 September 1975.
31. *Ibid.*
32. See *Daily Telegraph*, 6 January 1970.
33. *The Times*, 7 January 1971.
34. See *The Times*, 5 August 1971.
35. Besides the public debate the Ministry of Defence in Britain was apparently considering the options available for a successor to Polaris throughout the 1970s. See 'Memorandum by Admiral of the Fleet Sir Peter Hill-Norton, GCB, *op.cit.*, p.205.
36. See *Daily Express*, 13 August 1971 and *Daily Telegraph*, 7 March 1972.
37. *Twelfth Report from the Expenditure Committee*, House of Commons, 399, February 1973.
38. *Ibid.*, p.28.
39. *Ibid.*, pp.5-25.
40. *Ibid.*, p.6.
41. *Ibid.*, p.5.
42. *Ibid.*, p.27.
43. *New York Times*, 10 April 1973.
44. Pierre, *op.cit.*, p.295.
45. *Ibid., loc.cit.*
46. The programme was code-named 'Operation Antelope'.
47. This was later reduced to one area.
48. *Sunday Times*, 2 March 1975.
49. *Daily Telegraph*, 6 February 1974.

50. An amendment to the 1958 Act (which had been agreed to in October 1969) came into force in April 1970 just after the Heath government took office. Lord Carrington also apparently discussed nuclear exchanges during his visit to Washington in February 1973.
51. See p.92.
52. Cmnd. 5976.
53. All nuclear tests after August 1958 were carried out jointly with the US. There were it seems two tests in 1962, one in 1964 and one in 1965. There were then no tests until 1974. Prior to being made operational each Royal Navy SSBN launched two Polaris missiles while submerged off Cape Kennedy, Florida (Atlantic Test Range). Three more launches were conducted at the Atlantic Test Range after 1973-4 to test missile reliability. See 'Memorandum by Mr Farouq Hussein, Research Associate, International Institute for Strategic Studies', *Sixth Report. op.cit.*, pp.194-5.
54. The 1958 Act had three components. See pp.219–220, Note 15.
55. *Amendment to the Agreement . . . for Cooperation on the Uses of Atomic Energy for Mutual Defence Purposes of 3 July 1958,* Treaty Series, No.85 (1969), Cmnd. 4119. See Appendix 13.
56. *Amendment to the Agreement . . . for Cooperation on the Uses of Atomic Energy for Mutual Defence Purposes*, Treaty Series, No.46 (1970), Cmnd. 4383.
57. *Amendment to the Agreement . . . for Cooperation on the Uses of Atomic Energy for Mutual Defence Purposes*, Treaty Series, No.65 (1975), Cmnd. 6017.
58. Article II of the 1958 Act dealing with the exchange of information could be terminated by either state giving one year's notice after ten years, and one year's notice at the end of each succeeding five years. See pp.219–220, Note 15.
59. See *The Times*, 10 May and 3 June 1976 and *Daily Express*, 17 May 1976.
60. *The Times*, 10 May 1976.
61. *Ibid*. The estimates for the cost of the new programme at Chapelcross vary from £7 to £10 million.
62. *Ibid*. In fact the duration of the different components of the Act varied. They were due for renewal in December 1979. See pp.219-220, Note 15.
63. See *The Times*, 3 June 1976.
64. See Chapman Pincher, *Daily Express*, 17 May 1976.
65. See *The Labour Party Manifesto*, 1979.
66. It has been suggested to the author that there may be no fully rational explanation. 'One important individual simply decided it was time to produce tritium ourselves.' *Interview*, June 1979.
67. See Appendix 15.
68. See 'Memorandum Submitted by the International Institute for Strategic Studies', *Sixth Report, op.cit.* p.81.
69. It has also been suggested that the decision to produce tritium and the decision in the spring of 1978 to buy a £6 million Cray-1 Computer is part of an attempt to pre-empt the decision whether or not to replace

Polaris by creating the infrastructure and momentum for a replacement which it will be difficult to reverse. See 'Memorandum submitted by Mr Robin F. Cook, M.P., together with Mr Dan Smith', *Sixth Report, op.cit.*

70. See p.31.
71. See *The Times*, 22 May 1973, *Daily Express*, 22 May 1973 and *Daily Telegraph*, 22 May 1973.
72. Bell, 'The Special Relationship', *op.cit.*, p.112. See also Pincher, *op.cit.*, pp.157-63. Pincher argues that '. . . the Anglo-American alliance on Intelligence and Security is every bit as vital to Britain's survival as a free country as the partnership in nuclear weapons'.
73. Interview.
74. See *Observer*, 11 March 1979; *Guardian*, 5 April 1979; and *Daily Telegraph*, 13 March 1979. According to these reports American U-2 and SR-71 ('Black Widow') spy planes continued to use British bases at Weathersfield, Essex and Akrotiri in Cyprus. It is reported that there 'is still an average of one spy flight a week from British territory. RAF pilots may also be involved in these flights'.
75. See pp.20-21. (Also Notes 38, 127 and 132, pp.206, 210. The US apparently has branches of four of its most important Secret Services based in Britain. These include the CIA, the National Security Agency (NSA), the National Reconnaissance Office (NRO) and the Defence Intelligence Agency (DIA). The NSA apparently works closely (through joint establishments) with the British Government Communications Headquarters (GCHQ) at Cheltenham. According to Chapman Pincher 'the prime joint purpose is the long-range electronic surveillance of Russia's clandestine activities. . .'. *Op.cit.*
76. *The Times*, 18 August 1971.
77. See *The Times*, 14 September 1978.
78. See Appendix 16.
79. Interview.
80. Letter to the author from Professor P. Nailor, 27 February 1979.
81. The size of the intelligence team amongst the BDSW also highlights the importance Britain, at least, continues to attach to cooperation in the intelligence field. In turn the CIA also mounts 'a substantial operation' in Britain from the US Embassy. See Note 75, p.229.
82. See the Report of 'The Central Policy Review Staff (CPRS) Review of Overseas Representation', HMSO, 1977; *Twelfth Report from the Expenditure Committee*, HMSO, 1975-6; and *Fourth Report from the Expenditure Committee*, HMSO, 1977-8.
83. CPRS, *ibid.*, p.126.
84. *Ibid., loc.cit.*
85. *Ibid., loc.cit.* For a survey of exchanges in the Defence Operational Analysis field, see *The Second Report from the Select Committee on Science and Technology, Defence Research*, 1969. Report Appendix 18.
86. 'Special' in the sense that they are particular, intimate and exclusive areas of cooperation. In some respects the author has changed his mind on this point as a result of his research, see 'The Anglo-American

Relationship in Defence' in J.Baylis, (ed.), *British Defence Policy in a Changing World*, p.83.

87. The fact that the agreements exist and *continue* to provide the basis for close cooperation in many areas of the defence field is the important thing.

CHAPTER 6: A STOCKTAKING AND PROSPECTUS

1. See pp.24–8.
2. See pp.55–6.
3. See pp.66–72.
4. See pp.57–63.
5. See pp.35–9.
6. Interview.
7. See pp.71–2.
8. Interview.
9. See M. Howard's Introduction to *Anglo-American Strategic Relationships* (Report on a Colloquium held at St Anthony's College, Oxford, 14-17 April, 1970).
10. In terms of the degree of intimacy involved and the exclusive nature of the relationship.
11. For a discussion of the 'over-stretch' of Britain's defence resources see Darby, *op.cit.*, pp.252-5.
12. See pp.93–6.
13. Gowing, *op.cit.*, pp.152-8 and pp.338-48.
14. Pierre, *op.cit.*, p.316.
15. Ball, *op.cit.*, p.107.
16. It might perhaps be argued that these were even more important as determinants in Britain's self-image.
17. See Ian Smart, *The Future of the British Nuclear Force, op.cit.*
18. See pp. 33–5.
19. Cmnd.7849, *Mutual Defence Assistance Agreement between the United Kingdom and the United States.*
20. Ironically, because Wilson put a great stress on close links with the US while he was in office. See Chapter 4.
21. H.Wilson, *In Place of Dollars* (London: Tribune Pamphlet, 1952). See also L.D.Epstein, *Britain – Uneasy Ally* (Chicago: University of Chicago Press, 1954).
22. See p.67.
23. See Appendix 15.
24. Pierre, *op.cit.*, p.316.
25. *Ibid., loc.cit.*
26. For some observers the critical question is whether a plausible scenario can be envisaged in which Britain would in fact launch her missiles independently. Some would find such a set of circumstances impossible to foresee. Others would see it as unlikely but nevertheless possible in an uncertain world. See 'Memorandum submitted by

Mr Robin F. Cook, M.P., together with Mr Dan Smith', *Sixth Report to the Expenditure Committee, Op.cit.*, p.139.

27. The phrase '"Airstrip One" relationship' is used by C.Bell in *The Debatable Alliance, op.cit.*
28. See 'Why we are the world's most valuable aircraft carrier', *The Sunday Times*, 13 February 1977.
29. See 'Memorandum submitted by Mr Robin F. Cook, M.P. together with Mr Dan Smith', *Sixth Report, op.cit.* p.140.
30. See *Guardian*, 10 May 1979.
31. See Bell, 'The Special Relationship', in Leifer (ed.), *op.cit.*
32. The argument here is, of course, based upon certain assumptions about what enhances British security which cannot be proved in any rigorous way. The same, however, is true of those who believe the American partnership detracts from British security.
33. The various sections of the Act remain in force until 31 December 1979 unless they are extended once again.
34. See *American Foreign Policy Current Documents, 1958, Western Europe* (Department of State Publication, 7522, 1862). Statement by Mr Frederick Jandrey, Deputy Assistant Secretary for European Affairs, Before the Sub-committee on Agreements for Cooperation, Joint Committee on Atomic Energy, p.647.
35. Such speculation is, of course, difficult to substantiate. It might be argued that the West European states including Britain would have been unwilling to 'pay the price' if the US had returned to isolationism after 1945. The concern of these states, especially Britain, in the 1940s and 1950s to maintain their defences, however, would seem to throw doubt on such a supposition. It would seem probable that the Brussels Pact would have been expanded with larger defence expenditure being incurred.
36. In his memoirs Harold Wilson suggests that there was no link between the defence and economic partnership between the two countries. See Wilson, *The Labour Government, 1964-70*, p.341. Richard Crossman, however, questions this view. See Crossman, *op.cit.*, Vol.I, p.456.
37. Pierre, *op.cit.*, p.318.
38. In relation to the Soviet Union the phrase is sometimes used to describe the exclusive SALT negotiations.
39. Ball, *op.cit.*, p.102.
40. *Ibid.*, p.93.
41. Nassau is seen as the third mistake in Anglo-American relations. The 1958 Amendments to the McMahon Act and the Skybolt Agreement are regarded as the other two mistakes. *Ibid.*, pp.98-108.
42. Ball argues that 'If we are serious about checking nuclear proliferation – as I am certain we are – then we should be extremely careful not to make for the fourth time the mistake of taking affirmative action to keep Britain in the nuclear weapons business.' *Ibid.*, p.108.
43. *Ibid.*, p.99.
44. *Ibid., loc.cit.*
45. The author believes that there is *some* truth in this argument.

46. Statement by Mr Frederick Jandrey, *op.cit.*, p.647.
47. Information about Chobham Armour was apparently passed on to the Americans under the Burns–Templer Agreements, and led to certain criticisms in Britain. See *The Sunday Times*, 7 November 1976.
48. 'Statement by Mr Frederick Jandrey. . .', *op.cit.*, p.647. See also the evidence about continuing cooperation between nuclear scientists in *The Sixth Report, op.cit.*, p.53.
49. This is not, of course, to argue that it is equally advantageous.
50. 'Obsolescent in terms of the life-cycle of the submarines.' For a general impression of the debate see *The Sixth Report, op.cit; Time,* 14 May 1979; *Daily Telegraph,* 10, 12 July 1979; *The Economist* 15 September 1979; *Observer* 30 September 1979; *The Sunday Express* 7 October 1979; *Guardian* 1 November 1979; *Daily Telegraph* 2 November 1979; *Guardian* 5, 7 November 1979; *The Economist* 10 November 1979; *Guardian* 16, 18 November 1979; *The Times* 27 November, 4 December 1979.
51. See, for example, J.Cox, *Overkill: The Story of Modern Weapons*, (London: Penguin, 1977).
52. 'Memorandum submitted by Mr Robin F. Cook MP, together with Mr Dan Smith', *Sixth Report, op.cit*. They also argued, however, that the decision to continue in the nuclear field had partly been pre-empted by the purchase of a £6 million Cray-1 computer by Aldermaston in the Spring of 1978, pp.228–9, Note 69.
53. See Ian Smart, *op.cit.*, p.3 and various letters to the *Guardian* 8 and 16 November, 1979.
54. Largely for the same reasons as those identified in earlier debates. See p.107. See also J.Baylis, 'French Defence Policy: Continuity or Change', *Journal of the Royal United Services Institute for Defence Studies*, March 1979.
55. See Memorandum submitted by Mr Julian Critchley, MP, *Sixth Report*, pp.151-5.
56. See in particular 'After Polaris', by Admiral of the Fleet Lord Hill-Norton, in *The Economist*, 15 September 1979. There were, however, those who argued that a 'new Nassau' would be very difficult to achieve. Ian Smart, for example, argued in January 1979 that '. . . . . .it would be difficult for a policy maker in Britain to assume a repetition of the Nassau Agreement. That was a most extraordinary event at a most extraordinary period. To assume a continuation of such co-operation over a full decade in the future, with the uncertainties of the United States as well as British politics would be difficult.' 'I think', he said, 'it is an option which might exist and, if it were to exist, might offer certain advantages. But if it is to be on that option that one relies to provide the whole of British capacity in this area for the future then one is taking very considerable risk in making such an assumption, over ten years about American politics.' *Sixth Report, op.cit.*, p.59.
57. See *Guardian* 5 November 1979 and 7 November 1979. See also the evidence given to the Defence and External Affairs Sub-Committee,

Sixth Report, op.cit. For an evaluation of ballistic missiles versus cruise missiles see Ian Smart, *The Future of the British Nuclear Deterrent, op.cit.*, and Lord Hill-Norton, *The Economist*, 15 September 1979.

58. It would seem, however, that while still in office Mr Callaghan had convened a small ad hoc committee of four Cabinet members to consider a replacement for Polaris regardless of the 1974 Party Manifesto which stated that 'We have renounced any intention of moving to a new generation of strategic nuclear weapons.' For a discussion of the 'committee of four' and the Duff and Mason working parties which supported it see 'Planning for a future nuclear deterrent' in *The Times*, 4 December 1979.
59. See *Guardian*, 14 November 1979 and *The Times*, 11 December 1979.
60. Despite certain reservations, Mrs Thatcher's government provided much firmer backing for the US position over the hostages in Iran and the Soviet invasion of Afghanistan than most of the other W. European states.
61. See Henry Brandon's article in *The Sunday Times*, 23 December 1979 and *Observer*, 16 December 1979.
62. The announcement was made on the 24 January 1980. See *Guardian* and *The Times*, 25 January 1980.
63. *The Times*, 25 January 1980. The programme was started by the Heath government and continued by the Wilson and Callaghan governments. It is also interesting to note that the British Polaris Staff in the United States continues to be housed in the same building in Crystal City (Washington) as the US Strategic Systems Project Office which deals with Polaris, Poseidon and Trident.
64. See for example *Guardian*, 26 September 1979; *Observer*, 30 September; *Sunday Express*, 7 October 1979; *Guardian*, 1 November 1979; and the *Daily Telegraph*, 2 November 1979.
65. See *The Times* and *Guardian*, 25 January 1980.
66. At a time of difficulties within the EEC over such things as Britain's contribution to the Community Budget, such a decision would be likely to confirm continuing French suspicions about Britain's 'special relationship' with the US. See *The Times*, 26 January 1980.
67. Despite the 'rumours of the imminent announcement of the purchase of Trident in late 1979 and early 1980 the implications of such large expenditure on other areas of defence and other sectors of the economy received very little consideration. This seemed particularly surprising given the pressures to cut public expenditure at this time.

Bibliography

PUBLIC DOCUMENTS AND GOVERNMENT PUBLICATIONS

1. *British Command Papers*

Cmnd. 6743. *Statement Relating to Defence: 1946*
Cmnd. 7042. *Statement Relating to Defence: 1947*
Cmnd. 7327. *Statement Relating to Defence: 1948*
Cmnd. 7849. *Mutual Defence Assistance Agreement Between the United Kingdom and the United States*
Cmnd. 7895. *Statement on Defence: 1950*
Cmnd. 8768. *Statement on Defence: 1953*
Cmnd. 8986. *The Future Organization of the United Kingdom Atomic Energy Project*
Cmnd. 9075. *Statement on Defence: 1954*
Cmnd. 9388. *The Supply of Military Aircraft*
Cmnd. 9389. *A Programme of Nuclear Power: 1955*
Cmnd. 9391. *Statement on Defence: 1955*
Cmnd. 9555. *Agreement for Co-operation Regarding Atomic Information for Mutual Defence Purposes*
Cmnd. 9560. *Agreement for Co-operation on the Peaceful Uses of Atomic Energy*
Cmnd. 9691. *Statement on Defence: 1956*
Cmnd. 124. *Defence: Outline of Future Policy: 1957*
Cmnd. 363. *Report on Defence: Britain's Contribution to Peace and Security: 1958*
Cmnd. 476. *Central Organization for Defence: 1958*
Cmnd. 537. *Agreement for Co-operation on the Uses of Atomic Energy for Mutual Defence Purposes*
Cmnd. 859. *Amendment to Agreement between the Government of the United Kingdom of Great Britain and Northern Ireland and the Government of the United States of America for Co-operation on the Uses of Atomic Energy for Mutual Defence Purposes of July 3, 1958 (signed on 7 May 1959)*
Cmnd. 952. *Report on Defence: 1960*
Cmnd. 1288. *Report on Defence: 1961*
Cmnd. 1639. *Statement on Defence, 1962: The Next Five Years*
Cmnd. 1936. *Statement on Defence: 1963*
Cmnd. 1995. *Polaris Sales Agreement*
Cmnd. 2097. *Central Organization for Defence: 1963*
Cmnd. 2270. *Statement on Defence: 1964*
Cmnd. 2592. *Statement on the Defence Estimates: 1965*

Cmnd. 2853. *Report of the Committee of Inquiry into the Aircraft Industry*
Cmnd. 2901. *Statement on Defence Estimates: 1966. Part I: The Defence Review*
Cmnd. 2902. *Statement on Defence Estimates: 1966. Part II: Defence Estimates: 1966-67*
Cmnd. 3203. *Statement on the Defence Estimates: 1967*
Cmnd. 3357. *Supplementary Statement on Defence Policy: 1967*
Cmnd. 3540. *Statement on the Defence Estimates: 1968*
Cmnd. 3701. *Supplementary Statement on Defence Policy: 1968*
Cmnd. 3842. *Amendment to Agreement between the Government of the United Kingdom of Great Britain and Northern Ireland and the Government of the United States of America for Co-operation on the Uses of Atomic Energy for Mutual Defence Purposes of July 3, 1958 (signed on 27 September 1968)*
Cmnd. 3927. *Statement on the Defence Estimates: 1969*
Cmnd. 4383. *Amendment to Agreement between the Government of the United Kingdom of Great Britain and Northern Ireland and the Government of the United States of America for Co-operation on the Uses of Atomic Energy for Mutual Defence Purposes of July 3, 1958 (signed on 16 October 1969)*
Cmnd. 4290. *Statement on the Defence Estimates: 1970*
Cmnd. 4592. *Statement on the Defence Estimates: 1971*
Cmnd. 4521. *Supplementary Statement on Defence Policy: October 1971*
Cmnd. 4891. *Statement on the Defence Estimates: 1972*
Cmnd. 5231. *Statement on the Defence Estimates: 1973*
Cmnd. 6017. *Amendment to Agreement between the Government of the United Kingdom and Northern Ireland and the Government of the United States of America for Co-operation on the Uses of Atomic Energy for Mutual Defence Purposes of July 3, 1958* (signed on 22 July 1974)
Cmnd. 5976. *Statement on the Defence Estimates: 1975*
Cmnd. 6432. *Statement on the Defence Estimates: 1976*
Cmnd. 6735. *Statement on the Defence Estimates: 1977*
Cmnd. 7099. *Statement on the Defence Estimates: 1978*
Cmnd. 7474. *Statement on the Defence Estimates: 1979*

2. *Other British and American government publications*
Great Britain:
Parliamentary Debates (House of Commons) 1945-79
Parliamentary Debates (House of Lords)
Report of the Committee on the Management and Control of Research and Development (London: HMSO, 1961)
Second Report from the Select Committee on Science and Technology: Defence Research, Session 1968-69, No. 213 (London: HMSO, 1969)

Twelfth Report from the Expenditure Committee: Nuclear Weapon Programme, Session 1972-73, No. 399 (London: HMSO, 1973)

Second Report from the Expenditure Committee: The Cumulative Effect of Cuts in Defence Expenditure, Session 1976-77, No. 254 (London: HMSO, 1977)

The Report of the Central Policy Review Staff Review of Overseas Representation (London: HMSO, 1977)

Sixth Report from the Expenditure Committee: The Future of the United Kingdom's Nuclear Weapons' Policy, Session 1978-79, No. 348 (London: HMSO, 1979)

United States:

United States Congress: Joint Committee on Atomic Energy. *Hearing to Amend the Atomic Energy Act of 1946*, 83rd Cong., 2nd Session

United States Senate: *Congressional Record*, 81st Cong., 2nd Session, Vol. XCVI, Part 7, 10 July 1950, 9762-3

United States Congress: Joint Committee on Atomic Energy. *Senate Report, 1954*, 85th Cong., 2nd Session

United States Congress: *Public Law* 763, 83rd Cong., 2nd Session

United States Department of State: 'Declaration of Common Purpose', *Department of State Bulletin*, Vol. XXXVII, 11 November 1957

United States Department of State: 'Exchange of Notes Concerning an Agreement for the Supply of Intermediate Range Missiles to the United Kingdom', *Department of State Bulletin*, Vol. XXXVIII, 17 March 1958

United States Department of State: *American Foreign Policy Current Documents, 1958, Western Europe*. No. 7522 (Washington, 1962)

United States Department of State: 'Joint Communiqué and Attached Statement on Nuclear Defense Systems'. *Department of State Bulletin*, Vol. XLVIII, No. 1229, 14 January 1963

BOOKS

Acheson, D., *Present at the Creation* (New York: Norton (W.W.), 1969)

Allen, H. C., *The Anglo-American Predicament* (London: Macmillan, 1960)

——, *Great Britain and the United States: A History of Anglo-American Relations* (London: Odhams, 1955)

Attlee, C., *As it Happened* (London: Heinemann, 1954)

Ball, G. W., *The Discipline of Power* (London: Bodley Head, 1968)

Barker, A. J., *Suez: The Seven Day War* (London: Faber & Faber, 1967)

Bartlett, C. J., *The Long Retreat: A Short History of British Defence Policy, 1945-70* (London: Macmillan, 1972)

Baylis, J. (ed.), *British Defence Policy in a Changing World* (London: Croom Helm, 1977)

——*et al., Contemporary Strategy: Theories and Policies,* (London: Croom Helm, 1975)

Bell, C., *The Debatable Alliance: An Essay in Anglo-American Relations* (London: Oxford University Press, 1964)
Bertin, L., *Atom Harvest: A British View of Atomic Energy* (London: Secker & Warburg, 1955)
Birkenhead, Earl of, *The Prof in Two Worlds* (London: Collins, 1961)
Blackett, P. M. S., *Atomic Weapons and East-West Relations* (Cambridge: Cambridge University Press, 1956)
——, *Studies of War: Nuclear and Conventional,* (New York: Hill and Wang, 1962)
Boardman, R., *Britain and the People's Republic of China 1949-74* (London: Macmillan, 1976)
Bowie, R. R., *Shaping of the Future: Foreign Policy in an Age of Transition* (New York: Columbia University Press, 1964)
Brogan, B., *American Aspects* (New York: Harper & Row, 1964)
Brown, N., *Arms without Empire: British Defence Policy in the Modern World* (London: Penguin, 1967)
Bryant, A., *Triumph in the West: A History of the War Years based on the Diaries of Field-Marshal Lord Alanbrooke, Chief of the Imperial General Staff* (London: Collins, 1959)
Buchan, A., *NATO in the 1960s* (New York: Praeger, 1963)
Bush, V., *Modern Arms and Free Men* (New York: Simon & Schuster, 1949)
Butler, J. R. M., *Grand Strategy,* Vol. II, *United Kingdom History of the Second World War* (London: HMSO, 1957)
Butler, J. R. M., and Gwyer, J. M. A., *Grand Strategy,* Vol. III, Part 2, *History of the Second World War* (London: HMSO, 1964)
Byrnes, J. F., *Speaking Frankly* (New York: Harper and Brothers, 1947)
——, *All in One Lifetime* (New York: Harper and Brothers, 1958)
Callahan, R., *The Worst Disaster: The Fall of Singapore* (London: Associated University Presses, 1977)
——, *Burma, 1942-45* (London: Davis-Poynter, 1978)
Churchill, W. S., *The Second World War,* Vol. I, *The Gathering Storm* (London: Cassell, 1948)
——, *The Second World War,* Vol. II, *Their Finest Hour* (London: Cassell, 1949)
——, *The Second World War,* Vol. III, *The Grand Alliance* (London: Cassell, 1950)
——, *The Second World War,* Vol. IV, *The Hinge of Fate* (London: Cassell, 1951)
——, *The Second World War,* Vol. VI, *Triumph and Tragedy* (London: Cassell, 1954)
Clark, R.W., *The Birth of the Bomb* (New York: Horizon, 1961)
——, *Tizard* (Cambridge: MIT, 1965)
Conant, J. B., *Anglo-American Relations in the Atomic Age* (London: Oxford University Press, 1952)

——, *My Several Lives* (New York: Harper & Row, 1970)
Crossman, R., *Diaries of a Cabinet Minister,* Vol. I (London: Hamish Hamilton and Jonathan Cape, 1975)
——, *Diaries of a Cabinet Minister,* Vol. II (London: Hamish Hamilton and Jonathan Cape, 1976)
Dalton, H., *High Tide and After: Memoirs, 1945-1960* (London: Frederick Muller, 1962)
Darby, P., *British Defence Policy east of Suez 1947-68* (London: Oxford University Press, 1973), pp.388-9.
Dayan, M., *Diary of the Sinai Campaign* (London: Weidenfeld & Nicolson, 1966)
——, *Story of My Life* (London: Weidenfeld & Nicolson, 1976)
De Kadt, E. J., *British Defence Policy and Nuclear War* (London: Frank Cass, 1964)
Divine, D., *The Blunted Sword* (London: Hutchinson, 1964)
——, *The Broken Wing: A Study in the British Exercise of Air Power* (London: Hutchinson, 1966)
Driver, C., *The Disarmers: A Study in Protest* (London: Hodder & Stoughton, 1964)
Eden, A., *Full Circle: The Memoirs of Anthony Eden* (London: Cassell, 1965)
Ehrman, J., *Grand Strategy,* Vol. V. *United Kingdom History of the Second World War* (London: HMSO, 1956)
——, *Grand Strategy,* Vol. VI, *United Kingdom History of the Second World War* (London: HMSO, 1956)
Eisenhower, D. D., *Mandate for Change, 1953–1956* (New York: Doubleday, 1963)
——, *Waging Peace 1956–61* (New York: Doubleday, 1965)
Epstein, L. D., *Britain – Uneasy Ally* (Chicago: University of Chicago Press, 1954)
——, *British Politics in the Suez Crisis* (Urbana: University of Illinois Press, 1964)
Feis, H., *Japan Subdued: The Atom Bomb and the End of the War in the Pacific* (Princeton: Princeton University Press, 1961)
Fitzsimmons, M. A., *The Foreign Policy of the British Labour Government, 1945–51* (South Bend: Notre Dame University Press, 1953)
Fletcher, R., *£60 a Second on Defence* (London: MacGibbon and Kee, 1963)
Fullick, R. and Powell, G., *Suez: The Double War* (London: Hamish Hamilton, 1979)
Gardner, R. N., *Sterling–Dollar Diplomacy* (Oxford: Clarendon Press, 1956)
Gelber, L. M., *The Rise of Anglo-American Friendship* (London: Oxford University Press, 1938)
Gore-Booth, P., *With Great Truth and Respect* (London: Constable, 1974)

Gowing, M., *Britain and Atomic Energy, 1939–1945* (London: Macmillan, 1964)

———, *Independence and Deterrence: Britain and Atomic Energy, 1945–52,* Vol. I, (London: Macmillan, 1974)

Gretton, Vice-Admiral, Sir Peter, *Maritime Strategy* (London: Cassell, 1965)

Groom, A. J. R. *British Thinking about Nuclear Weapons* (London: Frances Pinter, 1974)

Groves, L. R., *Now it can be Told: The Story of the Manhattan Project* (New York: Harper and Brothers, 1962)

Gwyer, J. M. A., *Grand Strategy,* Vol. III, Part I. *United Kingdom History of the Second World War* (London: HMSO, 1964)

Hagan, K. J. (ed.), *In Peace and War: Interpretations of American Naval History 1773–1978* (London: Greenwood Press, 1978)

Hall, H. D., *North American Supply* (London: HMSO, 1955)

Hall, H. D. and Wrigley, C. C., *Studies of Overseas Supply* (London: HMSO, 1956)

Hancock, W. K. and Gowing, M., *British War Economy* (London: HMSO, 1949)

Harrod, R. F., *The Prof: A Personal Memoir of Lord Cherwell* (London: Macmillan, 1959)

Heren, L., *No Hail, No Farewell* (London: Harper & Row, 1970)

Hewlett, R. G. and Anderson, O. E., *A History of the United States Atomic Energy Commission,* Vol. I, *The New World, 1939–1946* (Pennsylvania: Pennsylvania State University Press, 1962)

Hewlett, R. G. and Duncan, F., *A History of the United States Atomic Energy Commission,* Vol. II, *Atomic Shield, 1947–1952* (Pennsylvania: Pennsylvania State University Press, 1969)

Higham, R., *The Military Intellectuals in Britain: 1918–1939* (New Brunswick: Rutgers University Press, 1966)

Hinsley, F. H. with Thomas, E. E., Ransom, C. F. G. and Knight, R. E., *British Intelligence in the Second World War,* Vol. I (London: HMSO, 1979)

Howard, M., *Grand Strategy,* Vol. IV, *United Kingdom History of the Second World War* (London: HMSO, 1972)

Huntington, S. P., *The Common Defense* (New York: Columbia, University Press, 1961)

Hyde, H., *The Quiet Canadian* (London: Hamish Hamilton, 1962)

Irwing, D., *The German Atomic Bomb: The History of Nuclear Research in Nazi Germany* (New York: Simon & Schuster, 1967)

Ismay, Lord, *The Memoirs of General the Lord Ismay* (London: Heinemann, 1960)

James, R. R. (ed.), *Winston S. Churchill: His Complete Speeches (1897–1963)* (London: Chelsea House, 1974)

Johnson, L. B., *The Vantage Point, 1963–69* (London: Weidenfeld & Nicolson, 1971)

Jones, R. V., *Most Secret War: British Scientific Intelligence, 1939–45* (London: Hamish Hamilton, 1978)
Kahn, D., *The Codebreakers* (London: Weidenfeld & Nicolson, 1974)
Kaufmann, W. W., *The McNamara Strategy* (New York: Harper & Row, 1964)
King-Hall, S., *Defence in the Nuclear Age* (London: Victor Gollancz, 1958)
Kingston-McCloughry, Air Vice-Marshal, E. J., *Defence: Policy and Strategy* (London: Stevens, 1960)
——, *Global Strategy* (New York: Frederick Praeger, 1957)
Kissinger, H. A., *The Troubled Partnership* (New York: McGraw-Hill, 1965)
Kleiman, R., *Atlantic Crisis: American Diplomacy Confronts a Resurgent Europe* (New York: Norton (W.W.), 1964)
Knorr, K. (ed.), *NATO and American Security* (Princeton: Princeton University Press, 1959)
Lash, J. P., *Roosevelt and Churchill, 1939–41: The Partnership that saved the West* (New York: Norton (W.W.), 1976)
Leahy, W.D., *I Was There* (New York: Whittlesey House, 1950)
Leifer, M. (ed.), *Constraints and Adjustments in British Foreign Policy* (London: Allen & Unwin, 1972)
Lewin, R., *Ultra Goes to War: The Secret Story* (London: Hutchinson, 1978)
Liddell Hart, B. H., *Defence of the West* (London: Cassell, 1950)
——, *Deterrent or Defence* (London: Stevens, 1960)
Lilienthal, D. E., *Change, Hope and the Bomb* (Princeton: Princeton University Press, 1963)
——, *The Journals of David E. Lilienthal,* Vol. II, *The Atomic Energy Years, 1945–1950* (New York: Harper & Row, 1964)
Lloyd, S., *Suez 1956: A Personal Account* (London: Jonathan Cape, 1978)
Love, K., *Suez: The Twice-Fought War* (London: Longmans, 1970)
Macdonald, I. S., *Anglo-American Relations since the Second World War* (Newton Abbot: David & Charles, 1974)
Maclean, D., *British Foreign Policy Since Suez* (London: Hodder & Stoughton, 1970)
Macmillan, H., *Tides of Fortune, 1945–1955* (London: Macmillan, 1969)
——, *Riding the Storm, 1956–1959* (London: Macmillan, 1971)
——, *Pointing the Way, 1959–61* (London: Macmillan, 1972)
——, *At the End of the Day, 1961–63* (London: Macmillan, 1973)
Mander, J., *Great Britain or Little England?* (London: Penguin, 1963)
Manderson-Jones, R. B., *The Special Relationship: Anglo-American Relations and Western European Union, 1947–56* (London: Weidenfeld & Nicolson, 1972)
Martin, L. W., *The Sea in Modern Strategy* (New York: Praeger, 1967)
Matloff, M. and Snell, E., *Strategic Planning for Coalition Warfare, 1941–42* (Washington: Dept. of the Army, 1953)
Mayhew, C., *Britain's Role Tomorrow* (London: Hutchinson, 1967)

McNeil, W. H., *America, Britain and Russia: Their Co-operation and Conflict, 1941–1946* (London: Oxford University Press, 1953)
Millis, W. (ed.), *The Forrestal Diaries* (London: Cassell, 1952)
Montgomery, Field-Marshal, *The Memoirs of Field-Marshal the Viscount Montgomery of Alamein, K.G.* (London: Collins, 1958)
Mulley, F. W., *The Politics of Western Defence* (London: Thames and Hudson, 1962)
Neustadt, R. E., *Alliance Politics* (New York: Columbia University Press, 1970)
Nicholas, H. G., *The United States and Britain* (London: University of Chicago Press, 1975)
Nieburg, H. L., *Nuclear Secrecy and Foreign Policy* (Washington: Public-Affairs Press, 1964)
Nixon, R., *The Memoirs of Richard Nixon* (London: Book Club Associates, 1978)
Northedge, F. S., *British Foreign Policy: The Process of Readjustment 1945–61* (New York: Praeger, 1962)
Nunnerley, D., *President Kennedy and Britain* (London: Bodley Head, 1972)
Osgood, R. E., *NATO: The Entangling Alliance* (Chicago: University of Chicago Press, 1962
Philby, K., *My Silent War* (London: MacGibbon & Kee, 1968)
Pierre, A., *Nuclear Politics: The British Experience with an Independent Strategic Force, 1939–1970* (London: Oxford University Press, 1972)
Pincher, C., *Inside Story: A Documentary of the Pursuit of Power* (London: Book Club Associates, 1978)
Pineau, C., *1956 Suez* (Paris: R. Lamont, 1976)
Porter, B., *Britain and the Rise of Communist China* (London: Oxford University Press, 1967)
Postan, M. M., *British War Production* (London: HMSO, 1952)
Roberts, H. L. and Wilson, P. A., *Britain and the United States: Problems in Co-operation* (New York: Harper and Brothers, 1953)
Rosecrance, R. N., *Defence of the Realm: British Strategy in the Nuclear Epoch* (New York: Columbia University Press, 1968)
Roskill, S. W., *The War at Sea,* Vols. I–III (London: HMSO, 1954–61)
Russett, B. H., *Community and Contention: Britain and America in the Twentieth Century* (Cambridge, Mass., MIT Press, 1963)
Schilling, W. R., Hammond, P. Y. and Snyder, G. H., *Strategy, Politics and Defense Budgets* (New York: Columbia University Press, 1962)
Schlesinger, Jr A. M., *A Thousand Days: John F. Kennedy in the White House* (Boston: Houghton Mifflin, 1965)
Sherwood, R. E., *The White House Papers of H. L. Hopkins,* Vol. I (London: Eyre & Spottiswoode, 1948)
______, *Roosevelt and Hopkins* (New York: Harper and Brothers, 1948)
Shinwell, E., *Conflict Without Malice* (London: Odhams, 1955)

Slessor, Sir J., *Strategy for the West* (London: Cassell, 1956)

———, *The Central Blue: Recollections and Reflections* (London: Cassell, 1956)

———, *The Great Deterrent* (London: Cassell, 1959)

Smith, M. E. and Johns, C. J. (ed.), *American Defense Policy* (Baltimore: The Johns Hopkins Press, 1968)

Snow, C. P., *Science and Government* (London: Oxford University Press, 1960)

Snyder, W. P., *The Politics of British Defence Policy, 1945–1962* (Columbus: Ohio State University Press, 1964)

Sorensen, T. C., *Kennedy* (New York: Harper & Row, 1965)

Stanley, T. W., *NATO in Transition* (New York: Praeger, 1965)

Stevenson, W., *A Man called Intrepid: The Secret War, 1939–45* (London: Macmillan, 1976)

Stimson, H. L. and Bundy, M., *On Active Service in Peace and War* (New York: Harper and Brothers, 1948)

Strachey, J., *On the Prevention of War* (London: Macmillan, 1962)

Strauss, L., *Man and Decisions* (New York: Doubleday, 1962)

Thomas, H., *The Suez Affair* (London: Weidenfeld & Nicolson, 1966)

Thorne, C., *Allies of a Kind: The United States, Britain and the War against Japan* (London: Hamish Hamilton, 1978)

Truman, H. S., *Memoirs,* Vol. I; *Year of Decisions* (New York: Doubleday, 1955)

———, *Memoirs,* Vol. II; *Years of Trial and Hope* (New York: Doubleday, 1955)

Turner, A. C., *The Unique Partnership, Britain and the United States* (New York: Pegasus, 1971)

Vandenberg, Jr. A. H. (ed.), *The Private Papers of Senator Vandenberg* (Boston: Houghton Mifflin, 1952)

Verrier, A., *An Army for the Sixties: A Study in National Policy, Contract and Obligation* (London: Secker & Warburg, 1966)

Waltz, K. N., *Foreign Policy and Democratic Politics: The American and British Experience* (Boston: Little, Brown, 1967)

Webster, Sir C. and Frankland, N., *The Strategic Air Offensive Against Germany, 1939–45,* Vols. I–IV (London: HMSO, 1961)

Wheeler-Bennett, J. W., *John Anderson: Viscount Waverley* (London: Macmillan, 1962)

Williams, F., *A Prime Minister Remembers* (London: Heinemann, 1961)

Williams, G. and Reed, B., *Denis Healey – the Policies of Power* (London: Sidgwick & Jackson, 1971)

Wilson, H., *The Labour Government 1964–70* (London: Penguin, 1974)

Winterbotham, F. W., *The Ultra Secret* (London: Weidenfeld & Nicolson, 1974)

Woodhouse, C. M., *British Foreign Policy since the Second World War* (London: Hutchinson, 1961)

Worcester, R., *Roots of British Air Policy* (London: Hodder & Stoughton, 1966)

Younger, K., *Changing Perspectives in British Foreign Policy* (London: Oxford University Press, 1964)

Zuckerman, Sir S., *Scientists and War: The Impact of Science on Military and Civil Affairs* (London: Hamish Hamilton, 1966)

ARTICLES

Baylis, J., 'French defence policy: Continuity or change', *Journal of the Royal United Services Institute for Defence Studies (JRUSI),* March 1977

Beaton, L., 'Facts about Skybolt', *New Scientist,* No. 275, 22 February 1962

_____ 'Labour's defence policy: Learning to love the bomb', *Statist,* Vol. CLXXXVII, No. 4530

_____ 'Men and/or missiles', *Crossbow,* Summer 1958

Brown, N., 'Britain's strategic weapons: 2, The Polaris A-3', *The World Today,* Vol. XX, August 1964

_____ 'British arms and the switch towards Europe', *International Affairs,* Vol. XLIII, No. 3, July 1967

Brundrett, Sir F., 'Rockets, satellites, and military thinking', *JRUSI,* Vol. CV, August 1960

Buchan, A., 'Britain and the bomb', *Reporter,* Vol. XX, 19 March 1959

_____ 'Britain and the nuclear deterrent', *Political Quarterly,* Vol. XXXI, No. 1, Jan.–March 1960

_____ 'Europe and the Atlantic Alliance: Two strategies or one?' *Journal of Common Market Studies,* Vol. I, No. 3, Spring 1963

_____ 'Nassau reconsidered', *New Republic,* 2 March 1963

_____ 'Partners and allies', *Foreign Affairs,* Vol. XLI, No. 4, July 1963

_____ 'The choice for British defence policy', *International Journal,* Vol. XVIII, No. 3, Summer 1963

_____ 'Wanted: A European deterrent', *Reporter,* Vol. XXI, 15 October 1959

Bull, H., 'The many sides of British unilateralism', *Reporter,* 16 March 1961

Bush, V., 'Churchill and the scientists', *Atlantic Monthly,* Vol. CCXV, No. 3, March 1965

Buzzard, Rear-Admiral Sir A. W., 'The H-Bomb: Massive retaliation or graduated deterrence', *International Affairs,* Vol. XXXII, No. 2, April 1956

Carlton, D., 'Great Britain and nuclear weapons: the academic inquest', *British Journal of International Studies,* Vol. 2, No. 2, July 1976

Church, F. C., 'U.S. policy and the "New Europe" ', *Foreign Affairs,* Vol. XLV, No. 1, October 1966

Cockburn, R. 'Science and war', *JRUSI,* Vol. CI, No. 601, February 1956
Cowley, Sir J., 'Future trends in warfare', *JRUSI,* Vol. LV, No. 617, 1960
Critchley, J., 'Ending the myth of nuclear independence', *Crossbow,* Vol. VIII, No. 31, April–June 1965
Crossman, R. H. S., 'The nuclear obsession', *Encounter,* Vol. XI, No. 1, July 1958
Dawson, R. and Rosecrance, R., 'Theory and reality in the Anglo-American Alliance', *World Politics,* Vol. XIX, No. 1, October 1966
De Weerd, H. H., 'Britain's changing military policy', *Foreign Affairs,* Vol. XXXIV, No. 1, October 1955
Edmonds, M., 'International collaboration in weapons procurement: The implications of the Anglo-French case', *International Affairs,* Vol. XLIII, No. 2, April 1967
Epstein, L. D., 'Britain and the H-Bomb, 1955–58', *Review of Politics,* Vol. XXI, August 1959
Field, T. F., 'Britain's deterrent and the decision to abandon the Blue Streak Missile', *Fifteen Nations,* Feb.–March 1962
Frankland, N., 'Britain's changing strategic position', *International Affairs,* Vol. XXXIII, No. 4, October 1957
Gibbs, N. H., 'Blue Streak, end or beginning?' *Air Force,* June 1960
——— 'The way ahead for the Western world's deterrent', *Fifteen Nations,* No. 15, Oct.–Nov. 1960
Goldberg, A., 'The Atomic origins of the British nuclear deterrent', *International Affairs,* Vol. XL, No. 2, July 1964
——— 'The military origins of the British nuclear deterrent', *International Affairs,* Vol. XL, No. 4, October 1964
Goold-Adams, R., 'Conventional forces and British defence policy', *Political Quarterly,* Vol. XXXI, No. 1, Jan.–March 1960
Gott, R., 'The evolution of the independent British deterrent', *International Affairs,* Vol. XXXIX, No. 2, April 1963
Groom, A. J. R., 'U.S.–Allied relations and the atomic bomb in the Second World War', *World Politics,* Vol. XV, No. 1, October 1962
Hartley, A., 'The British bomb', *Survival,* Vol. VI, No. 4, July–August 1964
Healey, D., 'Interdependence', *Political Quarterly,* Vol. XXXI, No. 1, Jan.–March 1960
——— 'The sputnik and Western defence', *International Affairs,* Vol. XXXIV, No. 2, April 1958
Hinton, Sir C., 'British developments in atomic energy', *Nucleonics,* Vol. XII, January 1954
Howard, M., 'Britain's defences: Commitments and capabilities', *Foreign Affairs,* Vol. XXXIX, October 1960
——— 'Strategy in the nuclear age, *JRUSI,* Vol. CII, November 1957
Just, W. S., 'The scrapping of Skybolt', *Reporter,* Vol. XXXVII, 11 April 1963
Martin, L. W., 'The market for strategic ideas in Britain: The "Sandys

Era" ', *The American Political Science Review,* Vol. LVI, No. 1, 1962

Neustradt, R. E., 'Memorandum on the British Labour Party and the MLF', *New York Review of Books,* Vol. XI, No. 10, 5 December 1968

Ovendale, R., 'The English-Speaking Alliance: The Anglo-American special relationship', *Interstate,* No. 2, 1975-6

Owen, Sir Leonard, 'Nuclear engineering – the United Kingdom: The first ten years', *Journal of the British Nuclear Energy Society,* January 1963

Pierre, A. J., 'Britain's defence dilemmas', in *The Atlantic Community Reappraised,* Proceedings of the Academy of Political Science, Vol. XXIX, No. 2, November 1968

_____ 'Reconciliation in Europe: A Western approach to the European Security Conference', *Interplay,* Vol. 3, No. 10, July 1970

_____ 'Nuclear diplomacy: Britain, France and America', *Foreign Affairs,* Vol. XLIX, No. 2, January 1971

Sainsbury, K., 'Second front in 1942: Anglo-American differences over strategy', *British Journal of International Studies* (*BJIS*) Vol. 4, No. 1, April 1978

Schilling, W. R., 'The H-Bomb decision: How to decide without actually choosing', *Political Science Quarterly,* Vol. LXXVI, March 1961

Sherfield, Lord, 'Britain's nuclear story: 1945–52: Politics and technology', *Round Table,* No. 258, April 1975

Simpson, J., 'Lessons of the British Polaris project: An organizational history', *JRUSI,* March 1969

Slessor, Sir J., 'British defence policy', *Foreign Affairs,* Vol. XXXV, No. 4, July 1957

_____ 'The revolution in strategy', *The Listener,* Vol. LI, No. 1302 and No. 1303

Sprout, H. and M., 'Retreat from world power: Processes and consequences of readjustment', *World Politics,* Vol. XV, No. 4, July 1963

Strachey, J., 'Is our deterrent vulnerable? – A defence in the 1960s', *International Affairs,* Vol. XXVI, No. 1, January 1961

Thomson, Sir G., 'Britain's drive for atomic power', *Foreign Affairs,* Vol. XXXV, No. 1, October 1956

Thorneycroft, P., 'Labour policy will destroy our only effective defence', *NATO's Fifteen Nations,* August–September 1964

Verrier, A., 'British defence policy under Labour', *Foreign Affairs,* Vol. XLII, No. 2, January 1964

_____ 'Defence and politics after Nassau', *Political Quarterly,* Vol. XXXIV, No. 3, July–September 1963

Walker, P. G., 'The Labour Party's defence and foreign policy', *Foreign Affairs,* Vol. XLII, No. 3, April 1964

Warner, G., 'The Nassau Agreement and NATO', *The World Today,* Vol. XIX, February 1963

Whitestone, Commander, N. E., 'Progress with Polaris', *Brassey's Annual,* London, 1966

Williams P., 'The United States and Western Europe: a conditional commitment', *Interstate,* Vol. 3, No. 2, 1978

Wilson, H., 'Britain's policy if Labour wins', *Atlantic,* Vol. CCXII, No. 4, October 1963

The World Today, Vol. 16, No. 8: 'Notes of the Month'

PAMPHLETS AND THESES

Beaton, L., 'The Western Alliance and the McNamara Doctrine', *Adelphi Paper,* No. 11 (London: Institute for Strategic Studies, 1964)

Bow Group (Conservative Party). *A Smaller Stage: Britain's Place in the World* (London: Bow Group, 1965)

Britain and the United States. (Council on Foreign Relations, New York and the Royal Institute of International Affairs, London, 1953)

Brodie, B., *The American Scientific Strategists,* RAND Memorandum, P-2979 (Santa Monica: Rand Corporation, 1964)

Brown, N., *British Arms and Strategy* (London: Royal United Services Institution, 1969)

Buchan, A., 'The Multilateral Force: An Historical Perspective, *Adelphi Paper,* No. 13 (London: Institute for Strategic Studies, 1964)

Bull, H., *Strategy and the Atlantic Alliance: A Critique of United States Doctrine,* Policy Memorandum No. 29 (Princeton: Center of International Studies, Princeton University, 1964)

De Weerd, H. A., *Britain and the Alliance*, RAND Memorandum, P-2779 (Santa Monica: RAND Corporation, 1963)

——— *Britain's Defence 'New Look' Five Years Later,* RAND Memorandum, P-2562 (Santa Monica: RAND Corporation, 1962)

——— *British Defense Policy: An American View,* RAND Memorandum, P-2390 (Santa Monica: RAND Corporation, 1961)

Ditchley Foundation, *The Nuclear Deterrent in the Context of Anglo-American Relations,* Report of a Conference held under the auspices of the Ditchley Foundation.

Fox, W. T. R. and A. B., *Britain and America in the Era of Total Diplomacy,* Memorandum No. 1, (Princeton Center of International Studies, Princeton University, 1952)

Heyhoe, D. C. R., 'The Alliance and Europe: Part VI. The European Programme Group', *Adelphi Paper,* No. 129 (London: International Institute for Strategic Studies, 1977)

Howard, M., *Anglo-American Strategic Relationships,* Report on a Colloquium held at St Antony's College, Oxford, 14–17 April, 1970

Imogighe, T. A., *War-time Influences Affecting Britain's Attitude to a Post-War Continental Commitment* (Ph.D. Thesis, University of Wales, October, 1975)

Kittredge, T. B., *United States–British Naval Cooperation 1940–45* (MS study on microfilm at the New York Public Library)

Marshall, General G., Report 'The Winning of the War in Europe and the Pacific' [Biennial Report of the Chief of Staff of the US Army, July 1 1943–30 June 1945, to Secretary of War]. (New York: Simon & Schuster)

Martin, L. W., 'British Defence Policy: The Long Recessional', *Adelphi Paper,* No. 61. (London: Institute for Strategic Studies, 1969)

Nailor, P. and Alford, J., 'The Future of Britain's Deterrent Force', *Adelphi Paper,* No. 156 (London: International Institute for Strategic Studies, 1979)

Northover, S. M. R., *The Global Strategy Paper: the Context and Significance of the Chiefs of Staff Paper, 1952, in British Defence Policy* (M.Sc. (Econ.) Dissertation, University of Wales, Aberystwyth, 1973)

Osgood, R.E., *The Case for the MLF* (Washington: Washington Centre for Foreign Policy Research, 1964)

Rose, R., *The Relation of Socialist Principles for British Labour Foreign Policy 1945–51* (D. Phil. Thesis, Oxford University, 1959)

Royal Institute of International Affairs *Atomic Energy: Its International Implications,* A Discussion by a Chatham House Study Group (London: Broadwater Press, 1948)

_____ *British Security.* A Report by a Chatham House Study Group (London: Oxford University Press, 1946)

_____ *Defence in the Cold War.* Report by a Chatham House Study Group under the Chairmanship of Major-General Sir Ian Jacob, London, 1950

Smart, I., 'Advanced Strategic Missiles: A Short Guide', *Adelphi Paper,* No. 63 (London: Institute for Strategic Studies)

_____ 'Future Conditional: The Prospect for Anglo-French Nuclear Cooperation', *Adelphi Paper,* No. 78 (London: The Institute for Strategic Studies, 1971)

_____ *The Future of the British Nuclear Deterrent: Technical Economic and Strategic Issues* (London: Royal Institute of International Affairs, 1977)

Williams, G., Gregory, F. and Simpson, J., *Crisis in Procurement: A Case Study of the TSR-2* (London: Royal United Service Institution, 1969)

Wilson, H., *In Place of Dollars* (London: Tribune Pamphlet 1952)

Index